D0528470

JAM WITH LAMB

JAM *with* LAMB

SEASONAL WEST COUNTRY COOKING

RICHARD GUEST

Foreword by
ROSIE BOYCOTT

BIRLINN

First published in 2007 by
Birlinn Ltd
West Newington House
10 Newington Road
Edinburgh EH9 1QS

www.birlinn.co.uk

Hardback ISBN 13: 978 1 84158 560 4
ISBN 10: 1 84158 560 2

Paperback ISBN 13: 978 1 84158 661 8
ISBN 10: 1 84158 661 7

British Library Cataloguing-in-Publication Data
A catalogue record for this book is available from the British Library

Edited by Alison Moss
Design by Andrew Sutterby

Printed and bound by 1010 Printing, China

Contents

Foreword

This is a book that we have been eagerly awaiting. Since moving to Somerset in 2002, we have been constantly struck by the enormous riches of the countryside. Within a radius of twenty miles from Taunton, there is an abundance of top quality produce, yet no one really knows about this and whenever a gastronomic area comes to mind, it's always one in France.

I well remember when my husband went into our local cheese shop and saw that the local brie was more expensive than the French one. He asked why. It's better, came the answer, and indeed it is. Not, I think, because it is intrinsically a better class of cheese, but because it is sold in perfect condition without any need to truck it several hundred miles from its place of origin. Yet we are still sadly conditioned to think that cheeses, breads, pâtés and pastries are all, somehow, better in France. Five years of living here have convinced me how wrong that belief is.

So there has been a desperate need for a cook book which draws on all these wonderful local ingredients and combines them in simple recipes that do not require the deft hands of a domestic goddess to guarantee success! A cook book that also does not necessitate rushing to the supermarket to buy esoteric ingredients which have been flown half way round the world (and which are often 'temporarily out of stock').

And who better to write such a book than Richard Guest, Michelin-starred chef at Taunton's famous Castle Hotel and a passionate believer in all things fresh, seasonal and local. In this book, Richard has given everyone the wherewithal to provide a genuine English cuisine for not only our dinner parties but also, my husband hopes, for every day of the year! Enjoy it as much as I have.

Rosie Boycott

Acknowledgements

I feel very lucky to have been given the chance to write a book about the subject I love. I wouldn't have been able to achieve this without the support of my wife Victoria who suffers for my love of my job. Many thanks to the producers of fine ingredients in the West Country, who give us cooks great variation and quality; Michael Raphael for referring me to the publishers, Birlinn, and to them for the opportunity to write the book; Nick Smith for the wonderful photography and patience with my poor directional skills as co-driver; to those from whom I have learned my skills over the years, and to Mr Chapman and the Castle for giving me the British brief and the space to enjoy the quality of produce the West Country has to offer. Also many thanks to Mary Gibbs for translating my illegible handwriting into type and Alison Moss for her prompt, efficient editing.

Preface

Thirty years ago Britain became mesmerised by a new gastronomic import from France. It was called nouvelle cuisine, and it inspired a generation of young chefs who missed the point and fell for the gloriously arty photographs that appeared in a rush of books written by the great architects of the movement. Suddenly food was sexy, chefs were raised onto pedestals, the glossies fuelled our appetites for fashionable eating and television cookery became a branch of show business.

Some of us were not so easily seduced. *The Good Food Guide* for a start described the nouvelle obsession as the *trompe l'oeil* school of cookery. And in Somerset I could not understand why it was so clever or desirable to fly in mange touts and haricots verts from Kenya or strawberries from California when the Castle was surrounded by orchards and pastures, uplands and meadows, gardens and smallholdings, which made my county the finest larder in England. And anyway, did I want my restaurant to deliver fancy menus identical with the rest? No! It made more sense to me to search out sympathetic chefs who might share my vision of rehabilitating the noble English culinary traditions and do it by working closely with local growers and suppliers. Slowly, slowly, we persuaded a green-fingered GP to grow fruits, vegetables and herbs for us in his Edwardian walled garden at Hatch Court, a mad farmer at a decommissioned RAF station on the Blackdown Hills to rear proper chickens, and many other wonderful people to join our campaign in praise of fresh local produce. More, we acknowledged their contribution to the cause – 'the English project' – by listing their names on the first page of our menu – and we still do.

Thirty years on and Richard Guest has done at last what I have longed to see. His book is an exuberant celebration of all that is best in England's West Country. He is the right man to do it for, although he is a canny Yorkshireman, his roots now reach deep into Somerset's soil. His wife Vicky comes from old farming stock in these parts and her family, the Barbers, make the starter for James Montgomery's renowned unpasteurized cheddar, Britain's finest and, without doubt, one of the world's great cheeses.

What I love about this book is that Richard's voice and his passions ring out on every page. You will find it a happy companion in your kitchen.

Kit Chapman
Proprietor, The Castle at Taunton
May 2007

Introduction

My first experience in a professional kitchen was at the helm of a big stainless steel sink in a rubber apron and Marigold gloves washing dishes at Hudson's Hotel in York when I was fifteen. It was here I got the taste for a life in kitchens. Impressed by cooks' stories and intrigued by their knife skills, I was drawn to the hot, tense and aggressive atmosphere created by the service. Like many other professional cooks I hadn't come from a family where the kitchen was the focal point of the house and it wasn't a passion for food that first got me addicted to kitchen life and cooking. It was the kitchens and the lifestyle itself. In my first full-time position in 1987 I was a YTS apprentice in a hotel called Elliott's, again in York, and I loved it. I thrived on the planning, the pace of work, the organising, the pressure of service – especially the last hour before service, which is vital for a smooth service, of arranging your section, 'the set up'. Making sure everything was in place: pans, seasonings, spoons, boards, spatulas, all in the same place every time, so no extra thought was needed during the service.

But it wasn't the love for ingredients and the skill of actually cooking that kept me interested, it was the sport of the job, even though I got a real thrill when I made my first béchamel sauce and my first pâté and I was always proud of my Marie Rose sauce for prawn cocktails. My dressing always tasted spot on, but that was more the avoidance of a clip round the ear from a sous chef than it was a passion for taste.

The real changing point in my career in kitchens came just before my eighteenth birthday. Two years into my YTS my mother recorded a television series called 'Take 6 Cooks'. At first I wasn't that interested by these 'airy-fairy' French guys romanticising about food, but then like a slap round the face came Marco Pierre White, a big scarecrow-like Northerner with a plum in his mouth. He was just exploding with angst and a kind of aggressive passion that blew me away. I thought instantly, 'Yeah that's it, I don't want to be one of those Masonic Francophile chefs with their names on their jackets and flags on their lapels. I want to be rock and roll like Marco', and the only place to do this was London.

So six months later I had finished my YTS and had arranged a trial in the Savoy kitchens under chef Anton Edelman. I really wanted to go to le Tante Claire, like Marco did, but I couldn't get a reply, so knowing the Savoy to be famous, I thought it was the next best thing! My two-day trial at the Savoy was more like an endurance test than a skill test. How long can a young man stand in one place with cold wet feet dicing carrots into small cubes without food and water before he gives in? But luckily there was so much going on around me in this massive and manic kitchen that I didn't notice the time going by. After two eighteen-hour days and a brief interview with the chef (he asked me if I thought I would like London and I replied that I didn't think I was going to see much of it, which amused him), he told me to get my hair cut and that I could start as a third commis in a month's time. At the time I felt honoured, but in reality they were probably just so desperate for more victims for their boot camp. Also I realised that my feet hurt that much they felt like they were going to start making a noise.

It was in these kitchens that I learned about truly top-quality ingredients imported with no expense spared from all over the world; nothing but the best. I also got to taste and use their glamorous ingredients such as truffle, fois gras and caviar – things that weren't often seen in York in the 1980s! But still it wasn't these things that engrossed me; it was still the thrill of the pressure and the sport of the service. You made sure your sauces were perfect all the time, not because you loved to make them but because you didn't want a verbal and sometimes physical flogging in front of the rest of the brigade, and you wanted to be respected for your hard work, speed and skill.

In 1992, after two and a half years of scraping my way through the Savoy kitchens I was enticed by a friend into my first actual Michelin starred kitchen. Bruno Loubet had left the Four Seasons and his look-alike, Jean Christophe Novelli, had taken over. He was apparently building a new team of movers and shakers of which a close friend was already a member, and soon I was on board. It started just how I liked it back then with long hours and a tense but exciting atmosphere. For the next three years the Four Seasons kitchen, which was the best equipped I had ever worked in, was where we slaved for the guidebooks, critics and food journalists and they all loved Novelli, and to a point we all shared the glory of his critical acclaim. It was the highest standard at which I'd ever had to cook. He pushed us all very hard and I matured a lot as a cook, but because we were in a third-storey kitchen using almost only French and imported ingredients there was still very little contact with the actual source of it. So to a degree the job was still about the chefs' cooking, the restaurant's floorshow and design rather than the raw ingredients.

But Novelli is a very expressive person and he allowed me to express myself through my cooking. From this I learned how to taste food properly and because of this I became very loyal to him, so when he moved on to open his own restaurant I followed shortly after for my first head chef's position. At the time, this was a risk for him but a great opportunity for me, and although at the beginning we were working without pay so the business could get up and running, it was still a fantastic time. The

kitchen was tiny and very poorly equipped, which made us feel a great sense of achievement just getting through the day, let alone getting good reviews and accolades. It was in this restaurant where I really learned the most about running a kitchen, as there was only a very small team and it became a very busy restaurant. It's amazing how much you learn from making mistakes when you have nobody to blame but yourself. The restaurant was called Maison Novelli and over the next three years the group expanded at an incredible rate to five restaurants. But this rapid expansion was to be the company's downfall. However, the years I cooked there made me a much better head chef now, by being such a bad head chef then. Suffice to say that in those days my people skills left a lot to be desired!

What first triggered my move from London to the provinces of England was a small hotel that Novelli was trying to buy. He sent me there in 1999 to get the restaurant up and running but unfortunately the deal collapsed. By this time, my wife Victoria and I had lost any will to move back to London. So the next best thing was to head further south to Somerset where Vicky's family lived.

I used the first few weeks of the new country lifestyle to fill my lungs with fresh air, catch up on my reading and organise some of my recipes and cook family meals, which is something I love to do but had very rarely had the chance. This was the first time since I was fifteen years old that I hadn't worked, and I was reaching a loose end and considering going back to London to work. Luckily fate stepped in. The kitchen at the famous Castle Hotel in Taunton had come up for grabs. After a few letters and some brief interviews I then had an incredibly intense interrogation for over two hours by the owner, Mr Chapman, who in the industry is renowned for being a bastion for British food. Also, great chefs such as Chris Oakes, Gary Rhodes and Phil Vickery had passed through his kitchens with great success. After my intense grilling he invited me to cook a dinner at the Castle for himself and a few of his foody friends to see if I was up to the challenge and although the event didn't go as perfectly as I would have liked, after a few days of deliberating, he offered me the job at the helm of his kitchens.

The message he gave me was I had to be all things great and British, which was a challenge I relished as I had just spent twelve years cooking in very French kitchens and it felt good to be cooking for my home colours. But still, even though over the next two years we would achieve a Michelin star and various other glossy accolades, I still feel now that I was cooking to impress them and not for the joy of cooking and pleasing customers. It wasn't until the visit of a well-known food critic, who had obviously come intent upon malice, but nevertheless had some just things to say, did I realise that I had all these wonderful suppliers and ingredients on my doorstep and years of fantastic training, yet I was still cooking, although at a high standard, for the wrong reasons.

It was the producers, growers and suppliers of the South West who helped me to firmly develop my style of cooking and menu composition. Their wonderful cynicism towards flashy food and pompous service and an almost flippant attitude towards precious chefs, are well earned through hard graft and the right outlook on food. One of the first farmers I really started to work closely with was John Rowswell of Barrington, a beautiful village in Somerset. He turned up one Christmas trying to sell mistletoe to Mrs Chapman, but with no luck there he talked his way into the kitchens to tell us about his other wares. When I found out that he grew a lot of his own vegetables as well as purchasing from local markets, a light went on inside my head and we started to plan out all the things for next year that he wanted to grow and I wanted to cook. It was from here that we started to let the seasons help us create our menus so they could evolve through the year.

Now I'm constantly looking forward to what next month will bring with almost a smug smile, knowing that my raw ingredients are so fresh and vibrant. From St Enodoc's Cornish asparagus, our first of the season which has a slight seaweedy taste, to Rosemary Moorehouse's in Lydeard St Lawrence that is so crisp it's beautiful just eaten raw as a crudity with its light, almost scallion, flavour. Then the fresh peas, although a fairly laborious task in a busy restaurant kitchen, it's worth every minute for the end result, and that emerald of the vegetable world, the broad bean. This is such a great vegetable it's so disappointing when they go on but we do tend to freeze as many as possible as I find they freeze particularly well and they can otherwise deteriorate very quickly. Then local tomatoes and runner beans and the fine beans follow. The list is endless throughout the year and living in the countryside is always a great inspiration for cooking. Just walking my dog through the local woods in Hatch Beauchamp I notice the wild garlic start to spring up in March. It's always a good marker that spring is just around the corner. When it forms its beautiful white blanket sprinkled with bluebells it just lifts your imagination. Every week the woods seem to change, which in turn tunes you in to the season.

Another great influence on my cooking has been my butcher, Steve Baker, who works tirelessly to a high standard and will only entertain British meat, if not purely that from the South West. He has a keen understanding of maturing on the bone and the importance of marbling in the eye of the meat. Good meat should always have a complex road map of speckled fat running through it to add flavour and moistness. I think, just as it is for restaurants, a good honest butcher is a really important part of a family's life. Good fresh eggs are another important and versatile ingredient and for these I go to Glebe Farm in Pitney where their eggs, with their rich yolk and thick white, come from happy chickens that have plenty of outdoor acreage to roam

around in. We also get our amazing pork from Glebe Farm; crossing Large Whites with Saddlebacks give great fat content for flavour.

All of these people work so hard to bring the fruits of their labour to our restaurant doors and far too often we chefs and cooks take all the credit when in reality it's usually the actual ingredients themselves that do most of the work. I tell you it takes a lot more skill to butcher down a cow and cut a perfect rib eye than it does to cook the steak. It's these skilled craftsmen that have helped me realise and relish in the joy of more simple cooking and it's a pleasure to work with these amazing ingredients that are so abundant in the West Country.

One of the first things I ever foraged from the woods to bring back to the kitchen was wild garlic. The moment I take a bag of the thick green leaves into the kitchen and the aroma drifts from the bag, everybody in the kitchen has a look of excitement as they know this almost marks the beginning of our culinary year. They know asparagus is just around the corner and the doldrums of the last month of winter are over. It is such a great feeling to collect ingredients yourself and return them home to eat, but take care to check with landowners and make sure you know what you're picking. I certainly wouldn't pick any mushroom unless I was 100 per cent sure what it was. My favourite place for picking garlic is in Lyme Wood in the village where I live in Hatch Beauchamp, a beautiful and carefully maintained forest that is always a perfect mirror for the seasons.

There are many food items linked with regional foods all over Britain and the West Country is no different, from breeds of cattle such as the North and South Devons or the Gloucester Old Spot pig and Dorset Horn sheep; regionally titled cheese such as Cheddar, Bath Soft, Dorset Blue Vinny, single and double Gloucester, Exmoor Blue just to skim the surface; then there's the confectioneries, Bath Olivers, the Colston bun, a Cornish saffron cake, and a Dorset Knob to name but a few. Other curious names include Bath Chaps, which sounds like a group of good old boys from Bath but is actually cured and boiled pigs jaws and jowls coated in breadcrumbs. All these nice little titles give the impression of a regional cuisine but in reality they are just titles given by their makers who have a sense of regional pride; it's not a regional style of cooking. I could make Yorkshire puddings on Sunday with local flour, eggs, and milk and call them Somerset batter puddings if I felt the urge but it wouldn't make them taste different to any other made with good flour and fresh eggs and milk, so to compare culinary techniques of different regions of Britain would be fairly pointless. There is a difference in productivity and the lush pastures, milder climate and fertile soils, along with the experienced, knowledgeable farmers and producers, means in the west we do have high quality products with which to do our cooking and we should sing loudly about our produce rather than scour history books in the hope of reinventing

our food profile to compare with other much larger European countries. We should just loose our chip and enjoy our produce with pride and whatever techniques we've acquired over the years.

The West Country is steeped in tradition when it comes to making a living from the land and its waters. Think of the withy men and their willow, the fishermen using age-old methods such as salmon butts and mudhorses, elverers who fish for elvers (baby eels on the River Parrett), eel combs to catch larger eels, cider-makers and peat producers, sheepskin tanners, cheese-makers, all still trying to make their livings while keeping traditions going. Even if some traditions are more cottage industry these days, they are still an important part of rural England and something that should give us a great sense of being. If we don't support these small producers another orchard gets ripped down for development and we stand to loose more than we know.

Why Buy Local?

The flavour and scent of fruits, roots, shoots and leaves that are imported today have one thing in common; they are all equally bland having been rendered characterless by industrial growing techniques that concentrate more on cloning their products to uniformity, and the conditions in which they are naturally grown aren't changed to benefit the end product but to increase the shelf life and prepare it for its long arduous journey to the other side of the planet. Some producers even resort to treating their fruit with radiation to make them sterile and prolong their shelf life! Others just crop them way before they have reached optimum ripeness, again to prolong shelf life, and so we at home buy rock hard fruit, such as avocados, and leave them in the fruit bowl hoping they will ripen until eventually we throw them away because they are black and horrible and then start all over again, so we end up having a constant supply of imported, inedible fruits on display.

When buying fruit and veg you need to feel the weight and firmness to assess if they are ripe and juicy and the aromas tell us what kind of flavour experience we can look forward to. All this isn't easy if it's wrapped in cellophane on a polystyrene tray. Although our supermarkets have improved tenfold, people have already been brainwashed into looking for uniformity as the standard rather than feel and smell. Alternatively shop for foods at your local markets, farmers' markets, growers, butchers and mongers, which I'm sure, if you look, you still have along your high streets and around your squares. Some people in the know have never stopped using these places for their shopping and surprisingly I find these people are actually the people who are living in the city centres who have no need to travel out to the big supermarkets, because all they need is within their community and on their walk home. It seems the people who rely on supermarkets are the folk who live further out in the countryside whose village shops have been shut down, not necessarily because of competition with supermarkets but for the fact that the shops are worth more as houses to sell for profit than the shop was making. People have been forced to go to supermarkets and even petrol stations, which seem to have taken over the role of village shops. But we still go shopping for other goods in town and go to work in town so we could just as easily shop for food from specialist individuals.

Buying fruit and vegetables is not just about buying things that are grown locally but being able to talk to the person you are buying them from, feel and smell and even taste the foods. Fruit and vegetable growers are obliged by trading standards to label where the items are from and they do so much more openly than supermarkets, with big bold writing on chalkboard signs among the fruit and vegetables so you know where it's from, can find out for yourself how it feels, smells and tastes, and you're much less likely to be disappointed. Buying local is not about trying to source Cornish pineapples or coffee grown in poly-tunnels in Dorset, it is about being able to correctly judge what you are about to hand over your hard-earned cash for. Purchasing locally can also benefit the community by keeping its money flowing through its own systems rather than those of multinationals on other continents.

As this is my first book what I'd really like to achieve is something user-friendly for people who love to cook, eat and entertain, but also to help them relax and enjoy the cooking without feeling under pressure with recipes too complicated for home kitchens. As I do all the cooking at home I'm aware that people don't have 100-litre stock pots to make veal jus so I've tried to keep the stocks and sauces as they should be, simple.

The dishes I have chosen are ones that throughout the year mark the seasons for me as a cook, things that I look forward to cooking and eating at home and at work, although you have to forgive me for occasionally being a bit showy in the presentation of some of the dishes, it's a hard habit to break!

SPRING

Springtime for cooks is a great time of optimism. The snowdrops have been and gone and the wild garlic and bluebells fill the woods. Asparagus takes pride of place on the menu and the mind turns to young shoots and the anticipation of the first new potatoes with their clean, earthy smell and the first tiny emerald broad beans that add their fluorescent green vibrancy to our dishes. Fish have long since spawned and have fattened up again and the spring lambs are plentiful. In short, it's a time that makes a cook smile again.

A Very Simple Wild Garlic Soup

What I love about this soup is its freshness. It has to be made and eaten straightaway to be really appreciated. I find the flavours deteriorate if it's chilled and reheated, although if you cool it down quickly on ice it makes a lovely chilled soup with a little crème fraîche; but I prefer it hot with crusty bread and a thick layer of butter. What I usually do is put the stock on before I pick the wild garlic so it's ready to make my lunch when I get back.

SERVES 4

1 chicken carcase
1 litre cold water
1 onion, peeled and halved
1 clove of garlic, peeled and split
small pinch of chilli flakes (optional)
500 g wild garlic
50 g butter (unsalted)
salt and fresh white pepper

Before you make the stock pour boiling water over the carcase in the pan and bring to the boil and drain. This gets rid of any nasties in there and makes for a more pure stock. Then pour over the cold water, add the onion, garlic and chilli flakes. Bring up to a slow simmer, skim off any scum that forms and leave on a lower simmer for 1½ to 2 hours. Strain the liquid and measure 700 ml into a clean pan.

Thoroughly wash the garlic leaves in cold water and drain. Remove the stalks and finely chop them. Add them to the stock and bring back to a rolling boil. Meanwhile, cut the garlic leaves into rough pieces and add to the stock with the butter and allow to boil for a further 2½ minutes then pour into a blender and blend for 3 full minutes.

Season with salt and white pepper to taste and pour into bowls and eat! Do not strain this soup or it will be watery.

Lamb Chops with Wild Garlic and New Potatoes
SERVES 2

10 small scrubbed new potatoes – any of the first of the new season will be good for this dish just as long as they're nice and fresh. Radiated imported ones won't cut the mustard
6 leaves and stalks of wild garlic
oil or lard for frying
4 lamb chops
75 g lamb trimmings (not too fatty)
100 ml water
50 g unsalted butter
1 heart of a spring cabbage
sea salt and fresh pepper

Boil the new potatoes in seasoned water with the stalks from the wild garlic. When the potatoes allow a fork to puncture the skin with ease, pull them off the heat and cover.
Meanwhile, in a frying pan heat some fat over a medium heat and add the lamb chops and trimmings. With a pair of tongs or 2 forks turn the chops and trimmings until they have a nice chestnut brown colour, then lower the heat and remove the chops, wrap them in foil, and put them in the oven switched on to pilot so they don't over cook but keep warm. Gather a few sheets of paper towels and crumple into a ball. Tilt the frying pan so all the oil tips to one end, then with the tongs and paper towels dab up all the excess fat. Return the pan to the heat, add the water, and with a wooden spoon scrape all the sediment from the bottom of the pan so no flavour is wasted. Add 25 g of the butter and stir in and reduce until they emulsify (come together as one liquid). Strain into a sauceboat and cover, and discard the lamb trimmings. Set aside the frying pan for later, but do not wash it as you will waste the flavour.
Bring the potatoes back up to boil then add the cabbage heart and garlic leaves to the pan. When it comes back to a rolling boil, drain the whole lot in a colander. Add the remaining 25 g of butter to the frying pan and heat until melted. Then tip in the potatoes and vegetables, season and toss together. Take the lamb chops from the oven and unwrap. Spoon the potatoes and vegetables onto two plates, put the chops on top, and pour the gravy at the table so it doesn't skin.

Lamb chops with wild garlic and new potatoes.

RISOTTO OF WILD GARLIC AND KING PRAWNS
Risotto! That's not British I hear you cry, but neither is a lasagne or pizza but when they're done right they are great. As far as I'm concerned a British cook, cooking in Britain, using the best of what's local and the best of what's imported, is cooking British food and I personally couldn't imagine cooking without some sort of inspiration from foreign lands. With risottos, for me the most important part of getting it right alongside using the right rice and a good stock is care and attention. Stay with it from the beginning, don't walk away from it for 1 minute or you'll get an uneven finish with some grains cooked and some not. Plus, it's how you learn about food and the cooking process by watching it change through stages. To see the rice, stock and fat – whether oil or butter – come together and bind the rice, and the nice shine when it's ready to eat, is a great process to work through. Important things to remember for risotto are: buy good quality Italian rice; make a good stock; take your time – if it starts to cook too quickly it may go stodgy – and serve the moment it's at its best and use hot plates. Generally use a good Parmesan to finish, but as we are using garlic and prawns for this dish we won't use Parmesan as it will become just another flavour.

As far as a perfect recipe for risotto goes, it is as long as a piece of string, because it depends on the kind of rice and its own liquid content as to how much stock you need. So I recommend you always have a lot more stock than you could possibly need and if there is any left over you can freeze it for another time. The three most popular types of rice from the Pavese area are Carnaloni, Arborio and Vialone Nano. Carnaloni is thinner and more delicate than Arborio, which has a bigger, fatter grain, and the Vialone Nano is smaller than both, almost like a pudding rice. It is the preferred type of grain used for seafood risottos, but if you can only find one of the other types I wouldn't worry too much; although there is a slightly different end product it won't be the end of the world.

SERVES 4 AS A STARTER OR 2 AS A MAIN COURSE

12 whole raw king prawns or tiger prawns
splash of dry white wine
1 litre water
4 or 5 wild garlic leaves, washed in cold water, stalks removed and leaves chopped
pinch of mild chilli flakes (Turkish are good as they are dried without seeds)
2 cloves of garlic, crushed
1 small onion, finely chopped
25 g unsalted butter
200 g risotto rice (risotto rice is pre-washed so unlike other rice you don't need to wash it)
salt and paprika

Peel the prawns and put aside all the heads and shells. Make a thin cut along the back, curved edge of each prawn, wash under cold water and refrigerate.

In a saucepan on a medium heat add a little olive oil then the heads and shells and slowly fry until they have turned completely pink, crushing them with a wooden spoon to release all the flavour from the heads. When it starts to colour on the bottom of the pan add a little white wine. Stir well then cover with 1 litre of water, add the stalks of the wild garlic and pinch of chilli flakes and the crushed garlic. Allow to simmer for 30 minutes before you strain the stock through a fine sieve and bring back up to a boil ready for the risotto.

Choose a pan with deepish sides to allow the rice to swell and a thick bottom: nothing too flimsy so it doesn't catch on the bottom. On a medium heat sweat the onions slowly in a little of the butter with a little salt so they don't colour as quickly, and use a lid in between stirring, which will also prevent them colouring. When they are translucent add the rice and stir thoroughly. When the rice takes on a shine start to add the hot stock a little at a time, stirring carefully but regularly and replacing the lid between stirring. Each time the stock has almost gone add another small ladle-full, keeping on a medium heat, and carefully stir the rice with a wooden spoon or a heat-resistant spatula so as not to damage the grains. With a metal spoon the hard edges tend to break up the grains releasing all their starch and making the risotto stodgy.

When the rice has started to swell and shine nicely, taste to make sure there's not too much bite then fold in the prawns and the chopped wild garlic leaves, a knob of butter or a little olive oil. Season to taste with salt and a little paprika, if preferred. The prawns will plump up nice and pink, and the moment they do serve straight away so they don't deflate and over cook.

Goat's Cheese with Wild Garlic and Carrot Marmalade

I have personally never been a great fan of cheeses with added bits such as herbs and fruit, especially unpasteurised cheeses made by craftsmen to be enjoyed in their own right and usually as an excuse to enjoy a fortified alcoholic beverage. So with this recipe I'm kind of breaking my own rules, but really it's more of a cheese spread to be enjoyed as a snack on some toast or biscuits, or as a starter with a chutney, or even as a sandwich filling. I'm including a recipe for carrot marmalade as its sweetness lends itself to the sharpness of the goat's cheese, and with a peppery leaf like rocket or watercress it makes a nice light lunch or starter. I personally prefer Golden Cross for its nice dry acidity but you can use any really.

However, bear in mind the harder the goat's cheese the more yoghurt you'll need to add and vice versa. To lift the goat's cheese flavour above that of the wild garlic I've added a little yoghurt to help keep its tartness.

SERVES 2

1 Golden Cross goat's cheese, cut into small pieces
3 wild garlic leaves and stalks, finely shredded
1 tbsp of goat's or Greek still yoghurt
salt and fresh pepper

Crumble the goat's cheese into a food processor with the wild garlic, yoghurt and seasoning and blend until the mix turns a pale green. Turn off and check the seasoning and if correct scoop the mix into moulds or roll in greaseproof paper to make a log that you can slice.

It is best eaten within the first three days or the garlic may start to deteriorate.

Carrot Marmalade

4 carrots, grated (as fresh as possible)
whatever the weight of the carrots add ¾ the weight in jam sugar
whatever the weight of the carrots add the equivalent in millilitres of water and about ¼ in white wine or cider vinegar: so 500 g of carrots = 500 ml of water and 100 ml vinegar
3 cardamom pods
1 peeled strip of orange peel finely sliced

Put everything in a pot and simmer until the carrot starts to go opaque and the syrup takes on a look of hot marmalade. It takes quite a while but don't be tempted to turn the heat too high and rush it as it easily catches and if over reduced it will crystallise. While still hot, poor into a sterile jar and seal. Once sealed it should keep for months.

EASTER SUNDAY STEW

If you're lucky enough to have Easter weekend off and the weather is crisp but with a bright blue sky this is a great family feast after a good walk across the fields or through the woods. A big lunch in preparation for an afternoon of the weekend papers!

SERVES 4 AS HEARTY PORTIONS

2 hind legs of rabbit
2 neck fillets of spring lamb
2 chicken legs
1 onion, peeled and quartered
2 cloves of garlic, peeled and split
1 stick of celery, roughly chopped
1 carrot, peeled and roughly chopped
2 bay leaves
1 sprig of thyme
1 litre of water
8 Pink Fir potatoes or Blue Congo (whichever blue variety), peeled
50 g butter
50 g plain flour
1 bunch of young carrots, peeled
2 small turnips, peeled and cut into wedges
1 bunch of spring onions, washed and trimmed of excess green and roots
10 young wild garlic leaves, washed
1 spring cabbage, stalk and outer leaves removed and remaining leaves cut into ribbons
salt and pepper

Put the meat, onion, garlic, celery, carrot and herbs into a stew pot or a large earthenware pot, cover with the water and add a little salt and pepper. Place on a low heat with a lid and allow the meat to poach very gently for 2½ hours. Gently simmer the potatoes for about 20 minutes until tender then cool down in cold water and cut into rough pieces.

Drain the contents of the stew pot through a colander and pick the meat from the bones. In the same pan melt the butter until bubbling then beat in the plain flour and cook until bubbling like hot sand. Slowly add the strained cooking liquor until you have a silky sauce. Add the young carrots and turnip and simmer for 2 minutes, then add the spring onions, wild garlic, cabbage and potato and flake in the meat and simmer for a further 2–3 minutes. Serve straight from the pot.

CHOCOLATE PECAN BROWNIES
MAKES 10 HUGE CHUNKS OR 20 DAINTY PIECES

225 g dark chocolate
4 whole eggs
300 g caster sugar
225 g butter, melted
75 g plain flour
75 g cocoa powder
½ tsp table salt
200 g chopped pecans

Preheat the oven to 150°C. Melt the chocolate in a bowl over a pan of simmering water or on low in a microwave. Meanwhile beat the eggs and sugar together then beat in the butter. Sift in the flour, cocoa powder and salt and fold together with a spatula. When the chocolate has completely melted, fold into the mix, and lastly, fold in the pecans. Spread on a baking tray lined with greaseproof paper and bake until a knife comes out clean, about 20–25 minutes. Cut while still warm and allow to cool before you pig out!

COOK'S TIP
The brownies will keep for 2–5 days in a sealed container in a dry cool cupboard.

Spring in the Air

One of the great turning points in my year, especially as far as menu planning is concerned, is the day when my first asparagus supplier phones me to say the first box will be arriving in two weeks. It's such a relief, like you've been marooned and there is a boat on the horizon. It truly is a turning point where all your favourite dishes come rushing back, as well as the ones you didn't get round to trying last season. The thing with asparagus is not to get too cocky with it. For myself I prefer the really thin-stemmed variety for its crispness and slightly 'oniony' flavour, which the Dutch hybrids don't come near: they are grown for speed and mass production, although they still make a good second best. Generally they need a little more of the skin peeling off, probably just above halfway, otherwise you have to over cook them to break down the fibrous skin. The thinner variety are delicate enough to eat raw so peeling is not needed and only 1 minute in boiling water is plenty long enough to cook them through. The longer you cook them the less interesting and more mundane the flavour becomes. So, like I said, the bigger they are the more you need to peel towards the spear so it will cook quicker and not affect the flavour. This mayonnaise recipe is perfect with little tiny raw spears of asparagus.

MAYONNAISE

juice and zest of 1 unwaxed lemon
2 tsp salt
1 tsp paprika
2 tsp honey
3 egg yolks
1 tbsp English mustard
250 ml grape seed oil or a mild olive oil

Put the juice, grated zest, salt and paprika in a small milk pan and dissolve together over a warm heat. Add the honey and when it has dissolved, remove the liquid from the heat and chill. Cool a round-bottomed mixing bowl and place inside a wet cloth rolled into a ring so it doesn't move when you whisk. Add the egg yolks and mustard and whisk together then add the chilled liquid and whisk to combine, then slowly mix in the oil until it comes together in a nice thick shiny sauce. If the mix starts to split add a little boiling water and whisk quickly. Hopefully this will balance the temperature and help the mixture emulsify. If this doesn't work throw it in the bin and mix some lemon juice, zest and paprika in some shop-bought mayonnaise and open a bottle of wine!

> COOK'S TIP
> When making any dressing or sauce that requires emulsification of oil or fats with liquids, such as mayonnaise or hollandaise, always dissolve your salt in the liquid first and then your sweetener, like honey or sugar if required, because salt doesn't dissolve in oils and fats so the seasoning is not dispersed evenly if you don't and if you add the honey or sugar at the same time as the salt it also makes the liquid denser and prevents the salt from dissolving.

ASPARAGUS WITH SMOKED SALMON AND RUNNY EGG DRESSING

This next recipe is more of a combination of things that work well together than a recipe, so the quality of the ingredients is of the utmost importance.
SERVES 2

The primrose flowers used as decoration place this dish firmly in spring.

Thinly sliced smoked salmon (if I don't smoke my own I buy them from Brown and Forrest in Hambridge but if possible look for a smoker who is local to you and is not driven by mass production)

12 spears of your local asparagus (peeled if it's thick)
2 fresh farm eggs
1 wedge of lemon
20 chives, chopped (with flowers or buds for garnish if possible)
Malden sea salt and fresh black pepper

Arrange the smoked salmon in ribbons in the centre of two plates. Put two pans of water on to boil, one for the eggs, one for the asparagus. When the water is boiling gently drop in the eggs and time for 3 minutes. When the timer has 2 minutes gone drop the asparagus into the other pan with a sprinkle of salt. When the timer goes off drain the asparagus, and put the eggs into cold water to prevent cooking just for 30 seconds. Then (if you wear a rubber glove it is not as hot to hold) cut the top off each egg and scoop the contents into a bowl and mix with a fork, season with salt and fresh ground black pepper and a small squeeze of lemon. Lay the warm asparagus on the smoked salmon, spoon over the runny egg mix and sprinkle with lots of chopped chives, and if you have them in the garden sprinkle over the flowers for garnish and eat as quickly after serving as possible.

> COOK'S TIP
> To add a touch of spring, finish with some primrose flowers for garnish.

Rosemary Moorehouse picking the first asparagus.

ASPARAGUS SOUP

Ask anybody who is in the business of buying and working with top quality ingredients and they will tell you how important waste management is, and this also translates to home, because if you've paid good money for something it is satisfying to get the most from it and the oldest trick in the book is making soups, something I really love to do.

There are lots of different ways of making and thickening soup but for this recipe I prefer the 'velouté' method using a flour and butter roux. This method fell out of favour a little as it takes a little more love than just chucking it all in a pan with potato and boiling it silly. It also contains the dreaded gluten, which seems to be the spawn of Satan at the moment, but I don't have a problem with gluten, so this is my preferred method.

SERVES 4

bones from one chicken, blanched for 30 seconds in boiling water
750 ml water
50 g unsalted butter
50 g plain flour
1 shallot, peeled and diced
1 clove of garlic, crushed
100–150 g asparagus peelings and trimmings (not the wood end bits). If you don't have enough trimmings you could make the weight up with English lettuce or even watercress
Malden sea salt and fresh white pepper
Cream or crème fraîche to taste

Cover the blanched chicken bones with the cold water and simmer very gently for 30 minutes then strain and discard the bones and keep the stock to one side.

In the same pan melt the butter over a gentle heat and slowly sprinkle over the flour and beat in with a wooden spoon or a spatula until nice and smooth and bubbling like a mud spring, then add the shallot and garlic and stir in for a few seconds. Slowly add the stock, ladle by ladle, stirring gently all the time until all the stock is incorporated and the velouté is silky smooth on the back of your spoon.

Chop your asparagus trimmings roughly and add to the velouté and simmer gently, stirring often for about 5 minutes, then blend in a food processor for 3 minutes. Strain through a fine sieve, season to taste with sea salt and freshly ground white pepper, and add a little cream or crème fraîche.

COOK'S TIP
If you cool the soup down in a bowl over ice, so it cools quickly, it can be stored for up to two days and reheated no problem.

Sautéed Monkfish with Pointed Cabbage and Cornish Rocket Potato in Rosemary Butter

Before cooking this dish read the method through and line up your ingredients on a tray in order of use before you start because this dish comes together all at the same time and being organised will help you not get flustered.

SERVES 2

6 chicken wings
300 ml water
10 small new potatoes, scrubbed (Cornish Rocket or Jersey Royals are good in May)
2 sprigs of fresh rosemary
pinch of seedless chilli flakes (it's milder when dried without seeds)
225 g monkfish at trimmed weight (ask your fishmonger to trim it)
40 g unsalted butter
1 small pointed cabbage, outer leaves removed and heart cut into sixths
sea salt and fresh black pepper

Chop the chicken wings and in a saucepan fry them in a little oil until golden brown. Remove the pan from the heat and dab away the fat with some paper towels. Put the pan back on a low heat, cover with the water and simmer gently. Cover the potatoes in water, add 1 sprig of rosemary and 2 teaspoons of sea salt, cover with a lid and cook slowly on a very gentle flame so they cook evenly. When a fork penetrates them with ease turn off the heat.

When the potatoes are cooked, strain the wings from the stock and in its original pan reduce the stock down to around 100 ml. Then add the chilli flakes, fresh black pepper and the other sprig of rosemary and reduce the heat to as low as possible.

Slice the monkfish into 2 cm thick medallions and in a sauté pan heat a little olive oil. Season the fish with sea salt and fresh pepper and lay the slices of fish into the hot oil and allow to colour a little on a medium heat then turn over. At this point turn up the heat under the stock to full and add the butter and the cabbage. Cover with a lid for 1 minute then pour the whole mix over the monkfish. Drain and add the new potatoes and like a stir-fry toss them all together and allow to reduce so the stock and the butter emulsify and glaze the fish and vegetables. Season to taste and adjust if necessary. Remove the rosemary sprigs and serve immediately.

COOK'S TIP

If you've got rosemary in the garden and it's flowering, pick some flowers to sprinkle over the dish as they will add a really punchy rosemary flavour as well as look pretty.

When using paper towels to remove fat if you have some tongs use them to hold the paper to reduce the risk of burning yourself. This method of removing grease from pans also reduces the risk of fat blocking your sink and making everything greasy during washing up.

STEAMED SEA BASS WITH HERB BRAISED LETTUCE, FRESH PEAS AND SCALLIONS

Once again this dish is all about timing so it retains it freshness. In the restaurant kitchen this kind of dish is referred to as a *la minuit* (French for minute) dish as it can only be cooked when the customer is ready for their main course. The only thing that can be done in advance is the stock, but at home I would make it all on the night so it all rolls together and makes the experience of cooking the dish more fulfilling.

SERVES 2

6 round-bottomed scallions (spring onions), trimmed and washed
1 stalk of basil, pick off the leaves but keep the stem
1 stalk of tarragon, pick off the leaves but keep the stem
1 clove of garlic, split
4 baby gem lettuces, washed and cut in half lengthways
100 g fresh peas, keep the pods (frozen petit pois are always a good alternative, see cook's tip)
100 ml water
2 110–150 g portions of sea bass, de-scaled and fin boned
40 g unsalted butter
sea salt, fresh black pepper and fresh nutmeg

Put a steamer on to boil. Cut the green stalks from the scallions and place in a saucepan with the basil and tarragon stems, the garlic, the outside darker leaves of the baby gems and, if you have them, the pea pods washed. Then cover the lot with the water and a lid and on a low heat bring to a simmer and cook for 15 minutes. Then strain and put the stock back in the pan and reduce down to around 100 ml before turning off the heat.

Rub the sea bass with a little olive oil and season with sea salt and freshly ground black pepper and wrap each portion individually in cling film. This helps the fish stay moist. Place in the steamer and set a time for 8 minutes.

Immediately put the lettuce, fresh peas and a quarter of the scallion bulbs into the stock with the butter on a full heat. Add the herb leaves torn up and a little fresh grated nutmeg and cover with a tight lid for 4 minutes. Then remove the lid and reduce the liquid until it comes together as a shiny butter sauce. If the 8 minutes is up before the sauce is ready just remove the fish from the steamer and leave on the side in the cling film. Divide the sauce between two bowls, unwrap the bass over the bowl so no juices are wasted, place on the sauce and eat straightaway. I personally like minted new potatoes with this dish but creamed potatoes work just as well.

COOK'S TIPS

If using frozen peas don't add them until the last minute. Also, make sure the lettuce is very fresh and moist. If the stalks look dry and a little reddish you will need to add a little water to the sauce because there won't be enough moisture in the lettuce to let down the stock as it reduces. If you see the butter start to bubble clear and crackle like water in hot oil quickly add a couple of tablespoons of cold water so it doesn't catch and burn.

JOHN DORY WITH A SORREL PURÉE AND BABY LEAVES, SHOOTS AND CRESSES

SERVES 4 AS A STARTER OR 2 AS A MAIN COURSE

400 g Maris Piper or Desiree potatoes, peeled and diced
500 ml whole milk
200 g baby spinach, washed
200 g sorrel, washed and stalk removed
2 300–400 g John Dory, filleted
2 tbsp virgin pressed rapeseed oil
1 punnet of pea shoots
1 punnet of baby sorrel
1 punnet of red mustard stalks
Maldon sea salt and pepper

Place the potato and milk in a sturdy pan and simmer on a very low heat until the potato is dissolving. Put the spinach and sorrel in a blender, pour over the milk and potato and blend for 3 minutes.

While this is blending heat a little cooking oil in a frying pan on a medium heat. If you think the pan may stick then lightly coat the fillets in a little seasoning flour first then gently fry until lightly coloured on the flesh side. Turn onto the skin side and cook for 1 more minute.

Season the purée to taste then spoon a little purée on each plate. Lay a fillet on top, drizzle rapeseed oil around the plate, sprinkle around some pea shoots, baby sorrel and red mustard and sprinkle a little Maldon salt on the plate for texture and seasoning.

Where Bread Comes From

The Romans? The baker? The supermarket? Or maybe the ancient Greeks! Where does bread come from? It comes from the same place as pastry. The mill. Flour produced in huge quantities from wheat bought from wherever is cheapest will do the job, but if you buy a mediocre product you'll only be able to make a mediocre product. Through my own ignorance I always used to buy French bread flour. It wasn't until one year I was at the Bath and West Show when I noticed one of the stalls had bowls of flour and stacked-up sacks. No gimmicks, no big flash photos and marketing, just brown paper bags full of brown flour and plain bowls filled with wheat and flour in the various stages of grinding. I thought to myself, they have either got no idea how to sell their product or it is so good it will sell itself. I sifted the flour through my hand and squeezed a tight fist and as I released my fingers the flour had set in a mould just with the warmth of my hand because it was so freshly milled and so full of life. The mill it comes from is called Burcott Mill, just outside Wells, and it has been involved in Somerset's flour industry for the best part of a thousand years, having been originally built for the Bishop of Wells in around AD750. Steam and the Industrial Revolution pushed it briefly into retirement for a few years around 1860 but it was soon in action again milling flour for a wealthy Victorian as a bit of a hobby. Then after a spell milling animal feeds for local farmers for about a century and after a complete restoration, which kept most of its machinery from 1864, including its impressive cast-iron water wheel, it now turns over 1 ton a week of stone ground wholemeal and spelt flour to sell all over Somerset. The miller behind its resurgence is the latest owner, Ian Burt, who, early in 2000, walked away from his city job as a high-powered and highly paid marketing exec. to join the growing force of good-life revolutionaries. Without a second's experience some might have thought it was a rather foolhardy move but with his will to learn the trade and a keen marketing eye he soon realised the growing trend towards organic and locally produced ingredients, so he sourced the very highest quality English wheat. The entire operation is now organic and like a true artisan he ensures every ounce of flour is milled, hand packed and hand labelled by him and him alone. There are now more than thirty farm shops and whole food stores throughout Somerset who sell his flour.

Basic Wholemeal Bread

Although the shelf-life of homemade bread is not that of shop-bought, sliced bread, even when it is too hard to make sandwiches it will always make better, crunchier toast. One hundred per cent wholemeal bread, with no chemicals and preservatives, can be a little heavy, but you can blend a little white bread flour in to lighten it slightly if you wish.

MAKES 1 500 G LOAF

500 g wholemeal flour (I use Burcott's extra fine)
10 g fresh yeast
10 g Malden sea salt
350 g water at room temperature

Crumble the yeast into the flour as if you're making pastry. Add the sea salt and mix in the water. The mix will be wetter than you expect but it will help lighten the bread. Using a plastic scraper, scrape the mix from the bowl onto a clean dry surface. Although it may stick a little, don't be tempted to throw flour everywhere, just use your scraper to scrape the mix together.

Making bread by hand has to be one of the most satisfying processes.

Lightly flour your hands and begin to work the dough fairly energetically so the starch absorbs the moisture, and keep working until it eventually forms a dough.

Roll into a lightly floured bowl, cover with a damp cloth and allow the dough to double in size. This will take anything from 45 minutes to 1½ hours depending on the temperature of your kitchen.

Tip the dough onto a very lightly floured surface, using a plastic scraper to help free it from the bowl, then lightly fold the dough. Don't be tempted to knead it with a heavy hand, this will knock out all the air: the term knocking back, which is often used at this stage, is a bit misleading, as you don't want to knock all the air out. When the dough feels springy and workable gently pat it down into a circle then fold and pinch the outside into the centre to make a bloomer shape so it is a kind of oval. Using your scraper to help pick it up, manoeuvre the dough onto a baking tray, cover with a dry tea towel and leave to prove until it has nearly doubled in volume – up to one hour.

Pre-heat the oven to 180°C. Spray water onto the dough – this will help the crust – and dust the surface with a little flour. Bake in the oven, spraying a little water while it's in the oven every now and then to help it crust, for about 30–40 minutes depending on your oven. You can tell if it's cooked as it will have a hollow sound when tapped. Leave to stand for 20–30 minutes before you smash into it.

PINK ROAST RUMP OF LAMB WITH GLAZED ROOTS AND DAUPHINOISE

SERVES 4

4 130–140 g lamb rumps
1 very small or ¼ of a large celeriac, peeled and diced
2 bunches of young turnips, peeled and halved or 1 medium turnip, peeled and diced
2 bunches of carrots, topped and peeled
1 small swede, peeled and diced
sprig of rosemary
200 ml water
50 g butter
2 tsp sugar
salt

Season the lamb rumps with just salt and brown together in a little lard on a medium heat in a pot with a lid that fits. Use tongs to brown the rumps so you get a good even colour. Turn off the heat, dab away the fat with paper towels, and replace the lid and allow to rest for 12–15 minutes. During this time the residual heat in the pan should allow the meat to cook nicely pink and not allow any juices to evaporate. Remove the rumps from the pan and add a tablespoon of water and a knob of butter. Stir well to make a little sauce from the pan juices. While the meat is resting prepare the vegetables.

Place the vegetables and rosemary in a large broad pan so they are not piled too high and cook evenly, or in a frying pan that has a lid, then add the water and bring to a rapid boil with the lid fitted for 1 minute. Remove the lid and allow the water to evaporate on a more medium heat. As the water evaporates the vegetables will finish cooking then the butter and sugar will glaze them as you gently stir them. Carve your meat and spoon a little of the pan juices over the meat so no flavour is wasted and serve with the Dauphinoise potatoes.

DAUPHINOISE

Dauphinoise is a classic accompaniment with roast lamb but over recent years restaurants have taken to serving it cut out in rings for presentation. This means it ends up with less cream, and less garlic and cheese, which is a shame, as for me part of the luxury of dauphinoise is the rich, creamy, overly garlicky cream that the potato is cooked in. At the Savoy we used to have to make it for literally hundreds of people. I remember on one occasion myself and another young cook, Simon Rogers, were placed in charge of making sure sixty or seventy chinas, each china serving ten people, while the sous chefs were running a book on how many we would burn! When you consider they were split between about ten ovens on two floors it wasn't very easy at all, and we had to patch a few up to get a hundred per cent – because they had so much cream and cheese, they would over glaze and burn easily.
Make the dauphinoise in advance if you're entertaining, that way you can keep an eye on it and if it's ready just before your guests arrive it fills the kitchen with a lovely smell.
SERVES 4

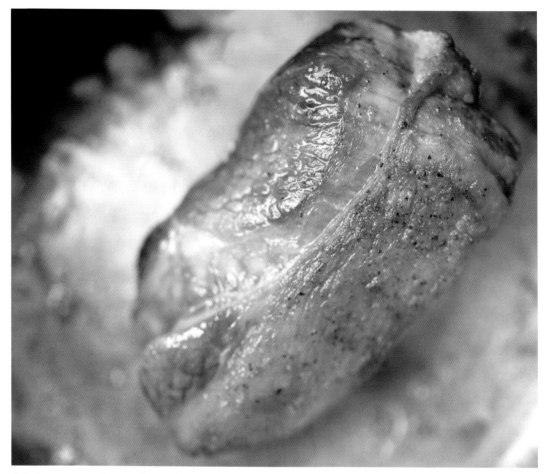

It is important to brown the lamb well to enhance its flavour before resting.

6 cloves of garlic
500 ml double cream
6 medium potatoes such as Maris Piper or
Desiree, peeled
200 g Jersey Shield, gruyère or emmental, grated
salt, black pepper and fresh nutmeg

Pre-heat the oven to 180°C. Smash 5 of the
cloves of garlic and simmer in the cream until it
has taken on a good flavour. Season to taste
with salt and freshly ground pepper and leave to
infuse. Slice the potatoes into fairly even slices
about ½ cm thick then rub the remaining clove
of garlic all over the surface of a pie dish.

Grate in some fresh nutmeg and a layer of
sliced potato, a small sprinkling of cheese and a
little seasoning. Repeat the process until the
dish is full then pour over the cream until it
comes to the surface. Give the dish a tap on the
surface to make sure the cream's gone right
through and add a little more cream if necessary. Sprinkle the remaining cheese over the
top, place the dish into a tray lined with a little
water so it doesn't catch on the bottom, and
bake in the oven. If it starts to over colour
before the potato is cooked, cover it with some
foil. It should take about 1½ hours, depending
on the potatoes and your oven.

Smoked Eel

When I first moved to Somerset and took on the Castle's kitchen, Mr Chapman, or the big wizard as he is respectfully known in the kitchen, used to continually cut out newspaper articles on West Country producers to make sure I was only buying from people who were the best.

One of the first of these discreet hints was a piece about a smokehouse called Brown and Forrest, where a chap called Michael was smoking eels. By all accounts they were a truly majestic product and something I should definitely try, especially as my experiences of the horrible, slimy, beady-eyed monster curling up my fishing line didn't represent the fondest of memories and or conjure up thoughts of something wonderful to eat. So I bought a whole eel via mail order and quite frankly it's never been off my menu since. Michael learned how to treat and smoke the eels in Germany in the 1980s before converting an old cider barn into a smokehouse at Bowdens Farm in Hambridge, a very beautiful and peaceful corner of the Somerset Levels where he hot smoked them over beech following the German method, but then added apple wood from local orchards to give the smoking a flavour of its own. The eels come from the chalk streams further south, the Itchen, the Test, the Avon and the Stour, where the river keepers catch them using an age-old method devised by monks. The trap is called an eel pack and is a metal structure like a giant comb set in areas of the rivers where the eels filter off downstream on their seasonal migration. They are completely wild fish which have grown to maturity in clear waters with plenty of food and are fattened up ready for their long journey ahead, which is what makes them perfect for hot smoking as the fat keeps them moist and gives a silky texture and succulent flavour. As Michael became more experienced he added

a cold smoker to the business to enable him to smoke salmon, poultry, cheeses, garlic and potatoes to broaden his produce range. In the late 1990s he attached a shop and restaurant where you can sample his goods with local ciders and wines. Four years ago Jess Pattisson and his wife joined Michael's business with a view to take over when Michael retired, which they have now done. Although Michael remains involved with the business he can now go home without the worries and I can tell you he has taught Jess well; I hope to be able to use his eels long into the future.

Steve Taylor preparing the eels for smoking.

SMOKED EEL PIE

This is made in the same way as a fish pie but because the eel is already cooked, no pre-poaching of the fish is needed. One small whole smoked eel should do for six good-sized portions.

SERVES 6

1 whole eel, skinned and filleted. Ask your supplier to send the bones and skin as well for the sauce if you're not preparing it yourself.
2 onions, peeled and halved
2 bay leaves
6 medium-sized potatoes such as Maris Piper or Desiree, peeled and halved
125 g butter
50 g plain flour
150 ml whole milk
3 medium-sized carrots, peeled and sliced
150 g spinach, washed
salt, fresh black pepper and fresh nutmeg

Cover the eel bones and skin and the onions with cold water. Add the bay leaves, bring to a simmer and gently cook for 30 minutes, skimming away any fat and scum on the surface. At the same time simmer the potatoes for the topping on a low heat so they cook evenly. When the stock has been cooking for 30 minutes turn off the heat and start your roux in a separate pan by melting 50 g of the butter until it's evenly bubbling. Stir in the flour to make a paste stirring constantly so it doesn't burn. Slowly strain in your stock one ladle-full at a time, making sure each one has been amalgamated before you add the next and stop when the sauce has reached a silky appearance on the back of your spoon. Cover with greaseproof paper and cook gently on a really low heat for 20 minutes.

Eels smoking on a rack over an apple wood fire.

Meanwhile, your potatoes should be soft enough to drain and pass through a food mill to remove any lumps. While it is still hot, beat in the rest of the butter and the milk with a wooden spoon or spatula then season to taste and cover with greaseproof paper. Boil the carrots in salted boiling water until they have not too much bite and refresh them in cold water. Blanch the spinach in the same boiling water for 30 seconds. Drain, refresh and squeeze out all the water. Flake the eel into your pie dish and mix with the carrot and spinach then pour over your sauce until the mix is just nicely covered. Chill for 30 minutes to let it set a little so you can spread or pipe on the potato topping.

Pre-heat the oven to 200°C. If the mash is cold, reheat it in a little hot milk and butter then spoon it onto the fish mix and spread it out so it completely covers the top. Use a piping bag and star nozzle if you prefer a fancier finish. I prefer to just brush the top with egg yolk and bake it for 15–20 minutes, but if you prefer you could sprinkle grated cheese over just before you put it in the oven to give a more savoury appeal. However, I find the eel does the talking and doesn't require many additions.

Carving an Eel

Carving an eel by hand takes skill and practice, so to be honest you are better off buying it pre-sliced or just buy a piece and flake it up by hand. Because eel carries a lot of very fine bones, we carve it ourselves at the Castle. We carve from the tail to the head, first peeling off the rubbery skin then filleting with a really sharp salmon carver. We cut thin slices of the eel almost like sushi, and every two or three slices we cut the end off so the slices don't have any trace of bones.

SMOKED EEL SALAD
SERVES 4

1 large carrot, peeled and grated or cut into spaghetti
2 tsp cider vinegar
1 tsp honey
200 g sliced smoked eel
red onion, peeled and sliced
1 bunch of watercress, thick stalks removed
horseradish cream
sea salt and fresh black pepper

A special technique is used when carving eel to avoid the pin bones.

Dress the carrot with a little salt and pepper, and marinate in the vinegar and the honey for a few minutes then gently toss with the eel, onion, and watercress. Arrange on your plates and finish with droplets of horseradish cream.

Smoked Eel with Scrambled Duck Egg and Spiced Oil

In my time at the Castle this dish has remained on the menu because I'm so fond of it. The eel from Brown and Forrest is an amazing product and, although eels are pretty mean looking creatures and not something people would automatically choose, once you've tried them there's no going back. I put this dish together with classic combinations of smoked fish and egg in mind, like smoked salmon and scrambled egg, kedgeree with its curry spices, and boiled egg and smoked haddock. The duck egg, with its richer taste and texture, the silky smoked eel and the spiced oil on a slice of crusty bread or toast, with or without a salad makes a great light lunch or supper.

SERVES 2

50 ml double cream
1 small shallot, very finely sliced
unsalted butter
2 fresh duck eggs or organic chicken eggs
slices of smoked eel
salt and fresh black pepper

FOR THE SPICED OIL
1 onion
4 cloves of garlic, chopped
250 ml rapeseed oil
1 tbsp ground cumin
1 tbsp turmeric
1 tsp cayenne
1 tbsp paprika
10 black peppercorns
1 tsp ground nutmeg
1 tsp ground ginger
1 tsp fennel seeds
1 tsp mustard powder

To make the spiced oil, sweat the onion and garlic in a little of the oil. Lightly toast the spices on a low heat in a dry frying pan until their aroma fills the room. Add the cooked onions and garlic and poor over the rest of the oil and stir gently. Leave on the lowest heat for 3 minutes. Remove the pan and allow to infuse for a few hours then strain through dampened kitchen paper and bottle. The oil will keep its flavour well for at least a month but keeps best refrigerated.

This method of scrambling eggs ensures the mixture doesn't go dry by allowing the egg to cook a little before we start to mix the ingredients. Bring the cream, shallot and a small knob of butter to a simmer and reduce them. Crack in the eggs on a very gentle heat until the white starts to cook a little. When it's about a quarter cooked, start to fold the mix together with a spatula or wooden spoon until it takes form. You will notice this method keeps little bits of the egg in chunks rather than a smooth purée: this helps keep it moist. Season to taste and spoon onto your toast, lay over some sliced eel and drizzle on some spiced oil.

Fried Smoked Salmon Parcels

These are a kind of pan-fried version of a toasted sandwich and they make a great starter or snack.

SERVES 2 AS A STARTER OR 4 AS A SNACK

8 slices of white bread, crusts off
100 g smoked salmon
butter
crème fraîche with a little orange zest and juice mixed in with it (optional)
fresh black pepper

Smoked eel with scrambled duck egg and spiced oil makes a great light lunch.

Place a slice of bread down on a clean surface and pat it down a little with the palm of your hand. Arrange a little circle of smoked salmon in the centre, leaving about 3 cm of bread uncovered around the edge. Season with freshly milled black pepper then lay a second slice on top. With the thick edge of a knife blade press down fairly hard around the edges to create a seal and trim off 5 mm excess of the rough edges to neaten them a little. Repeat until you have four parcels almost like giant ravioli. Fry them two at a time in butter until golden and serve with some crème fraîche that has a little orange zest and juice mixed in it.

Fillets of Huss in a Spring Vegetable and Herb Broth

Huss comes from the shark family and is sometimes seen on fish and chip boards as rock-salmon: it is also known as dogfish. It's a wonderful fish that keeps its moisture well and has a nice meaty flavour. There are different varieties, but good fishmongers tend to go for the spur dog rather than the smooth hound, or the even less appetisingly named 'stinker'.

This broth is finished with a herb purée, which gives it a vibrant green colour and a fragrant aroma. You should make more than you need, otherwise it will sit beneath the blade in the blender and won't purée smooth. Any left over can be used to flavour pasta or other soups and will keep refrigerated for up to 3 days. You can also freeze it in cubes to use again for the same dish.

SERVES 4 AS A STARTER

FOR THE HERB PURÉE
500 ml water
1 tbsp sea salt
1 bunch of flat parsley leaves (stalks retained for the stock)
30 tarragon leaves
30 basil leaves
30 coriander leaves
1 bunch of chives
3 wild garlic leaves (optional)

FOR THE STOCK
8 chicken wings
750 ml cold water
2 cloves of garlic, split
1 small onion, peeled and chopped
parsley stalks (from the herb purée ingredients)
6 white peppercorns

FOR THE BROTH
75 g carrots, peeled and finely diced
75 g swede, peeled and finely diced
75 g turnip, peeled and finely diced
4 75 g fillets of huss, all skin and bone removed
100 g plain flour (for coating the fish)
8 spring onions, trimmed and cut into quarters
6 spears of asparagus, trimmed of woody root and sliced into thin rings
mild-flavoured oil for cooking
sea salt and fresh black pepper

You will need to make the herb purée before the broth. Bring the water and salt to the boil, add the herbs and boil for 2 minutes. Drain quickly and blend on full power for 2 minutes then pour into a cold bowl and chill immediately.

Put the chicken wings in a sturdy pot, boil a full kettle of water and pour it over the wings. Quickly bring back to the boil on a high heat then drain away the liquid and cover the wings again with the cold water. Add all the other stock ingredients and bring to a simmer for 30 minutes. Allow to sit off the heat for 10 minutes then strain and discard the solids.

In a sturdy pot start to gently sweat the carrots, swede and turnip in a little oil until they start to soften, then pour over 400 ml of the stock and bring to a simmer. Meanwhile coat the fish fillets in a little salt and roll in the flour. Heat a frying pan with a little oil and fry them gently until golden on both sides. Then put them on to paper towels to drain. Add the spring onions and asparagus to the broth and boil for 1 minute. Place the fish in the centre of four breakfast bowls, add 4 teaspoons of the herb purée to the broth, season to taste and spoon over the fish and serve straight away.

COOK'S TIP
If you can't get huss then use the same weight of red gurnard, which is always a good cheap alternative.

SMOKED SALMON SCOTCH EGGS
MAKES 4 EGGS

4 free-range or organic eggs
300 g smoked salmon
flour, beaten egg and breadcrumbs for coating
fresh black pepper

Boil the eggs for 6 minutes. Drain, peel and cool down at room temperature. Chop the smoked salmon in a food processor and season with freshly ground black pepper. Lay a sheet of cling film down on your work surface and pat out about a quarter of the salmon mix. Place an egg in the middle and then, using the cling film, wrap the salmon around the egg and set in the fridge. Repeat with your other eggs. Leave in the fridge for 1 hour then peel away the cling film

and carefully roll each one in flour then beaten egg and then fine breadcrumbs. Leave to set for 10 minutes then deep fry until golden.

AIR-DRIED BARROW BOAR
Curing meat is no longer a common thing for anybody to do in professional and home kitchens as there are many other quicker and easier ways of preserving meats. For most of us, having pieces of salted meats wrapped in cloth hanging around in pantries and larders is not ideal. But for me it was a great way of getting more people to try the boar, as the saddle is a very expensive cut of the beast. By curing it and air drying I can slice it very thin like Parma ham or Coppa and thus offer it more reasonably priced to a broader public, whereas a roast joint would be a very expensive option. I recommend you don't try this in summer when your kitchen or larder will be too warm.
SERVES 6–8

1 kg boneless boar saddle
1 kg sea salt
500 g sugar
50 g crushed black pepper
50 g crushed fennel seeds
50 g crushed caraway seeds
a little apple brandy

Mix the dry ingredients together very well so the salt and sugar is evenly mixed then pack the loin in the mix until totally covered. Cover with something fairly heavy to press the cure in the meat and refrigerate for 2 days.

Wash off the meat and dry and brush with a little apple brandy then wrap in muslin cloth and tie. Allow to air dry for 10 days in a cool pantry. This is fantastic as a starter with fruit, cheeses, or as a light lunch with fried or scrambled egg on toast.

A Simple Pork Pâté

Potted meats, pâtés and parfaits are all variations of using up by-products of offal, excess fats, tough, sinewy cuts, and trimmings in the same principle as making sausages. By the same token prime cuts don't lend themselves to these sorts of preparations, although once again we professional cooks have been guilty through overt snobbery of using prime cuts blended with fat to create smoother mixes that are better on the eye – but not taste- and texture-wise. With experience you learn that appearance is not the main aim with what should be rustic preparations like these and there are various different methods. Some require you to cook the meats first and then bind them with eggs and cream but I find you loose the flavour of the meat juices and the little pockets of jelly created if you cook the pâté from raw. I don't recommend you go out and buy a mincing machine unless you love your gadgets. Instead, ask your butcher to mince for you. Instead of the normal terrine mould we might use at work you can use a bread tin or an oval or round china casserole dish. Traditionally cured fat sliced paper-thin is used to line the moulds but as this is not easy to obtain for home use instead you can use streaky bacon.

SERVES 10

500 g pork neck or shoulder, diced
250 g pork belly with no skin, diced
250 g pure pork fat, diced
100 g pig's liver, trimmed and diced
1 pig's kidney, trimmed and diced
½ nutmeg, grated
2 tsp garlic salt
2 tsp onion salt
3 tsp salt
5 tbsp apple brandy
18 slices of dry cured streaky bacon
150 g pork fat diced into small cubes but not to be minced
3 bay leaves
fresh back pepper

FOR THE STOCK

100 g pork and bacon trimmings
1 small onion, peeled and chopped
2 bay leaves
sprig of thyme
250 ml water
casserole dish that holds just over 1 kg of water when full

Start the process about 2–3 days in advance so it has time for the flavours to mature and the juices to settle.

Mix the pork neck and shoulder, belly, pure pork fat, liver and kidney with the nutmeg, garlic salt, onion salt, normal salt, apple brandy and 12 twists of fresh black pepper. Mix well and chill overnight.

On the same day lay the strips of bacon, two at a time in between 2 sheets of greaseproof paper and roll them out with a rolling pin so they spread out thinly. Line the mould so the ends meet in the middle of the bottom surface and there is enough overhang to pull over the pâté when the mould is filled later. Chill until needed.

Make the stock by frying the trimmings and onion until brown, then add the herbs. Pat away the excess fat with paper towels and pour over the water. Simmer for 30–40 minutes. Allow to cool naturally without straining, then strain and chill.

The next day mince, or have your butcher mince, your marinated meats on a medium

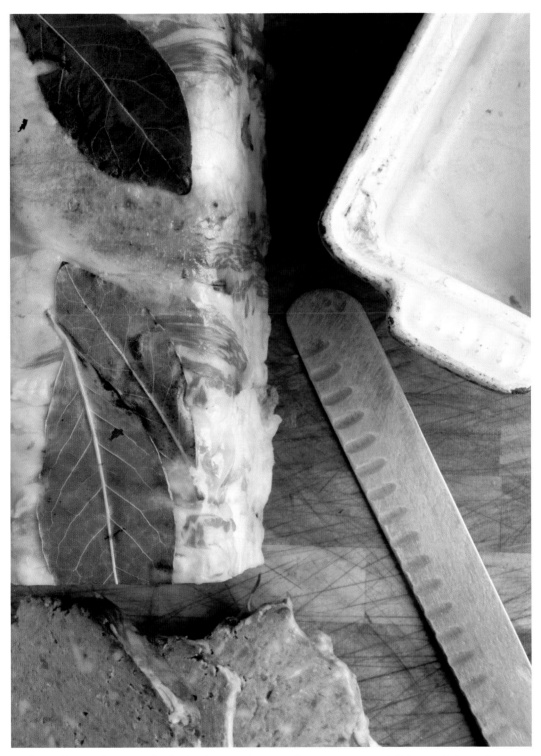

Pork pâté is a perfect example of using less popular cuts of meat to create a delicious and cheap dish.

grind, not too fine and not too coarse. If you're lucky enough to have a mixer that has a mince attachment make sure the meat is very chilled before you mince it and pass a sheet of grease-proof paper through at the end to push the rest of the meat through. If you have a hand mincer, cut the meat up into small pieces and chill before you mince so it's not such hard work and put a piece of greaseproof paper through afterwards to push out all the meat. Mix in the diced pork fat. Then mix by hand really thoroughly and make sure that your hands are scrupulously clean. Mix the stock in thoroughly and then take a little piece of the mix and make a tiny burger so you can fry it off and test the seasoning and adjust if you wish.

Pre-heat the oven to 170°C. Fill your lined mould, making sure not to have any air pock-ets, to about 1 cm below the top and fold over the bacon and cover with 3 bays leaves and the lid. Half fill a roasting tray with boiling water from the kettle and lay in an old tea towel and place the dish on top (this will prevent the cut side of the mix over cooking). Bake in the oven, checking after about 1 hour with a skewer. If the skewer is hot on your lip after being inserted into the middle of the pâté, remove and leave to cool for an hour. If the mix is still cold put it back in and check every 10 minutes. Once the pâté has cooled slightly you can either press down with a weight if you want to de-mould the pâté and slice, or leave it and just scoop it from the mould after it's matured for a day or so. Although in England we like our pickles and chutneys, some crusty bread and a few gherkins and pickled onions will be just as good. Nevertheless, I've included an apple chutney for the diehards on page 193.

The Fish Cake Phenomenon

Part of my duties at the Castle was to take on and run its popular brasserie, Brazz, as it's called. But for my first three or four years the Castle's restaurant took up all of my time and the brasserie ran itself. But as time went on and we became a sounder, more organised unit in the Castle, the more time I could spend trying to bring Brazz up to speed. It was during that time spent there that I witnessed the phenomenon that is people's obsession with fish cakes. We sell literally thousands; in fact we actually have a guy, Sall 'the fish cake' Fonsela, who just makes them because they take up so much time. On occasions in the past we've run out of them and people have got up and walked out! You can have fish and chips, grilled Dover sole, moules marinière, fish pie – all English favourites – and fish cakes will still outsell them.

The recipe we use only includes salmon, as I find other white fish can go dry. Also, importantly, we do not use too much potato; it should be 60–70 per cent fish to 30–40 per cent potato, as the potato is the binding agent not the main ingre-dient. We also do not put in too many other ingredients to muddle the flavour. Herbs such as dill, chervil and coriander are far too overpow-ering and too much of them can ruin a dish when all you need is good ingredients and accu-rate seasonings. The salmon is the same as we use for smoking and the one that Jess at Brown and Forrest uses for his smoked salmon. It comes from Loch Duart at the top of Scotland, well known for sustainable farming methods.

FISH CAKES
SERVES 2

200 g salmon fillet
100 g mash using potatoes that have been sim-

mered slowly, skin on and peeled while hot and mashed with a hand masher to retain a little texture
3 spring onions, finely sliced
Malden sea salt, fresh white pepper and a pinch of cayenne
Plain flour, beaten egg and milk, and fine bread-crumbs in separate bowls for the coating

Season the salmon and sear in hot olive oil in a pan that won't stick. When it's golden on both sides but still raw in the middle, lift the fish into a bowl and allow to cool down. The residual heat will allow the fish to finish cooking in the bowl and still keep pink and moist. When cool mix with the mash, onions, a pinch of cayenne and salt and pepper to taste. Mix everything gently with your fingertips so you don't pound the fish too small and you'll get a better texture. Separate into 75 g balls and shape into little cakes using a little flour and a palate knife. Roll each one through the flour then the egg then the crumbs then back through the egg mix and again through the crumbs. Reshape with a palette knife.
They can then be either deep-fried until golden and flashed through a medium oven, or pan fried in fairly deep oil or butter and again flashed through the oven for a few minutes. The two most popular accompaniments at the restaurant are lemon butter or tartare sauce.

Lemon Butter

4 tbsp water
juice and zest of 1 lemon
1 tsp sugar
3 tbsp double cream
75 g cold butter, diced
salt and cayenne pepper

Reduce the water, juice and zest of the lemon,

and the sugar down until there's only a little liquid left. Add the double cream and reduce by half. Season with a little salt and cayenne pepper and whisk in the butter until you have the consistency of runny custard then strain and serve. Do not boil the sauce, as all the fats and liquids will separate and you'll have a greasy mess.

Tartare Sauce

3 egg yolks
2 tbsp cider vinegar
1 tbsp English mustard
200 ml rapeseed or grape seed oil
1 tbsp washed and chopped gherkin
1 tbsp capers
1 tbsp finely chopped shallots
1 tbsp fresh chopped parsley

Whisk together the egg yolks, cider vinegar and mustard in a bowl on a cloth so the bowl doesn't wobble. Slowly whisk in the rapeseed or grape seed oil until you have a mayonnaise then the gherkins, capers, shallots and parsley and mix well. You could add a grated boiled egg as well but with fishcakes I find it makes the sauce a bit heavy.

Fish Pie

To make a really good fish pie, like shepherd's and cottage pie, as with most simple rustic dishes, they do require a bit of love, care and attention in preparation but they are great dishes to make in advance for informal suppers or lunches as all you have to do is reheat.
SERVES 6

6 Maris Piper or Desiree potatoes, scrubbed
200 g salmon, skinned
200 g cod, skinned
fresh parsley

Fish pie is understated but can be delicious when made with fresh, local produce.

fresh tarragon

2 small onions, peeled and diced

1 clove of garlic

30 scrubbed mussels

100 g butter

50 g plain flour

150 ml whole milk

200 g prawns

100 ml double cream

2 egg yolks

salt, fresh white pepper and cayenne pepper

Put the potatoes on to boil just as you start to prepare the dish. Bring a pan of seasoned water to the boil and drop in the salmon and cod, turn off the heat and leave to stand for 1 minute. Take the fish from the liquor and chill on a plate covered with cling film. Bring the liquor up to a boil and skim away any scum. Add a sprig of parsley and tarragon, the chopped onion and garlic then simmer for 10 minutes. Using a little of the stock, steam the mussels in a pan with a tight lid until they are all open then drain the juice back into the stock. Remove the mussels from the shell and refrigerate. Melt 50 g of the butter and stir in the flour over a low heat until it bubbles evenly then slowly add the unstrained stock a ladle at a time until you have a sauce that coats a spoon. Allow to cook for 20 minutes and strain through a fine mesh sieve and cool to room temperature.

While this is cooling you can finish the topping. Pre-heat the oven to 175–180°C. Drain and peel the skin from the cooked potatoes using rubber gloves to protect from the heat and then pass the potato through a food mill. Melt the rest of the butter in the milk and pour over the potato and beat together and season to taste then spoon into a piping bag. If you put

the bag in a jug first, allowing the bag to overhang the lip of the jug, it will be easier to fill. If you haven't got piping bags you will have to spread it on. Break up the salmon and cod into flakes and mix with the prawns and mussels, picked tarragon leaves and chopped parsley (don't chop the tarragon or it will be too strong). Add the double cream, pour over some of the sauce and mix well, but not too much sauce, just enough to bind. Season to taste with salt and fresh milled white pepper and a little pinch of cayenne and spoon the mix into a pie dish and smooth it over. Pipe or spoon over your creamed potato. Lightly brush the surface with egg yolk and bake in the oven: make sure the oven temperature is not too high or the top will burn before the mix is hot. If you're making the pie in advance and heating it from the fridge it will need a little longer to heat through. Serve the remaining sauce separately, finished with the herbs and seasonings, for those who like extra sauce.

FILLETS OF COD WRAPPED IN DENHAY HAM WITH SPINACH PURÉE AND BAKED POTATO
SERVES 4

4 130 g cod fillets

8 slices of Denhay air-dried ham

8 sage leaves

4 medium baking potatoes, scrubbed

1 litre water

2 tbsp salt

200 g baby spinach, washed

butter

salt, fresh black pepper and nutmeg

Pre-heat the oven to 180°C. Wrap each piece of fish in 2 slices of the ham with 2 leaves of sage in between the fish and the ham and refrigerate until needed.

Prick the potatoes, oil them very lightly so salt will stick and season. Bake until the skin is crisp and they are soft to a fork (about 1½ hours) then turn the oven right down to keep them warm.

Bring the water and salt up to a boil. Add the spinach and boil for 1 minute then drain in a colander and into a blender. Blend the spinach for 3 minutes then place into a shallow bowl and put in the fridge to cool quickly.

Lightly fry the fish enough to crisp the skin then remove the potatoes from the oven, raise the oven temperature to 200°C and put the fish in for 4 minutes. Meanwhile, cut the potatoes in half and scrape the potato into a bowl. Add a few knobs of butter, season with salt and pepper and mash with a fork. Heat the spinach purée up in a little melted butter and season to taste with salt and nutmeg. Spoon a circle of purée onto the plate then potato in the middle and then the fish on top and drizzle over any pan juices.

West Country Cheeses

Cheese-making to mere mortals like myself is a bit like electricity. I know basically where it starts but the rest of the process might as well be magic; it just happens in a mystical way. But in reality very clever people make electricity and very clever people make cheese and it would seem that there are quite a few of these people in the West Country, and over the last twenty years or so the cheese-makers around here have really dusted themselves off and decided to give the rest of Europe a run for its money.

One of the most important cheeses is Montgomery's cheddar made by James Montgomery at his farm in North Cadbury, Somerset. It is arguably one of the best cheeses in the world and I can tell you Mr Chapman would put himself forward as a self-confessed Monty's addict. It has a delicious nutty flavour that, because it isn't a standardised product, changes like a good wine. Every batch you try may differ from day to day and all are rigorously tasted and quality checked. James also makes a cheese using milk from his mother's Jersey herd called the Jersey Shield, which is one to watch out for in the future as it is an excellent cheese. It is also used by Bill Oglethorpe who washes it in brine to create a washed rind called Ogle Shield. It's difficult to find but specialists like the famous Neil's Yard Dairies, or Longmans Cheese, Paxton & Whitfield, and the Bath Fine Cheese Co. would be worth a try. There are many other dairies producing cheddar, a few using unpasteurised milk to compete with Montgomery's. Those who keep James's standards so high because of their own are people like the Keen family from Moorhayes Farm in Wincanton, Somerset, whose Keen's Cheddar is slightly sweeter than Monte's and is equally coveted as it resembles cheddar made by Richard Calver who also makes an excellent red Leicester-type cheese dyed with the annatto nut known as Westcomb Red.

Soft cow's milk cheeses that have a Francophile feel to them have also been mastered. Sharpham's Elmhirst, a very rich mould-ripened cheese that has a gooey runny centre when fully ripe is one of my favourites with crusty toast or oatmeal biscuits. The Sharpham Estate, which also produces some great wines, make Sharpham Rustic, a young semi-hard cheese with a nice creamy texture and fresh flavour. The Sharpham cheese similar to brie, such as Elmhirst, is beautifully rich and to be enjoyed with crusty bread and good wine. They also make the goat's cheese Ticklemore for Sarie Cooper and Robin Congdon who couldn't make it any more because his own blue cheeses affected its ripening. Goat's cheese is not generally thought of as a blue cheese and

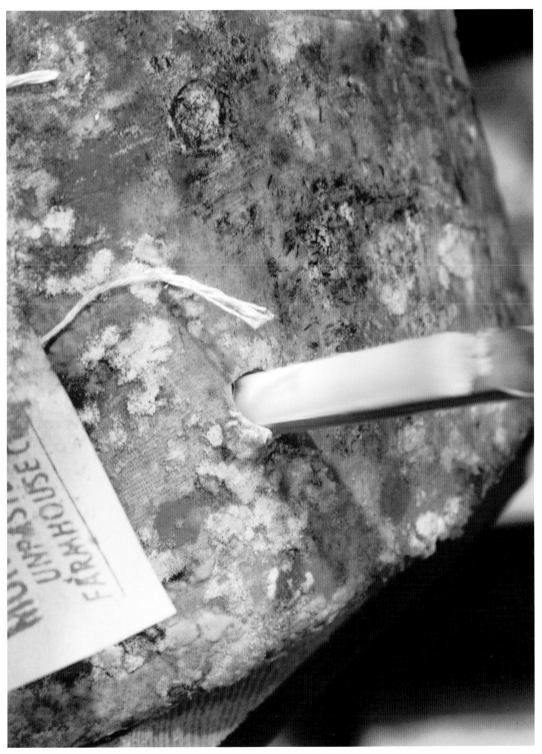

Montgomery's unpasteurised cheddar, one of the world's best cheeses.

The West Country now competes with the rest of the world for the finest cheeses.

is frowned upon by French cheese-makers, but Robin Congdon and his cheese-maker, Rick Trant, have done just that with their Roquefort-like Harbourne, made in Beenleigh just outside Totnes by incredibly inventive people who, to recreate the cave-like ripening process of Roquefort, buried a wine tank in a big hole. Their better-known blue is their ewe's milk Beenleigh Blue, which is their original cheese. This is a unique cheese worthy to compete with any French blue-veined cheese. Other unusual blue-veined cheeses well worth trying are Mike Davies' Dorset Blue Vinny made at Woodbridge Farm, Sturminster Newton, Dorset, which has a similar flavour to a good Stilton but to my mind it's a little more interesting, and another blue, the Exmoor Jersey Blue from Willett Farm, Lydeard St Lawrence, Taunton, which is a seasonally changing cheese from soft to firm and can be very buttery when soft. They make several other blues that are all good but the Exmoor to me is their best.

Goat's and ewe's milk cheeses are becoming ever more popular in an age when food fads have caused cow's milk to fall out of favour, along with wheat and gluten – so some good can come from fads. Barbara Johnson, a cheese-maker in the Cotswolds village of Cerney near Cirencester, makes the Cerney ash pyramids coated in oak ash and moulded like little pyramids, which have a wonderful, dry, smooth texture and an acidity good enough to win supreme champion at the 2000 British Cheese Awards above 700 other entries. Another cheese-maker who makes pretty special goat's cheese is Mary Holbrook, who now works for Neal's Yard watching over their maturing cheeses and is considerably respected for what she achieved with her great British goat's and ewe's cheeses such as Little Ryding,

and another ash-coated pyramid, the Tymsboro, both superb cheeses. She also invented the Tyning and Emlett and Old Ford cheeses named after her fields.

Each of these cheese-makers share an obsession with taste and experimenting with dairy products. Stinking Bishop is a perfect example of a kind of Gloucester cheese that's been washed in perry cider (a cider made with pears) and has a rather heady aroma and lovely orange colour and a surprising smooth and mellow flavour. It's made by Charles Martell using milk from his Gloucester cows. He also makes double and single Gloucester of which any artisan would be proud.

Other successes are Graham Padfield's Bath Soft and the Wyfe of Bath, Kelston Park and Bath Blue, which he created through trial and error over the years with great success. Then there is Annette Lee's Woolsery, a spreadable soft cheese and Catherine Mead's Cornish Yarg, similar in texture to a Caerphilly, except it's cleverly wrapped in nettle leaves to make it distinctive, and if you're talking about Caerphilly you have to mention Duckett's Caerphilly made in the Mendip hills, which has a special, slightly salty flavour.

I could just go on and on about all these really innovative people who mess around with mouldy milk to bring flavour to our inexperienced palates, and there are more and more great cheese-makers popping up, so it's up to us as consumers to experiment more with our eating habits and try as many different types as we can to keep the diversity flowing. Hopefully these special old and modern cheeses will keep going strong, along with many more than I've mentioned here just in the West Country. We shouldn't have to buy a foreign made cheese for quite some time.

Fried Ham and Cheese Sauce Parcels

These are a kind of handmade Breville toasty. They make a really moorish snack and quite smart little starters. The only downside is they only work with sliced white bread: wholemeal doesn't stick together and with seeded bread the seeds burn before the bread crisps.

SERVES 4

25 g butter, melted
25 g plain flour
250 ml milk, warmed
1 tsp English mustard
100 g strong cheddar
8 slices of good quality cooked ham (sliced off a joint not from a cellophane packet)
16 slices of white bread per person, crusts removed (this will give you 2 parcels each)
salt and fresh black pepper

Melt the butter until bubbling then stir in the flour until you have a paste that's bubbling. Slowly pour in the milk until you have a thick silky sauce. Add the mustard and the cheddar and stir until the cheese has melted into the sauce. Season to taste and leave to cool in a bowl. Cover the sauce with cling film so it doesn't skin over.

Fold the ham into squares about 5 cm x 5 cm. To make one parcel, pat a slice of bread down a little with the palm of your hand then place a piece of ham in the middle. Place a spoonful of the cold cheese sauce on top then lay another slice of bread on top and press down so the edges meet. Seal the edges of the sandwich with a rolling pin or the flat edge of a knife all the way around so it is sealed like ravioli. Repeat with the other parcels. Trim away the very edge of the parcels so they have no frayed edges. Heat a little butter in a frying pan until evenly bub-

bling then, only doing 3 or 4 at a time, fry until golden and crisp on a medium heat so as not to burn the butter. When the bread is crisp the cheese sauce inside should be molten and gooey so be careful when you bite in that it doesn't drip down and burn your chin.

Smoking Mackerel

Early spring is the best time for smoked mackerel as they are at their oiliest, so they stay moist and juicy and retain their flavour well. The easiest way to hot smoke at home is using a barbecue rather than splashing out on a smoking machine. At the Castle we use an old aluminium pot to burn the oak chippings over a gas ring with a wire rack on top. When it starts to smoke we put the brined fish on the rack, lay a sheet of greaseproof on the fish and then cover with tin foil and a lid. When the lid gets too hot to touch, the fish is done, but at home you don't have the extraction to suck away the excess smoke so a barbecue in the garden is much more sensible.

FOR 6 SMOKED FILLETS

200 g salt
100 g sugar
500 ml water
2 bay leaves
6 mackerel fillets

Simmer the salt, sugar, water and bay leaves until all the salt and sugar has dissolved then cool down. When cold, brine the fillets for a couple of hours then pat them dry. While they are brining don't just sit and wait, get the barbecue burning as you normally would. When it's burnt down to the coal embers sprinkle over fine oak shavings until they are covered and as they start to blacken and smoke lay the mackerel fillets skin side down on the rack and cover with the lid. Allow to smoke for about 30 minutes until the flesh is golden and cooked through. In a proper smokehouse this takes a few hours but the fish are much higher above the heat so the heat is not as intense as it is in a barbecue. If you don't want to smoke your own just go to Brown and Forrest and buy some.

Warm Smoked Mackerel with Spring Leaves, Potato, Shallot and English Mustard Dressing
serves 2

6–8 waxy potatoes (Pink Fir or Ratte potatoes), peeled
1 clove of garlic, finely crushed
1 tbsp cider vinegar, preferably Kingston Black
1 heaped tsp English mustard
1 tbsp honey
4 tbsp rapeseed or grape seed oil, or a mild olive oil
2 large smoked mackerel fillets
50 g soft butter
1 shallot, peeled and finely sliced into rings
1 sprig of parsley, chopped
2 small or 1 large spring lettuce such as Oakleaf, or baby gem, cored and washed in very cold water and spun
sea salt and fresh black pepper

Put the potatoes on a simmer in salted water. Whisk the garlic, vinegar and mustard with a little salt and fresh pepper until the salt has dissolved then add the honey and mix well. Slowly whisk in the oil until you have an emulsified dressing and put to one side.

When the potatoes are soft enough for a fork to penetrate turn off the heat and drain. Smear the mackerel with butter and grill until the butter is bubbling and crackling but not burnt. Then in a large salad bowl break up the potatoes with the back of a fork and mix in the shallot rings and a tablespoon of the dressing. Flake in the mackerel and add all the butter and sediment from the tray and gently toss together with the parsley. Arrange the lettuce in the centre of your plates and drizzle with some dressing then spoon the mackerel and potato mix in the centre. This simple dish is lifted with a nice cold glass of decent cider.

COOK'S TIP
Don't dress the soft leaves in a bowl like other more sturdy leaves as they will bruise and wilt.

SUMMER

The summer months bring us an explosion of colours and flavours that give us more variation in local ingredients than at any other time of year. Red berries and cherries make lighter desserts with a brighter appearance and a more natural sweetness. I also find people's attitude towards food changes. It is no longer just fuel but mood food that more suits people's cheery outlook through the summer holiday season, which in turn makes us feel better about what we're cooking. Lighter food is less laborious and quicker to prepare and everything seems that little bit more healthy and bright, which helps us through the long hot days in the kitchen.

Roast Beef – Not Just for Sunday

Towards the end of May when the wild garlic is
turning yellow and the blossoms have all but
gone from the trees and, if you're lucky, the
growers are cutting the last bit of asparagus,
summer is already in people's minds. Holidays
abroad are booked but there's still the hope that
the great British summer will arrive. We start to
get out our garden furniture and sit outside
wrapped in coats enjoying the lighter nights and
pretending it's warmer than it is. Everybody's on
a diet so that they can break out the shorts and
bikinis, so this is an ideal time for making use of
the amazing selection of vegetables and fruits
that we produce through these months. I do,
however, like to lower the tone a little with plenty
of butter and double cream, but these are
nothing a good walk through the fields in the
last of the daylight won't sort out.

Summer 'garden parties', if the weather holds
out, always turn out to be great occasions and a
summer roast always goes down well. My prefer-
ence is for a nice fat rib of beef roasted rare, but
if you prefer your beef well done without having
to endure grey, tough meat, choose a joint that
lends itself to slow cooking instead of ones that
are better served moist and pink such as sirloin,
rump, fillet and rib eye. Slow-cooking boned
and rolled brisket, chuck or the skirt rolled up
and then cooked for a long time on a low heat,
will be lovely and tender, but the leaner cuts will
just go dry and chewy; even topside is too lean
for eating well done. So I strongly recommend
not using prime cuts for eating well cooked as it
is a waste of money, time and effort and will
invariably lead to disappointment. Allow at least
30 minutes extra before serving the meat to
allow it to rest. If you carve it straight from the
oven all the moisture will run out from the centre and you run the risk of it being dry.

RARE RIB OF BEEF WITH PAN JUICES AND SUMMER SALAD

When choosing the meat for this dish, South
Devons and North Devons are good breeds, but
in reality you want it to have been hung on the
bone for at least three, preferably four, weeks so
it matures properly. Keeping it on the bone
helps retain moisture: as there's no direct heat
on the bone, the heat doesn't penetrate the meat
in that area and force the moisture out.
Although people assume it's blood that's running out, it's mainly water. Also, when choosing
the joint you want to see as much marbling of
fat through the eye of the meat as possible,
almost like lightening strikes of fat: these help
keep the meat moist, tender and tastier.

SERVES 6

1.5 kg rib of beef on the bone
3 onions, peeled and cut in half
75 g butter, cut into small cubes

FOR THE HORSERADISH DRESSING
4 egg yolks – boil the eggs for 10 minutes then
peel and separate the whites from the yolks and
retain the whites for the salad
1 heaped tbsp creamed horseradish
3 tbsp white wine vinegar
1 clove of garlic, crushed
250 ml single cream
salt and fresh white pepper

FOR THE SALAD
2 English lettuces, washed and outer leaves and
core discarded
2 oak leaf lettuces, washed and outer leaves and
core discarded
1 small red onion, finely sliced
6 English radishes, finely sliced
200 g fresh peas – if they are small and tender

don't cook them, but if they're a little bigger blanch in boiling water for 1 minute and refresh in cold
4 egg whites from the boiled eggs, chopped

Pre-heat your oven to its maximum temperature. Put the egg yolks, horseradish, vinegar, garlic, and salt and pepper in a food processor and blitz together. Add the cream and blitz until smooth, then chill.

Rub the beef all over with a little oil (this helps the salt stick) then season liberally with salt. Create a trivet in a roasting tray with the onion halves and lay the meat bone side down. Place in the hot oven and allow to colour for around 15 minutes. When it is oak brown in colour, reduce the heat to around 180°C and pour water into the tray so it doesn't burn (enough to cover the bottom of the tray) and allow to cook for another 15 minutes. Turn the heat up to 200°C and cook for a further 30 minutes (1 hour in total), then remove from the heat and leave to rest for 30 minutes on a wire rack so the air can circulate and the meat rests evenly. All the water should have evaporated from the tray so add a little more and with a wooden spoon rub all the sediment from the bottom of the tray into the water. Add the butter and stir around until all the flavour from the roasting tray is in the butter sauce, then strain and cover with a lid so it doesn't skin over.

Mix all the salad ingredients together and dress with the horseradish dressing to taste.

Carve the beef pouring any expelled juices into your butter sauce and drizzle over the meat. Pink Fir Apple potatoes or Charlottes simmered very slowly with a big sprig of mint, tarragon and chives and plenty of salt then dropped in loads of butter work wonderfully with this dish.

COOK'S TIP
You will hear lots of ifs and buts about browning meat before you roast and seasoning with salt before or after cooking with all sorts of scientific bumph, but at the end of the day seasoning the outside of the beef and browning it makes it taste nice so who cares, although I don't use pepper if roasting at high temperature because I find it burns and goes bitter.

Chips

One of my fondest memories of snack food as a kid is a chip sandwich, although it's something to be frowned upon in this day and age. But for me, mum's chips were the best, squeezed between two heavily buttered slices of bread, with too much salt and occasionally vinegar. We even had a lad at school nicknamed 'chip butty' because it was all he would eat! I think mum's chips were good because she used a pan rather than an electric fryer, which meant the oil heated gradually as the chips cooked so they cooked evenly and crisped at the end, but with hindsight the danger of a pan of boiling oil on an open gas flame makes me cringe. These days chips have been divided into different camps due to the arrival of fast-food chains and ultra crispy processed French fries, which are a far cry from the old chip shop favourites doused in malt vinegar and salt. From the first few that were hot and crispy down to the ones at the bottom all soft and soaked in vinegar, your bag of humble chips involved a variety of eating experiences. Along with French fries come so-called wedges, which are just rustic chips, deep-fried with the skin on. In reality these are just a lazy habit taken up by greedy pub chains who don't want to pay somebody to peel the potatoes – not that I have a problem with potato skin on a jacket potato or a fresh Jersey Royal, but it has no place on a chip. Over recent years in restaurants around England it has become a bit of a mission to cook a chip that will retain its crispiness from the kitchen to the table and all through the meal. I know that Heston Blumenthal of the world-renowned Fat Duck restaurant went to great lengths to create his thrice cooked chips that are first blanched at a regulated temperature in water for a precise time, then in fat at a low temperature for a precise time to evaporate the liquids, then finished in hot oil to crisp them up, and again the potato will be a specific variety that will change through the year depending on where they are from. At home I have found the best way is to almost replicate the method used in roasting potatoes using Yukon Golds, Maris Piper or Desiree, but not waxy potatoes or jackets. Peel them and cut into segments like large fruit segments then carefully simmer in salted water, paying lots of attention so that they don't cook past breaking point and fall to pieces. And don't pack too many in the water as they won't cook evenly and some will be raw when others are crumbling. When the potato segments are soft enough to break with a spoon fish them out carefully with a slotted spoon and place them on a kitchen towel. Then roll them gently on the towel to puff up the starch on the surface. Don't worry if a few break up because they will be the crispiest. Pre-heat beef dripping to 180°C and fry until golden and crispy. If, for health reasons, you prefer vegetable fat to dripping, the potatoes will crisp up just as well but I find that the flavour is not quite as good.

GLOBE ARTICHOKES WITH SALAMI AND COPPA HAM, PINK FIR POTATOES AND MELTED JERSEY SHIELD CHEESE
SERVES 4

8 large Pink Fir Apple potatoes, peeled
2 sprigs of rosemary
4 large globe artichokes, peeled down to the heart
½ lemon
bay leaf
sprig of thyme
thinly sliced cured meats, such as Deli Farms salami, Coppa ham or Denhay ham, or a combination and be fairly generous
Slices of Montgomery's Jersey Shield (if you can't get Jersey Shield, substitute with the Irish cheeses Durrus or Gubbeen, or use a good quality cheddar but slice it more thinly)

The combination of salami, artichoke and potato was inspired by the French Raclette.

Pre-heat the oven to 180°C. Simmer the potatoes in salted water with a sprig of rosemary until tender, then strain. Scrape the choke away from the artichokes with a spoon and then simmer in salted water with the lemon, bay leaf, sprigs of thyme and rosemary until tender. Turn off the heat and add a few ice cubes or some cold water to stop the cooking process and leave to cool. (Store the artichokes in the liquid if you are not using them straightaway.)

Thickly slice the potatoes and lay them in a serving dish. Quarter the artichoke hearts and add to the dish and then the slices of cured meat and salamis layered all over the top and bake in the oven for 5 minutes to start the fats melting a little. Remove from the oven, cover completely with the sliced cheese and grill until the cheese is molten and bubbling. Serve straightaway with crostinis of stale bread or some crunchy bread sticks. It's quite nice eaten with a cold cider but not too cold, as it will make the cheese hard to digest.

Know your Butcher

My favourite job when it comes to preparation is the butchery. I seem to learn something new about the meat itself and my own technique every time, and for me it's an absolute pleasure to watch a skilled master butcher at work. Their knowledge of where the seams, muscles and tendons lie within the meat is almost that of a surgeon. They are hard-working, skilled people, who work in a cold, damp environment and for long hours but still raise a smile and good manners for their customers. With the environmental officers visiting them much more than restaurants they now have our health and well-being to look after as well. If your purse string is a bit tight they will always recommend cheaper cuts as they need to sell the whole beast not just the prime cuts and they can help you in other ways as they are equipped with tools such as slicers and mincers, which people don't tend have at home. A good country butcher won't have just

Always look for lots of marbling as this helps to keep the meat moist and adds flavour.

decided to buy local for marketing reasons, he will have always known where his meat came from and had a working relationship with the farmer and the abattoir.

I had to choose the butcher for the Castle very carefully as I needed someone who could give me full traceability and deliver the consistent standard of hanging, marbling and, for the brasserie bespoke cuts, meat cut by hand not by band saw. Steve Baker of S. & C. Meats (Steven and Claire's Meats) has always come through for me as he understands the importance of communication with his customers and his own suppliers. Although most butchers who supply the catering industry are detached from their customers and their processes are much more factory led, Steve keeps his business as large as he can without it getting so big that he cannot deal with his customers personally and on a daily basis.

All the beef we use comes from David Jasper's South Devon cows farmed on the Devon/Cornwall border in Tredbury where he has his own abattoirs so he can keep the whole process from the rearing to the killing as close as possible so the animals don't have the stress of travelling. The South Devons are not as fashionable to market as say the North Devons, Ruby Reds or the Aberdeen Angus, but because they are a docile cow and easy to handle and pasture, they have a good rate of growth, and good mothering, milk producing and excellent beef qualities, which makes them ideal for a farmer who cares about the end product. Watching the way David moves around the cows without them flinching – one even broke a headlight while scratching his head on David's car – feeding them corn from a bucket, shows he has good herdsmanship and I can see why Steve gets all his beef from David. These are like-minded people who love

and care about what they do and what they produce. If you cook for enjoyment or you cook purely for nourishment but care about what you eat, then I suggest you get to know your butcher.

Garden Party

Every year at the end of June there is a very grand lunch at the Castle in the Norman Garden, hence its title the Garden Party. Seventy to eighty customers turn up in linen summer suits and panamas and ladies in their prettiest shoes and shades, and we put on a good spread while they listen to the steel band or a ragtime jazz. They usually start with a light salad to wet the appetite, followed by seafood with lobster, langoustine, oysters and other crustaceans and molluscs. Then we have the meat course where each table of around eight to twelve people get their own joint carved at the table with new potatoes, dug that morning, fresh peas and broad beans and any other vegetables always cropped first thing that day. One year we had roast fore ribs of beef; another the sirloin; but most recently we opted for something a bit more classical and made Beef Wellingtons, one for each table. We wrapped them in brioche instead of puff pastry, which was a bit nerve-wracking, so I will stick to puff pastry in the future just for my own blood pressure, although the result was fantastic. For the dessert we made summer fruit jelly terrine in sandcastle moulds, so we had eight giant wobbly jelly castles with ice-cream kept cold in bowls we made of ice, with sweet pea flowers set in. Luckily it didn't rain until everyone was leaving! Puff pastry is one thing that you can buy in shops that is generally as good, if not better, than most people can make at home. One I tried recently was the lightest and fluffiest I've ever come across made by a lady called Moira Black at Dorset Pastry, where she uses organic local flour and butter. She tells me the flavour and texture of the pastry changes throughout the year according to when the flour was milled and butter originally churned, but nevertheless I've included a recipe so you can have a go at making your own. Puff pastry is made up of layers of flour dough and fat, and during the cooking process the fat separates into its layers and essentially fries the thin layers of dough. It rises because of the water evaporating from the dough and the butter, creating steam. This recipe, although fairly laborious is by no means the most complicated. Some can be almost mathematical in the angle of the folds and the number of turns and double turns. I will say that, as with any buttery pastry recipe, every-thing has to be cold: even the flour should be cold and your workbench too – maybe use a few ice cubes from your freezer to cool it then just wipe it dry before you flour.

Puff Pastry

500 g strong white flour such as Skipton Mill or Doves, plus extra for dusting
500 g good quality butter
1 tsp table salt
2 tsp white vinegar
475 ml ice cold water

Rub 75 g of the butter into the flour. Dissolve the salt in the vinegar and add the water then gradually work the water into the flour until you have a dough. Slice the remaining butter lengthways into 12 slices, not fridge cold but not room soft. Flour your work surface well and roll the dough into a square about 4 cm thick. Place 1 slice of butter in the middle then fold the outer edges into the centre over the butter. Flour and roll out and repeat the

process until all the butter has been used, and then for good measure chill it down for 10–20 minutes and repeat the rolling and folding a few more times. Wrap in greaseproof paper and chill.

Beef Wellington
serves 6

Ask your butcher for a larder-trimmed fillet about 1 kg in weight, which will have the tail, the chain and the head removed and all the sinew cut away.
10–12 sheets of cured ham such as Denhay or a Prosciutto or Parma
1 egg, beaten
Puff pastry (see recipe above)

for the mushroom stuffing
2 kg button mushrooms
250 g raw chicken breast meat, diced
2 eggs
500 ml double cream
2 large onions, finely chopped
6 cloves of garlic, chopped
lots of fresh chopped parsley
salt and fresh white pepper

for the gravy
500 g of a cheap cut of beef, diced
500 g mushrooms, the cheap mis-shaped mushrooms are fine
1 rasher of smoked bacon or a piece of trimming from the butcher
1 large onion, diced
1 large carrot, diced
75 ml water
1 sprig of thyme
1 bay leaf
150 g cold unsalted butter, diced

Fry the mushrooms very slowly in a little oil, adding a little more if the pan goes dry, but not much as the mushrooms soak it up, and cook without salt so they don't bleed and will colour better. When they are completely golden and smell nice and nutty, place them in a food processor and finely chop them down. Chill. For the next stage you'll need to cool down the bowl of the food processor until it is freezing cold then add the diced chicken and blend to a paste. Add the eggs and blend again to a paste; go around the sides with a spatula and blend again to make sure all the egg is incorporated. Slowly, with the blade turning, add the cold cream, stopping every few seconds to scrape a spatula round the sides so it is mixing properly and repeat until you have the consistency of stiffly whipped cream. Turn into a mixing bowl and chill it down. Sweat the onions and garlic with a little oil and butter and a sprinkle of salt so they don't colour. When they are translucent pour onto a plate and cool down. When the mushrooms, onions and chicken mousse are fridge cold fold them all together, season with table salt, white pepper, fresh chopped parsley and leave in the fridge. Season the fillet with sea salt and pre-heat a pan on a medium heat with beef fat up to a depth of about 1 cm. Then using tongs to manoeuvre it, brown the fillet evenly around its circumference, which takes about 5 minutes, and place on a wire rack to allow an air flow and an even rest. Pre-heat the oven to 180°C. Roll out the puff pastry into a large rectangle on a well-floured surface. Keep a ruler handy so you can measure to see when it is big enough to roll around the whole fillet with about 3 inches extra at either side to allow for the filling. On a sheet of greaseproof paper or tin foil lay the sheets of ham in a flat rectangle and spread them with the mushroom and chicken stuffing, about 2 cm thick. Place the fillet in the middle and, using the paper, roll the stuffing and the ham around the fillet to form a cylinder then roll it from the paper into the centre of the pastry. Dab a little water onto the pastry ends so they will seal and fold the sides up to meet in the middle and scrunch between your fingers so you get what looks like a giant Cornish pasty. Make a few pricks in the top for steam and brush with a little beaten egg. Bake in the oven until a skewer comes out nicely warm on the back of your hand. Make sure you push the skewer right into the middle when testing. Allow the Wellington 10 minutes to rest before serving.

Meanwhile make the gravy. Flour the meat and brown with the mushrooms on a medium heat in a little beef fat. Add the bacon and vegetables and colour them a little. Dab away the fat with paper towels, add the water, thyme and bay leaf and simmer until it is reduced right down so that there is just a little liquid left. Turn down the heat to very low and stir in the butter slowly. Turn off the heat and leave to infuse for 10 minutes then strain. Do not boil if you're warming it through as it may split. If it does split try whisking an ice cube in. As the cube dissolves and cools down the fat and liquids, it will help them emulsify.

RUBY CHARD AND COURGETTES WITH CREAM CHEESE AND TORBAY SOLE

Torbay sole is another name for sand sole, which is similar in appearance to a Dover sole but with a sandy colour. It is called the Torbay sole as they seem to land more around that coast. If you cannot get sand sole, go for megrims or plaice, all of which are lovely fish and cheaper than Dover sole.

SERVES 2

2 350–400 g (whole weight) Torbay sole or megrims, head and black skin removed

The magnificently coloured and aptly named ruby chard.

100 g plain flour, seasoned with 2 tsp table salt (for coating the fish)
2 medium-sized courgettes, washed and sliced into 1 cm rounds
6 stems and stalks of ruby chard, stalks cut into 2–3 cm strips and the leaves separated, washed and torn into rough pieces
1 clove of garlic, peeled and crushed
50 ml double cream
75 g full-fat soft cream cheese
6 basil leaves, torn
sea salt and black pepper

Heat a little oil in a pan that you're confident it won't stick, then lightly flour both sides of the fish and carefully lay them into the pan on a medium heat and allow to colour until golden. Turn and repeat on the other side. Meanwhile, in a separate pan heat a little oil and shallow fry the courgettes over a medium heat and turn when golden. Add the chard stalks and colour a little. If at this point the fish is golden on both sides remove them from the heat while you finish the vegetables. Add the garlic, cream, cream cheese and chard leaves to the pan with the torn basil leaves and a little salt and pepper and simmer until the cheese has melted into the cream and is nicely coating the vegetables.

To serve, run a knife down the centre of the top two fillets of each fish and push the fillets gently to each side to reveal the bone. Gently lift the bone out and discard. Spoon the chard and courgettes onto your plates and lay the fish fillets on top.

COOK'S TIP
It is best to cook smaller flat fish on the bone to keep them moist and prevent over cooking.

Pan Fried Halibut with Potato Gnocchi and Summer Greens with Smokey Bacon Butter

I love this dish, but most Italians would get very upset because gnocchi is usually served very simply in a butter sauce or olive oil. I have Anglicised it by making the gnocchi the starch of the dish. Making the gnocchi, stock and blanching the vegetables in advance would be sensible to reduce pressure on yourself and allow you to just concentrate on getting it nice.

SERVES 2

2 100–120 g skinless fillets of halibut
4 slices dry cured back bacon, cut into strips
100 g butter, diced and chilled
1 tbsp chopped fresh parsley

FOR THE GNOCCHI
400–450 g potatoes (Desiree and Maris Piper are good)
ground nutmeg
1 small egg
50 g type '00' durum wheat pasta flour. You can use plain strong flour but the result will be second rate. Most big supermarkets stock durum wheat in their specialist food area and having it in your cupboard also means you could have a go at fresh pasta, as the same thing applies to its end result.
salt and fresh white pepper

FOR THE BACON STOCK
6 chicken wings
3 slices dry cured smoky bacon
800 ml cold water

FOR THE VEGETABLES
50 g shelled fresh peas, boiled in seasoned water for 1 minute and refreshed in cold water

100 g fresh broad beans, boiled until tender to touch (about 2 minutes), refreshed in cold water then squeezed from their skins
1 heart of spring cabbage, stalk and stems removed, boiled for 1 minute and refreshed
1 small leek, trimmed, diced and washed, boiled for 1 minute

Use the same water for all the vegetables, just cook them one at a time and remove with a slotted spoon so you don't have to keep draining and filling the pan. When all the vegetables are blanched refrigerate in a colander on a plate so they carry on draining.

To make the gnocchi, simmer the potatoes on a very low heat with their skins on. The low heat allows even cooking, if you boil them too quickly the mix will be grainy. When the potatoes will allow a blunt point like a spoon handle through with ease, they are ready. Rinse in a little cold water to make them easier to handle. Peel off the skin with a small knife and pass the potato through a ricer (potato mill) – if you don't have one push the potato through a sieve. You need 300 g of passed potato. Place in the fridge until cool then season with ground salt, fresh ground white pepper and a little nutmeg.

Crack the egg into a dish, making sure there's no shell (if it's a medium-to-large egg discard half the white) then add to the potato and mix well with your fingertips. Sift in the flour and mix together to form a very soft dough. Flour your bench and cut the dough into three even pieces. Gently, using the flat palms of your hands, roll each one out into an even sausage about 2 cm thick. Cut into 2 cm long pieces, flour lightly and roll into little balls. To shape the gnocchi recipes usually suggest a fork, but a better tool to use would be butter paddles – the little grooved wooden paddles used for rolling butter into

patterned balls – so if you see them in a cook shop grab a pair as they are usually cheap.

Before you shape the gnocchi put a pan of water on to boil with some salt added to taste. Then flour your butter paddle or fork or, if you're lucky, your gnocchi board, well. Slowly, with a little pressure from your thumb, roll each ball into a shell shape and onto a floured sheet of greaseproof paper. When they are all done, tip them into the boiling water and as they float to the surface spoon them off into cold water to stop them cooking. Then gently place on an oiled tray or plate, cover in cling film and refrigerate until needed.

To make the bacon stock, boil the kettle and pour enough water over the wings and bacon in a pan to cover them. Bring back to the boil on a medium to high heat. When a scum forms drain them off, cover with the cold water and bring to a gentle simmer. After 30 minutes strain and reduce by half and either use straight away or cool down as quickly as possible and store in the fridge.

Before you bring your ingredients together to finish the dish, put a pan of water on to boil to reheat your vegetables and gnocchi. In a frying pan that you know doesn't stick, warm a little olive oil over a medium heat. Season the fish and lay the pieces skin side down and fry gently until golden, then turn. Allow to colour a little then

COOK'S TIPS
This is a really satisfying dish to cook and wonderful to eat but I don't recommend to do this for more than two people at home as it would be quite demanding. Also when tossing the vegetables, gnocchi and sauce together you might find it easier to transfer them to a warmed bowl so it doesn't spill over the sides.

remove with a fish slice and place onto a baking tray and transfer to the oven set at its lowest possible heat so as not to over cook. In the same frying pan add the bacon lardons and fry until crispy. Then drain away the grease with paper towels and add the stock and butter and stir with a wooden spoon. Meanwhile add the vegetables to the boiling water and then the gnocchi for 30–40 seconds and then drain well in a colander. Add the chopped parsley to the sauce and then the vegetables and gnocchi and toss them all together. Taste for seasoning, adjust if necessary then spoon into bowls and lay the fish on top.

Roast Chicken with a Salad of New Potatoes, Fresh Peas, Broad Beans and Monty's Cheddar

The sediment in the roasting tray and the juices from the carving tray are integral to the dressing for this dish so no flavours are wasted.

SERVES 4

1 medium sized free-range chicken, preferably dry plucked (ask your butcher to remove the wish bone for ease of carving)
200 ml water
18–20 small new potatoes such as Charlotte or Jersey, scrubbed
2 cloves of garlic, split
4 baby gem lettuces, outer dark green leaves discarded, washed and drained
100 g fresh peas, blanched in boiling water with a good pinch of salt for 1 minute then cooled quickly in cold water
150 g small broad beans, blanched in boiling water with a good pinch of salt for 2 minutes then cooled in cold water and the beans popped from their rubbery jackets
70–100 g Montgomery's cheddar, or Keen's, Quick's or Green's

FOR THE DRESSING
4 tbsp cider vinegar
1 tbsp whole grain mustard
1 tbsp runny honey, such as Sedgemoor Farm
1 tsp table salt
2 tbsp mild olive oil or virgin rapeseed oil

Have all these ingredients ready as we make the dressing last minute when the chicken is cooked.

Pre-heat the oven to 200°C. Lightly oil the skin of the chicken and sprinkle with salt. Place in a roasting tray and pour the water in. Cover the chicken with greaseproof paper to stop the foil from sticking then completely cover the tray with tin foil and seal the edges well so not much steam can escape. Bake for 45 minutes then carefully remove the foil and paper and continue to roast for another 45 minutes until the skin is golden and the juices run clear. Transfer the chicken to a carving tray and prop the legs up at about 45 degrees so the juices flow back into the breasts and they don't dry out.

While the chicken is resting, cook the new potatoes in simmering water with a good pinch of salt and the garlic. Cook very gently until you can puncture them with a fork with ease then turn off the heat and leave to stand in their cooking liquor so when you serve they will be just warm but not so hot as to wilt the lettuce leaves.

When the chicken has had 15 minutes resting drain the potatoes, cut them in half and mix with the peas, beans and lettuce in a big salad bowl. Carve the chicken and tip any juices from the carving tray back in the roasting dish. Add the vinegar, mustard, honey and salt and give it a good stir with a wooden spoon. Tip into a dish and whisk in the oil and drizzle over the salad. Spoon the salad around the chicken and grate over the cheese.

Roast chicken with a salad of new potatoes, fresh peas, broad beans and Montgomery's cheddar.

STUFFED COURGETTE FLOWERS AND SAUTÉED COURGETTES AND A TARRAGON VELOUTÉ

This recipe requires you to buy your chicken from a butcher or a farmers' market, because you need the giblets inside the chicken, which you don't get in big stores. You can use the crown one night and then this recipe another. It also requires you to either grow your own courgettes or buy from a vegetable box scheme or market; in July time the finger-sized courgettes are in flower and we can use the flower as a kind of sausage skin, thus less of the vegetable is wasted.

Courgette flowers were stuffed with all manner of mousses during the nouvelle cuisine era of the 1980s but to make a mousse out of lobster or any perfectly good prime fish or meat is in my mind complete madness, for mousses, stuffing, sausages and the likes should be made from off-cuts, fats, and offals, to make use of all the edible parts and to make good use of every part of a creature that lived and died for our nutrition. When you buy your chicken ask the butcher to take off the legs for you if you do not know how, but it is fairly straightforward. If you manoeuvre the chicken around with your hands you can feel where the joints are and almost pull the legs off just using a knife to cut away the skin and connecting tissues.

SERVES 4

12 courgettes
salt, sugar and fresh black pepper

FOR THE STUFFING

All the meat of 2 chicken legs, skin and bone removed (and kept for stock) and finely diced chicken liver, heart and kidneys, trimmed and diced
6 slices of streaky bacon, finely diced

2 slices of bread crusts, moistened with a little milk and made into a firm paste with your hands
pinch of garlic salt
fresh grated nutmeg
salt and fresh black pepper

FOR THE VELOUTÉ SAUCE

neck, leg bones and wings from the chicken
1 small onion, chopped
1 clove of garlic, crushed
3 tarragon stalks (leaves picked to finish the sauce)
50 g butter
50 g plain flour

To make the stuffing put everything in a food processor or mincer and blend into a paste. If you're using a processor rather than a mincer stop every few seconds and give it a stir so it blends evenly: it should come together like coarse sausage meat. Then in a hot pan fry off a little piece of the mix in a little oil and taste it so you can adjust the seasonings. Then chill down for 1 hour while you prepare the sauce and the courgettes.

To make the sauce, pour boiling water from the kettle over the stock bones in a pan and bring to a boil then drain away this scummy liquid and refill with fresh water, enough to cover by around 4 cm. Add the onion, garlic and tarragon stalks and bring to a gentle simmer. In a separate pan melt the butter. When it is bubbling away add the flour and stir in with a wooden spoon or heat-proof spatula until a paste has formed. Remove from the heat until the stock has simmered for about 30 minutes then put back on a low heat and slowly add the stock stirring little by little so you get a smooth sauce. At first the mixture will just expand but as you slowly add the liquid it will take form as a sauce, and don't worry if any bits from the stock go into the

sauce as we are going to pass the sauce later. When the sauce has reached a stage where it looks like liquid silk, it's ready but to allow the flour to cook out cover the pan with a lid, turn the heat to as low as possible, or even better place on a heat diffuser, and allow to cook for another 20 minutes.

Separate the flowers from the courgettes, remove the stamens, wash and check for bugs. Cut the courgettes in half lengthways and season with salt, sugar and fresh black pepper and leave in a colander for 10 minutes to drain and allow the seasoning to penetrate. Pre-heat an electric steamer. Take the stuffing from the fridge, cup each flower in a slightly open fist and spoon in the meat and mould with your hands. You'll probably fill

about six large or eight small flowers. Then roll them individually in oiled and seasoned cling film and steam for 10 minutes. Meanwhile, sauté the courgettes in a little olive oil until golden. Strain the sauce through a fine sieve and add picked but not chopped tarragon leaves. Squeeze the cooked flowers from the cling film into a serving dish (if you use rubber gloves it won't feel so hot) then sprinkle over the golden courgettes and spoon over the sauce. All in all this dish will probably take about 2 hours from start to finish if you follow the flow of the recipe and multi-task a little. This may sound like a long time but you'll find it very rewarding not to waste anything and you will have created a great-tasting and nutritious dish.

Use young courgettes (and their flowers) for this dish to take advantage of their fresh, nutty flavour.

Breaded Lamb Sweetbreads with English Mustard Mayonnaise, Peas and Broad Beans
serves 4 as a starter or 2 as a main course

8 decent-sized lamb breads, blanched in salted boiling water for 30 seconds then plunged into ice water. This way you can peel off any sinew, which retracts and goes chewy when cooked.
dish of seasoned flour
2 whole eggs, beaten
dish of fine breadcrumbs, if you don't have breadcrumbs you can use semolina
handful of fresh peas, boiled for 2 minutes and refreshed in cold water
handful of broad beans, boiled for 2 minutes and refreshed in cold water then skins removed
1 English lettuce, washed, spun and stalks removed
1 small bunch of chives, chopped

for the mayonnaise
3 egg yolks
3 tsp English mustard
2 tbsp cider vinegar

250 ml grape seed oil or mild olive oil
2 tbsp boiling water
salt

Flour the lamb breads then coat in egg and roll in the crumbs.

To make the mayonnaise, whisk the yolks, mustard and vinegar in a bowl secured on a wet cloth until well mixed then slowly add the oil until it comes together. (It helps if someone else adds the oil so you can concentrate on whisking.) When it all comes together add a couple of tablespoons of boiling water and whisk in. Refrigerate until needed.

To deep-fry the lamb breads I prefer to use beef fat; in fact I prefer beef fat for deep-frying anything, including fish and chips. It makes them taste how they should, not of vegetable grease or palm oil! If you have an electric fryer then just pre-heat and drop them in at 170°C until golden brown then drain on paper towels and season. Mix the peas, beans, lettuce and chives with your desired amount of mayonnaise. Season to taste with freshly milled salt and portion out on to plates with the lamb breads.

June Salad
SERVES 4 AS A STARTER OR 2 AS A MAIN COURSE

4 poached eggs (see cook's tip below)
75 g pine nuts
8 slices of dry, cured streaky bacon
1 oak leaf lettuce, outer leaves and stalk removed, washed and spun
2 handfuls of young spinach, washed and spun
100 g fresh peas, boiled for 2 minutes in salted water and refreshed in ice water
100 g broad beans shelled, boiled until tender between (2 and 3 minutes), refreshed in ice water and skins removed
1 small bunch of chives cut into 8 mm lengths
nasturtium petals to garnish

FOR THE DRESSING
juice of 1 lemon
1 tbsp honey
150ml avocado oil
salt and fresh black pepper

Toast the pine nuts and while still warm add ¼ tsp of honey. Roll the nuts gently in a paper towel to remove the excess honey and sprinkle with a few twists of freshly milled salt (the honey just allows the salt to stick). Pre-heat the oven to 180°C. Place the bacon between two sheets of greaseproof paper and then roll out as thin as possible with a rolling pin. Bake on a non-stick tray in the oven until very crispy then drain on paper towels and flake into pieces.

To make the dressing, gently warm the lemon juice with salt and black pepper. When the salt has dissolved add the honey and dissolve then remove from the heat and chill. Whisk in the avocado oil. The dressing will need to be whisked or shaken well before use.

Taking two separate bowls, in one lightly dress your salad leaves then arrange on plates; in the other dress the peas, beans and pine nuts and sprinkle over the salad. Crumble over the crispy bacon, snipped chives and top with the poached eggs. Garnish with nasturtium petals at the last second.

COOK'S TIPS
Nasturtiums are loved by small creepy crawlies so check them first and very gently dip in cold water and shake them off. Poaching an egg does not require bizarre techniques, as some will have you think. You don't need to spin the water; you don't need to add vinegar, unless you like the taste. All you need is plenty of boiling unsalted water, nice fresh eggs and a slotted spoon. When the water is at a rolling boil gently crack the egg into the water and do no more than two at a time. As the egg floats to the top spoon it above the surface to check firmness. When it's as you require spoon either onto a draining cloth and serve, or into ice water to stop the cooking so you can reheat in boiling water when needed.

Poached Salmon (HOT OR COLD)
The best way to enjoy a poached salmon, hot or cold, is to make sure the ingredients you are eating with it are as fresh as possible. New potatoes such as Charlottes, little bunches of carrots and broad beans and little breakfast radishes – all must still have the smell of the earth they come from to really work well with and lift the salmon.

Poach the salmon with just a hint of shiny

orange colour left through the flesh so it's not dry, and serve with hot, buttered potatoes, boiled with masses of mint and a little too much salt, the broad beans and carrots as young as you can get them with little peppery radishes, more molten butter and fresh chopped parsley, and perhaps a hollandaise for hot or a mayonnaise for cold. But you shouldn't need much sauce if the salmon's not over cooked and if you are lucky enough to have a fishmonger who gets wild salmon between May and August.

There is a lot of history with wild salmon around the Levels using salmon buts (willow traps) or flatners, flat-bottomed row boats with dipping nets, but sadly through over fishing from large trawler nets, poachers and pollution, wild salmon are expensive and hard to come by. So if you're buying farmed fish make sure the colour is not too luminous, because this indicates it has been fed too much carotene to colour the flesh. The flesh itself should be firm like a tense muscle and not greasy to touch.

If you are poaching individual pieces of salmon, which is much easier, especially if you don't have a fish kettle in which to cook a whole fish, buy steaks on the bone rather than fillets; the monger will cut right through the circumference of the fish to give you a kind of Barnsley chop – but of salmon. Because it's on the bone it will stay more moist than a fillet. If you prefer boneless fillets, I suggest wrapping them in cling film and steaming them or searing them in a pan. For the poaching liquor don't be tempted to glug in too much wine and vinegar or citrus: too much of these will overpower the flesh and leave you with warm pickled fish.

SERVES 6

2 shallots, sliced
20 white peppercorns
1 flat tbsp sea salt
good sprig of parsley
sprig of celery leaf
1 litre water
6 120–140 g salmon steaks

Place the shallots, peppercorns, sea salt, parsley and celery leaf in a pan with the water. Simmer together for 5 minutes then leave to infuse. When all your vegetables are prepared and ready to be cooked and the new potatoes nearly there bring the liquor back to the boil and drop in the fish and turn off the heat. While it cooks you can boil your vegetables so they will be ready together. Let the fish cook in the residual heat for 8–10 minutes then gently spoon them out into a dish and spoon over a little of the cooking liquor so they don't dry out. If you're eating them cold don't cook for any longer than 8 minutes then spoon out onto a plate and leave to cool at room temperature. Don't serve straight from the fridge: if they're fridge cold they're not nice.

> COOK'S TIP
> If the thought of running around at the last minute sounds daunting use timers to help, and split the jobs so somebody else can watch the vegetables while you watch the fish. Cooking doesn't have to be done in total solitude, it can be as sociable as the lunch itself.

Seared Scallops with a Vinaigrette and June Vegetables
SERVES 4 AS A STARTER OR 2 AS A MAIN COURSE

2 heads of baby fennel, cut into quarters

lengthways, or 1 small bulb, cut into 8 pieces lengthways with its stalk removed

6–8 small bunch carrots, peeled and halved lengthways

6–8 breakfast radishes, leaves removed and halved lengthways

20 shelled broad beans blanched for 1 minute refreshed and skins removed

8 spring onions, the green discarded and trimmed

8 new potatoes, slowly simmered in salted water until tender then refreshed, peeled and cut into quarters

8 large or 10 medium scallops, trimmed (I personally prefer to remove the orange coral but if you like it, leave it on)

2 tbsp cider vinegar

1 tbsp local honey (I use Sedgemoor honey from Creech St Michael in Somerset as it has a mild floral flavour and it's not too overpowering)

75 ml avocado oil

10 small basil leaves (as small as possible)

sea salt and fresh black pepper

Once you've prepared all the vegetables and got all the ingredients together on a tray this becomes an all-at-once dish so you will need to warm your plates. Put a pan of salted water with a lid on to boil and pre-heat a non-stick pan on a medium heat with a little olive oil. Drop the fennel and carrots in the water and put back the lid. After 1 minute add the radishes. Carefully lay the scallops into the non-stick pan and season with freshly milled salt and pepper. Then put the beans, spring onions, and new potatoes in the water. When the scallops have coloured turn them over using tongs to cook the other side. Drain the vegetables in a colander and return the pan back to the heat. Add the vinegar, seasoning then add the honey on a

high heat. When the vinegar has almost evaporated add the vegetables and toss together, then pour over the avocado oil and sprinkle in the basil leaves. Spoon the vegetables onto the warmed plates with a slotted spoon and place the scallops on top and spoon over the rest of the dressing.

COOK'S TIPS
As with any shellfish the scallop has to be as fresh as possible. Only buy from a fishmonger who buys them himself in the shell and opens them when you are there. If they don't they will be buying them in tubs of water third or fourth party and the end product will inevitably be second rate.
Use 100 per cent avocado oil as it's not at all bitter and has a lovely smooth flavour and vibrant green colour.

Where the Best Cherries Come From

I'll tell you where they come from, Pixford Fruit Farm in Bishops Lydeard, Somerset. Until I moved here I would have argued that good cherries, like peaches and apricots, would need to be imported, but how wrong I was – and now I wait all year for these beauties. First we get the white and pink ones that look like shiny china marbles and are slightly sharper in taste. Then come the deep burgundy variety, which just explode in your mouth, and once you get over the incredible stomach cramps from gorging yourself senseless on them, you can start to put them to use in the kitchen. I have to say though, sitting outside in the sunshine (if you're lucky) with your eyes closed eating the best cherries you've ever tasted certainly takes some beating.

The People Behind the Fruit

Mervyn and Heather Ellison Nash have been at Pixford Farm since 1978. At that time Mervyn's late uncle grew dessert apples and blackcurrants. They then expanded into cider apples growing for Taunton Cider, which is now Gaymers. Now they have twenty varieties of eating and cooking apples, eight different varieties of plums, ten different cherries with varied levels of sweetness, and damsons. They also have mulberries, figs, walnuts and hazelnuts and all their fruit is picked when totally ripe and ready to eat on the day of sale. People come from near and far who are in the know to get their fill and I feel honoured to be one of the only restaurants in the country to get to use the fruits of their labour. I remember asking Mervyn what he did through winter in between the seasons and he looked at me like I was an idiot and said calmly: 'we prune 20,000 trees'. Needless to say I felt very small.

CRISPY DUCK LEGS WITH WARMED CHERRIES AND SAUTÉED POTATO, CUCUMBER AND SHALLOT
SERVES 4 AS A STARTER, 2 AS A MAIN COURSE

4 duck legs, lightly oiled and seasoned with fresh milled salt
6 Pink Fir Apple potatoes, scrubbed
12 nice plump cherries, stalks removed but left whole until the last minute (see cook's tip)
5 cm of cucumber, peeled, halved, deseeded and sliced
1 shallot, peeled and sliced into thin rings
sea salt

Prepare the duck in advance. Pre-heat the oven to 175°C. Lay the duck in a small deep roasting dish, skin side up, with just enough water to cover the bottom of the tray to a depth of about 1 cm. Cover with greaseproof paper and then tin foil and seal tightly. Bake in the oven for 2–2½ hours; the skin and flesh should be very soft to touch. Allow to cool for 10–15 minutes and very carefully, with a fish slice, pick each one up and turn it on to a tray and refrigerate. Set the fat left in the roasting tray in a bowl in the fridge. Pre-heat an oven to 180–200°C. Simmer the potatoes slowly in salted water until a fork penetrates with ease, then refresh, peel and slice in half lengthways. In a non-stick pan on a medium heat add a tablespoon of the duck fat then add the duck legs skin side down and gently fry until crispy and golden then turn and repeat on the other side. Remove the duck, add the potatoes to

Mervyn Ellison Nash with his first crop of cherries.

the pan and put the duck back on top, skin side up. If you don't have an ovenproof pan, transfer to a non-stick roasting dish or a roasting dish lined with greaseproof paper and place in the oven until the potatoes are nicely coloured then remove from the oven and portion on to warmed plates. Drain the fat from the pan into paper towels and discard. Cut the cherries in half and add to the hot pan over a medium heat. Roll them around just to warm them through and accentuate their flavour. Spoon around the duck and sprinkle over the shallots and cucumber, and add a little sea salt to the potatoes.

COOK'S TIPS

If you pre-cut the cherries they will oxidise and turn brown.

The reason we cook the duck first in water and cover it is so the skin stays soft. If we cooked them crispy straight away when we came to reheat them the skin wouldn't re-crisp, it would just go chewy and burn. This way the skin retains some moisture and fat and goes nice and crispy when we fry it.

Dark Chocolate Custard Tart with Cherry Compote

This recipe makes quite a large tart and is very rich but worth every calorie. You will need very good quality dark chocolate – look for 76–78 per cent cocoa solids; anything less will not give you the right result.

SERVES 10

FOR THE SWEET PASTRY

500 g soft flour
300 g baking margarine
1 small pinch of salt

3 small eggs, beaten
125 g caster sugar

FOR THE CHOCOLATE CUSTARD

250 ml double cream
130 ml whole milk
350 g dark chocolate, chopped
4 egg yolks

18cm x 4 cm flan ring

To make the sweet pastry, sieve the flour and gently rub in the salt and margarine until you have a sandy texture. Make a well in the centre. Dissolve the sugar in the beaten eggs and pour into the well. Gradually incorporate together until you have a smooth dough. Roll out to about 1 cm thick and refrigerate on a tray lined with greaseproof paper and chill for about an hour. On a floured surface roll out the dough to about 5 mm thick. Roll the pastry over your rolling pin and then over an upside down bowl that has a slightly smaller circumference than the flan ring then gently turn into the ring and mould into the edges until the mould is completely lined with a little overhang to allow for shrinkage: don't worry if you have to patch up holes as this is very delicate pastry. Line with greaseproof paper and baking beans. If you don't have baking beans just use some rice or lentils and bake at 180°C for 15 minutes then remove the beans and bake for a further 15 minutes to seal the pastry.

Meanwhile, boil the cream and mix in the milk on a medium heat. Put the chocolate in a bowl, pour over the hot liquid and stir until all the chocolate has melted. Place the egg yolks in a separate bowl and slowly pour over the chocolate. Whisk thoroughly and leave to stand.

While the pastry is still hot, pour in the chocolate

Dark chocolate custard tart with cherry compote – a rich, indulgent dessert.

custard, turn the oven down to the lowest it will go and slowly bake for about 2 hours until it has lost its wobble. Then allow to cool for 30 minutes before refrigerating.

Before serving, warm the tart in a low oven (the tart should have been out at room temperature for 1 hour) for 5 minutes so that the filling will be soft, smooth and rich. Serve with a spoonful of the cherry compote next to it and a dollop of whipped cream.

Cherry Compote

1 kg cherries, stoned (stone just before you need them)
750 g jam sugar
1 vanilla pod, split

In a heavy duty pan put the cherries on a low heat with a lid for 2 minutes to allow a little moisture to escape then add the sugar and vanilla and stir well until the sugar has dissolved. Then turn the heat up a little stirring with a wooden spoon constantly as the fruit breaks down. Watch

carefully: if it starts to bubble really quick and spits, turn down the heat. Keep stirring until it reaches jam (105°C on a sugar thermometer or when the mix is opaque) and spoon some on a cold plate and chill. You don't want it to set like jam. rather a nice thick syrup covering the cherries. When ready, store in the fridge in a sterile container with a tight lid. This mix also makes a great filling for bakewell tarts or a black forest gateau and eats really well with a panacotta.

Cherry Bakewell

The French love their cherry clafoutis but I'd rather have a fresh-baked bakewell any day.
SERVES 8

FOR THE PASTRY
500 g plain flour, sifted, plus extra for dusting
250 g icing sugar, sifted
400 g butter at room temperature, diced
4 egg yolks

FOR THE ALMOND FILLING (FRANGIPANE)
250 g ground almonds
250 g icing sugar
250 g soft butter, diced
4 eggs, beaten
70 g plain flour
cherry compote (see recipe above)

25 cm x 3 cm flan ring

Rub the flour, sugar and butter together with your fingertips or in a food processor until it resembles breadcrumbs then make a well. Slowly mix in the egg yolks to form a dough. Knead a little then on a tray lined with greaseproof paper and then floured, roll the pastry about 1 cm thick and refrigerate.

Mix the almonds and icing sugar together then rub in the butter. Slowly mix in the eggs, making sure to mix thoroughly with no lumps and set to one side.

Place the flan ring on a non-stick tray or line a tray with greaseproof paper. Take the pastry from the fridge, flour your surface, turn out the pastry and peel off the greaseproof paper. Roll until approximately 5 mm thick. Roll carefully onto your rolling pin to enable you to manoeuvre it without tearing and gently roll over the flan ring and mould into the sides patching up any holes as you go. Spoon in your cherry compote and spread about 5 mm thick but making sure there are plenty of cherries evenly distributed. Chill for 10 minutes. Pre-heat the oven to 170°C. Pour over the almond mix and bake for 40–50 minutes until a knife will come out clean. Allow to cool for 30 minutes before you delve in.

The northerner in me leans towards custard but here in the south a dollop of clotted cream is the general consensus. This tart also eats well cooled down, or even cold with a fresh pot of tea. If you don't have the time or the inclination to make the cherry compote, use a decent jam or, in autumn, some poached pears or quinces sliced and spread across the pastry.

COOK'S TIPS

If you really want to be clever dip some cherries in caramel as if making toffee apples and when the sugar sets place on top of the tart.

If you want to freeze the tart (it freezes very well) makes sure it's well chilled and then for ease, cut into 10 equal triangles and wrap in cling film.

WILD CHERRY BRANDY

Although non-cultivated cherries aren't very big and don't eat as well as their cultivated cousins, they do have their uses and some of the darker ones have a lovely almondy flavour, especially if you suck the stone. One nice way to use them is to flavour alcohols in much the same way you would use sloe berries later on in the year, and cherries are much more abundant. I don't recommend picking them if the trees are on a roadside as I don't think the carbon monoxide will do much to enhance the flavour, but if you look carefully you can see them everywhere – in parks, golf courses, etc. I pick mine from the trees in Lyme Wood in Hatch, where they have been planted to provide the wood for commercial use. I don't recommend wearing your best clothes as it can be a rather messy job. This recipe takes about a month for the flavour to mature and is an ideal warmer for late summer, while sitting in the garden of an evening. A few shots of this makes you feel like the sun is on the back of your neck, but go steady!

1 kg cherries
1 litre cheap brandy or gin
750 g sugar
1 vanilla pod, split (optional but worth it)

Wash and stalk the cherries. Dissolve the sugar and alcohol together over a gentle heat. Wrap a rolling pin with cling film and in a bowl mush the cherries a little and pour over the liquid and the vanilla pod. Transfer the whole lot to a jar and leave to stand for 1 month in a warmish place – maybe somewhere that gets a little sunshine in the daytime. Then pass the liquid through a double muslin cloth to remove any sediment and bottle.

Pickled Cherries

500 g brown sugar
500 ml cherry vinegar if you can get it, or raspberry vinegar if not
10 turns of fresh mild black pepper
2 star anise
1 kg firm fresh cherries, stalk removed and washed but leave the stone in for its almondy flavour

Dissolve the sugar in the vinegar on a low heat with the black pepper and star anise. Tip in the cherries and bring up to a boil. Carefully remove the cherries with a slotted spoon from the liquid onto a flat tray then reduce the liquid by half. Put the cherries into a sterilised jar, pour over the liquid then seal. Leave either in your fridge or a cool cupboard for a few months before serving with pâtés, cheeses or cured meats.

COOK'S TIP

To make a cherry vinegar if you're stoning any cherries for compote or jam, just put all the stones in red wine vinegar to infuse. Generally I fill a bottle about a third full then pour over the vinegar and leave in a warm area of the kitchen for around a month before use.

Gooseberries

Unless you count strawberries that are grown under polythene in May as one of our first fruits – which I don't – then the humble and not always favoured gooseberry takes that title. The early small, hairier and sharper ones are good for cooking as the later sweeter varieties break down more and don't hold the sugar as well. These are better for crumbles and cheesecakes.

Fillets of Mackerel in Oatmeal with a Gooseberry purée

Classically this dish was done with herring but it works well with any oily fish, as it is the sharpness of the gooseberry that cuts through the fish's oily flavour.

SERVES 4 AS A STARTER

4 100 g fillets of mackerel, fin bones removed
2 eggs, beaten with a splash of milk
200 g porridge oats
100 g breadcrumbs or semolina blended together to make a semi-smooth powder
200 g flour, seasoned with fine milled salt
watercress or lamb's lettuce to garnish

Cut each fillet in half across the middle then dip individually in the flour then the egg then the oatmeal so each piece is nicely coated. (Remember to use one hand for the egg and the other for the flour and oats so you don't get all gummed up.) Chill until needed but no longer than 2 days. To serve, pre-heat some olive oil or clarified butter in a pan that isn't well known for sticking. When the oil runs just around the pan add the fillets of mackerel and fry on a low heat and turn when golden (always turn away from yourself so the fat doesn't splash you) and continue to cook on a low heat until equally coloured then remove from the pan onto paper towels (don't pour or the fat will soak the paper and defeat the object of draining). Then simply spoon a little gooseberry purée onto the plates (see below) and place the fish next to it. Garnish with watercress or lamb's lettuce.

Gooseberry Purée

1 kg small green gooseberries, topped, tailed and washed

250 ml water
1 kg sugar

Put the water and gooseberries in a pan with a lid on a low to medium heat and cook until the fruit softens slightly. Add the sugar and stir gently with a wooden spoon until it takes on a jam-like consistency and a light pinky colour then while still hot very carefully pour into a food processor and blend for 1 minute. Pass through a sieve and store in sterile jars.

> COOK'S TIP
> This recipe can be used in fools or to make dressings or even as a condiment with roast duck, so it's fairly versatile.

Gooseberry Preserve
This is excellent with cheeses like Spenwood and Sussex pecorino and Montgomery's cheddar, as well as with pâtés, parfaits and cured meats.

500 g firm early season gooseberries, washed, topped and tailed
500 g Demerara sugar
⅓ fresh nutmeg
spice bag made up of 2 cardamom pods, 10 white peppercorns, ½ star anise, sprig of mace all wrapped in muslin or a J-cloth and tied with string
salt

In a very clean sturdy pan warm the gooseberries over a low heat with the lid on to allow a little moisture to seep out and the berries to soften slightly. Add the sugar and grate over the nutmeg and allow the sugar to dissolve. Add the spice bag and turn up the heat slightly, stirring fairly regularly. Allow the berries to cook down until pinky brown in colour and of a jam-like consistency then finish with a good pinch of salt. Allow to cool slightly then sterilise a jar in boiling water and poor in the mix. Brush a little strong alcohol on to prevent bacteria then cover with greaseproof paper and the lid. It will keep for months in a cool storage area but if you're like me and you like your cold meats and cheese for supper it won't be around for long.

Gooseberry Dressing
This is good with breaded fish or the classic mackerel in oatmeal and with king prawns as a dip.

75 ml gooseberry purée (must be cold)
175 ml grape seed oil or a mild olive oil
a small amount of vanilla beans scraped from a pod (optional)
icing sugar to taste

To purée the gooseberries warm them in a pan then blend in a processor and pass through a sieve. To complete the dressing, simply blend the oil into the purée slowly with the vanilla and chill. Add a little icing sugar to sweeten if necessary.

Gooseberry Fool
SERVES 4

600 ml double cream
vanilla pod
50 g icing sugar
200 ml gooseberry purée (see Gooseberry Dressing)

Whip the double cream to a stiff peak with the seeds from the vanilla pod. Fold the icing sugar into the cream then gently fold through the gooseberry purée to create a rippled effect. For added texture fold through some crumbled up shortbread biscuits or even Hobnobs

Gooseberry Crumble

This crumble recipe is from Kevin Knapper, a Yeovil boy with real West Country tastes. Although crumble topping recipes are two a penny this one is great because it cooks so crunchy. The only argument we have is whether to serve with cream, ice-cream or custard.

SERVES 4

115 g butter
175 g plain flour
20 g Demerara sugar
88 g porridge oats
500 g later season plump gooseberries, washed, topped and tailed. The red hybrid varieties are good for crumble but it's a good idea to eat one first to judge how much sugar you will need.
4 tbsp granulated sugar
unsalted butter

Pre-heat the oven to 160°C. Rub the butter and flour together then mix in the sugar and oats. Transfer to a roasting dish and bake gently, stirring every few minutes until it is very lightly coloured and crunchy. Then set aside to cool down. You can store the mix in a sealed container in a dry cupboard for up to four days.
Turn the oven up to 180°C. Cover the bottom of your crumble dish with the gooseberries. Sprinkle over your desired amount of caster sugar and mix a few knobs of the butter into the berries. Cover with a 2 cm thick layer of crumble mix and bake until golden in colour and the sugars are bubbling up the sides. If the mix starts to colour too quickly turn the oven down to 160°C.

Strawberries

Over the last ten years strawberries have been abused. Growers are constantly trying to get the season to start that extra few weeks early or stretch it out that bit longer and who can blame them, because if they didn't take such measures, people would just go out and buy Dutch ones anyway.

It's such a shame that in this country we sometimes have such a lack of duty towards the special things we have and a constant yearning to have our cake and eat it all year round, that it takes organisations set up in other countries, such as the Slow Food Movement, to notice and promote the potential of small producers. There's something so vague and pointless about eating forced watery strawberries with sugar and cream when a really good strawberry, sweet with syrupy juice, makes you close your eyes with pleasure and always gives me a sensation of pride.

So be patient; let the tourists eat the first lot and wait to savour the outdoor varieties. A morning down at a pick-your-own fruit farm is also good therapy for the soul.

The Castle's Strawberries and Cream
SERVES 4

Hull and wash enough strawberries for four people. Roll the strawberries in the strawberry syrup (see the recipe below) and spoon onto the shortbread (see the recipe below). Next to this add a good dollop of the Crème Chantilly (whipped double cream with a few vanilla seeds scraped from the pod and icing sugar to taste) and drizzle over a little more syrup. If you want to be a bit flash you could garnish it with spun sugar or sheets of melted sugar, but it's not really necessary.

Fresh strawberries rolled in strawberry syrup and served with elderflower panacotta.

STRAWBERRY SYRUP

250 g over-ripe strawberries
50 g caster sugar

In a heat-proof bowl place the strawberries and sugar and cover with cling film. Bring a pan of water to the boil, turn down to a very low heat and put the bowl over it and leave to cook for 30 minutes. Turn off the heat and leave for a further 30 minutes. Then let it strain through a sieve without forcing any pulp and put the liquid in a small pan, and reduce down over a low heat until it coats the back of a spoon and set aside to cool. This syrup will keep for weeks in a very clean container.

SHORTBREAD

225 g butter at room temperature
250 g caster sugar, plus extra for dusting
10 g plain flour
60 g semolina

Pre-heat the oven to 160°C. Combine all the ingredients in a food mixer to form a dough. Chill the dough down for 30 minutes then roll out to 2 cm thick and cut out 8 cm rings. Place on a lined baking tray and bake until very lightly coloured. Allow to cool slightly and dust with caster sugar.

ELDERFLOWER PANACOTTA

Elderflower as a flavour has made a comeback over the past few years through organic drinks and cordials and makes its fashionable appearance in shabby-chic weekend supplements. Nevertheless it's been used in cooking for hundreds of years and comes into flower ready to complement strawberries and gooseberries beautifully. Like anything picked from hedgerows

for consumption don't take it from the roadside as car fumes probably don't make a great flavour for anything. Also, wash well in cold water and be mindful of hedgerows in fields that farmers may have sprayed. For this recipe you will need a good quality double cream – something nice and rich: whipping or single won't give the same result.
SERVES 6

500 ml double cream
½ vanilla pod, split
5 heads of elderflower, green stalk removed and washed
2 gelatine leaves (just to make sure)
75 g sugar

In a heavy-bottomed saucepan on a low to medium heat bring the cream, vanilla and elderflower to a gentle simmer for 15–20 minutes. Soak the gelatine in cold water until it goes soft, drain and dissolve in the hot cream and leave to infuse for 30 minutes covered with a lid. Strain through a fine sieve into a measuring jug. Lightly oil six individual moulds with a little vegetable oil. Fill each mould with an equal amount, cover with cling film and chill for at least 4 hours but preferably overnight.
To de-mould, rub your hands on the mould to remove the chill then gently with your fingers loosen the edges and flop out onto plates.

COOK'S TIP
A panacotta like this will lend itself to anything fruity – cherries, strawberries, gooseberries. If you want to garnish the dish, drop some washed elderflowers in egg white and caster sugar, shake off the excess, leave to dry on a rack for a few hours and place on top.

Summer Vegetable Panaché

Vegetables can unfortunately be overlooked or even snubbed in some restaurants but they remain a staple of rural England's diet. One of the things I've noticed always get comments when I'm entertaining at home is how nice and colourful the vegetables are and what fresh flavours. This at first bewildered me: why did the vegetables always get more praise than all the fancy stuff I've tried to impress with, but so many people don't give the vegetables that little bit of extra attention they need. So often they are boiled or even microwaved until whoever's cooking has got time to drain and they are stuck in the bottom of the oven until everything else is ready, usually for about 20 minutes. This means they are around 25 minutes overcooked. I've seen many a recipe in well-thumbed home cookbooks giving a cooking time for asparagus tips of around 20 minutes. In reality, if you're boiling or steaming your vegetables they should be the last thing you cook while your meat or fish rests. Once again pre-preparation is the key, so there's no panicking last minute: not advisable when sloshing big pans of boiling water around!

serves 6 or 4 greedy

20 young bunch carrots, trimmed and peeled
3 golden beetroots, peeled and cut into 1 cm dice
18 breakfast radishes, washed, green removed and halved lengthways
10 young courgettes, washed and halved lengthways or sliced if bigger
175 g shelled fresh peas
175 g shelled broad beans, as small as possible so you don't have to remove the little outer skins, but if they are bigger I suggest you boil for 2 minutes then refresh and pop from their outer skin to reveal the little green bean

10 spring onions, trimmed, peeled and halved lengthways
2 pointed cabbages, outer leaves removed, de-stalked and cut into strips
50 g butter or olive oil
Malden sea salt and white or black pepper

Put a big pot of water on a simmer in advance so when everything else is ready you can just add salt to taste. I suggest a tablespoon of Malden sea salt to a litre of water. Keep each vegetable separate once prepared so they can be added to the pot individually. A timer or a clock showing seconds is helpful, and a tight lid. When you're ready (top the pan up from the kettle if necessary), bring the water up to a rapid boil then add the carrots and beetroot to the pot. Cover for 2 minutes then add the radishes, courgettes, peas and broad beans. Cover for a further minute then add the spring onions and cabbage and cover for another 1½ minutes. Drain in a colander and melt the butter in the same pot over a medium heat. When it starts to bubble and crackle pour in the drained vegetables and season with fresh pepper. Stir gently to coat with the butter and serve straightaway in a hot dish.

To add a simple extra dimension, add some fresh tarragon sprigs to the butter before you add the vegetables.

Lynmouth Bay Lobster with a Lobster Marie Rose Sauce

Exmoor coast lobsters come from very rocky headlands like Hiveer Point, Wring O Peak, Lynmouth Foreland and the 'Valley of the Rocks' – the highest sea cliffs in England. The tides and eddies are some of the strongest in the world, which keeps the waters fresh and attracts fish. It is also ideal for shellfish. From late spring to

Summer vegetable panaché showcases the best of summer vegetables.

mid-July the lobsters stop filter feeding and come out to feed on the decomposing fish used as bait in the pots positioned to catch them. The Oxham family have run boat trips around Lynmouth for generations and their detailed knowledge of the coast allows them to fish during the calmer summer months when they are not generating electricity for the bay in their little station where the hydro-electric turbines are fuelled by the power of the West Lyn river. Lobster, like most crustaceans, is quite a decadent treat for the English, so I always wait for our summer months and for the pots in Lynmouth to start bursting at the seams before I put them on the menu. I also believe shipping them in from Canadian farms all year round means lobster can become a mundane menu item instead of generating the special grand entrance that it deserves. Its absence allows the heart to grow fonder. The only downside to cooking shellfish is it has to be alive right up until the moment you cook it. In fact, the less time it spends out of the sea the better, which makes this a task I don't relish as I've never been the sort of cook who likes to look his food in the eye before it is put out of its pending misery. If you're worried the creature will squeal and further your guilt, don't, as this is a myth. I've cooked thousands of lobsters and crabs over the years and I've never heard a peep out of any of them.

The best way to prepare this dish is to ask a fishmonger if he has any lobster or prawn heads (they usually freeze them and sell them for stock or bisque), otherwise you'll have to prepare it in advance which is fine but lobster eats so much better when it is just cooked; the meat can go a little firm after a few hours in the fridge. They change colour to red when cooking because the heat breaks down protein and allows the carotenoids to reveal their true colour.

SERVES 4 AS A STARTER OR 2 AS A MAIN COURSE

2 500 g lobsters
3 tbsp sea salt
1 tbsp sugar
4 tbsp white wine vinegar
Lobster Marie Rose Sauce (see recipe on page 81)

Add the salt, sugar and vinegar to a large pan of boiling water and return to the boil. With a large chopping knife push the blade through the cross marking on the top of the lobster's head. (Although I am not a biologist I am told this ends it quicker than the pot.) When this deed is done drop them into the boiling water for 10 minutes: if they are slightly bigger allow 15 minutes. Pull them out of the pan and plunge into cold water for 1 minute to stop the cooking process and make them easier to handle.

If preparing for a dinner party you'll probably have to de-shell the flesh first, then share out the meat onto fresh flat leaf lettuce with a dollop of the Marie Rose Sauce on the side and a wedge of lemon. If it's just the two of you I prefer to leave them in the shell and, with some sturdy kitchen or poultry scissors to aid release and a napkin tucked in your shirt, break it from the shell at the table and drop into the sauce.

I find a bowl of fresh new potatoes and some crisp English lettuce help to digest all this decadent protein and smashing it at the table, although not as easy as it sounds and quite messy, does create rather a sense of occasion. If you serve them on a chopping board covered with a tea towel it makes it easier to crack the claws with the blunt edge of a chopping knife, and to get the tail flesh out cradle it in a tea towel or napkin and crack together between the palms of your hands and then pull apart using

Matthew Oxham on his boat October Morning *fishing off the Lynmouth coast.*

When buying lobster pick the liveliest one: the livelier the lobster the better the meat.

the cloth to cover the sharp bits of the lobster's armoured plating. However, be warned; if using your best napkins this will stain them so an old tea towel would be better.

Lobster Marie Rose Sauce

This recipe makes quite a bit but doesn't really work well with piddly little amounts and, like Simon Hopkinson says in *Roast Chicken and Other Stories*, if you try to make a small amount in a food processor it doesn't blend it just splashes up the sides. Besides you can always use it for prawn cocktail tomorrow. First we need to flavour the oil. If you don't manage to get lobster heads, prawn shells will do and remember to keep the shells from the lobsters you cook for further use.

FOR THE LOBSTER OIL

500 g lobster heads and shells
pinch of chilli flakes
500 ml grape seed oil or any other impartial oil

Put the heads and shells in a sturdy pan and with a rolling pin wrapped in cling film smash the shells to a pulp. (People will tell you to remove the feather shaped gills from the head for various reasons but I've never found it affects the end product so I leave them be when making oil.) Once smashed down put them on a medium heat and stir until all their proteins start to catch on the bottom of the pan and turn brown. Add the chilli flakes and the oil and stir well to remove the sediment from the bottom of the pan. Let the oil come up to a simmer then pull off the heat. Skim away any scum that's surfaced and leave to infuse for an hour or so then strain through a fine sieve and chill.

FOR THE SAUCE

6 egg yolks (freeze the whites for meringues, soufflés, consommés, etc.)
1 heaped tsp tomato ketchup
2 dashes of tabasco
1 tsp sweet paprika
4 tbsp white wine vinegar
3 tsp sea salt
2 caps of brandy/cognac
500 ml lobster oil (see recipe above)

Put all the sauce ingredients except the oil in a blender or smoothie-maker and blend for 30 seconds then slowly drizzle in the oil. When half the oil is in, turn off the machine and scrape down the sides with a spatula so you get an even mix. Turn back on and add the rest of the oil – it should come to the texture of a loose mayonnaise – then refrigerate. You may not need to add all the oil.

July Salad

This salad uses a few special ingredients such as candy-striped and golden beetroot, which are not readily stocked in grocers. However, with market gardens becoming ever more popular there is no reason why you shouldn't ask one of your local growers to germinate and grow a few for you. I'm sure they won't mind as it will give them a different product to sell and broadens their range. That's exactly what I did with John Rowswell in Barrington at Bakers Farm, who now grows and sells tons of specialist vegetables, from purple and green cauliflowers to rainbow carrots. All these things help to bring colour and cheer to mealtimes.

SERVES 2

1 small golden beetroot, peeled and sliced very thinly

July salad - by just using ingredients within their season a salad will almost create itself.

1 small candy-striped beetroot, peeled and sliced very thinly

8 small bunch carrots, peeled and halved lengthways and blanched in salted boiling water for 1 minute then refreshed in ice water

6 baby courgettes, yellow and green, washed and sliced

6 baby turnips, peeled and quartered and blanched in salted boiling water for 1 minute then refreshed in ice water

4 round spring onions, trimmed and quartered

handful of broad beans, blanched for 1 minute, refreshed in ice water and squeezed from their shells

2 soft English lettuces, cored and washed in cold water

Malden sea salt and mild black pepper

cornflowers or nasturtiums for garnish

FOR THE DRESSING

2 tbsp cider vinegar

2 tbsp mild honey

1 tsp fresh mild coriander seeds

1 cardamom pod, split

avocado oil

Warm the vinegar, honey, coriander seeds and cardamom pod together on a gentle heat for a few minutes then turn of the heat and leave to infuse and cool.

In a large bowl place all your prepared vegetables, but not the lettuce, and season with fresh mild black pepper and a good couple of pinches of Malden sea salt. Mix them well and leave to stand for about 5 minutes to allow the salt to penetrate and break down the vegetables. Then strain over your infused liquid, mix well and again leave to stand for a few minutes. Dress with avocado oil and toss together. Lay out the best leaves of the lettuce on two plates and

Candy-striped beetroot turn a pretty blush pink when cooked in their skin.

spoon over the vegetables and dressing and, if you're out to impress, garnish with a few washed nasturtium flowers for added summer colour.

Although this recipe is vegetarian it also eats really well with warm fish, especially oily fish such as mackerel and pilchards or red mullet, and also with crumbly cheese such as Caerphilly.

COOK'S TIP

If you don't like the crunch of uncooked vegetables in salads you can always cook the vegetables before you slice them but I find this dilutes their goodness and flavour.

Tomatoes

When buying tomatoes, although this may seem an odd thing to say, perfect shapes and even colour is not what you should be looking for, as this generally means they've been grown in a laboratory-type environment. Outdoor tomatoes are a lot more inconsistent in appearance and it's the scent and flavour that really counts. A strong and fresh scent is a clear indication of a better flavour and a good weight will mean it is nice and juicy rather than hollow and dry. The majority of the flavour is in the jelly-like liquid around the seeds. I spent years blanching and peeling tomatoes then discarding the seeds and juice into stockpots so I could dice the flesh into nice little cubes of flesh to garnish sauces and salads. It wasn't until later in life that I realised I was discarding most of the flavour. Although the skin is pretty indigestible I never discard the jelly-covered seeds now.

This next recipe for a tomato syrup is something I worked on with Jean Christophe Novelli at the Four Seasons and it has become a mainstay in my kitchen. It's fantastic for dressing salads or pastas, cold or hot, and for adding zing to fresh crab or prawns. It's even great on chips and turns a tomato salad into something special. If you have a market in your town see if they have any over-ripe tomatoes going cheap for this recipe, but they should not be furry, obviously.

Tomato Syrup

1 kg ripe tomatoes, cut in quarters

3 cloves of garlic, peeled and smashed

2 shallots, peeled and sliced

good pinch of sea salt

8 turns of fresh milled black pepper

2–3 sprigs of fresh basil

1 tbsp sugar

Place all ingredients in a big bowl and cover tightly with cling film. Half fill a large pan of water and bring to a simmer. Place the bowl on top and leave on a lower simmer for around 1½–2 hours to allow all the juices to be released from the tomato. Then leave to stand for another hour. Prick the film with a fork to allow some steam to escape then carefully remove the cling film. Line a colander with a tea towel or muslin cloth, drain the water from the pan and place the colander over it. Pour in the tomato compote and fold over the edges of the cloth and put some plates on top to weigh it down for a few hours so all the juice can run through but not the tasteless pulp, which will remain in the cloth. This can now be discarded. Reduce the liquid on a low to medium heat until it coats the back of a spoon then pour into a sterilised jam jar and refrigerate. As it has been heated and reduced it will keep for months in the fridge.

Seared Red Mullet with Fine Beans, Young Courgettes and Brandy Wine Tomatoes

I use brandy wine tomatoes for this because they're grown outdoors and their sweetness lends itself perfectly to the red mullet. However, you can use any good fresh variety and it's quite nice to use varied colours like yellow and orange as well as red to add summer sunshine to the dish. The fine beans need to be, well, fine, and again if you can get a variation in colour in the beans and courgettes, the yellow and green all help to brighten things up. I use avocado oil for this dish but if you prefer olive oil then just substitute with the same quantity.

serves 2

1 clove of garlic, peeled and smashed

2 tbsp cider vinegar

4 tbsp avocado oil or olive oil

Tigerella tomatoes have an incredible fragrance when still on the vine, which influences the flavour.

2 or 3 fat ripe tomatoes, scored and plunged into boiling water for 20 seconds then refreshed in ice water and peeled and dried on cloths
a handful of fine beans, stalks removed and washed
6 baby courgettes, washed, topped and tailed and halved lengthways
3 100–150 g red mullets, filleted and fin boned
1 banana shallot, peeled and thinly sliced
1 tbsp fresh chopped flat parsley (chopped last minute)
a drizzle of Tomato Syrup (see recipe on page 84)
fresh ripped basil leaves
sea salt and fresh black pepper
a little sugar to season

Once you have assembled your ingredients, have ready a pan of salted boiling water for the beans and courgettes, a non-stick pan and oil on a low heat, warming up ready for your fish, and another sauté pan for the tomatoes.
Into the sauté pan add the crushed garlic and vinegar and slowly reduce the vinegar to almost nothing. Season with sea salt and then add the oil and remove from the heat. Cut the tomatoes into wedges and season with salt, fresh black pepper and sugar and lay them in the pan. Then drop the beans in the boiling water and after 1 minute add the courgettes and boil for a further minute. Drain in a colander. In the non-stick pan, carefully lay in the fish fillets, red skin down and season in the pan with salt and pepper. When golden, turn with a palette knife or tongs: don't shake them as this makes their juices come out and prevents colouring, which results in dry flesh. When turned, return the pan with the tomatoes to the heat and turn them. Then turn off the heat under the fish and add the beans, courgettes, shallot and parsley to the tomatoes and gently baste them with the oil and

then share onto two plates with the fish fillets. Drizzle over the tomato syrup and basil leaves.

> COOK'S TIP
> This is a dish for which you need to be pre-organised with the ingredients and utensils, so you don't panic last minute. If you find it easier, pre-cook the beans and courgettes and just boil the kettle and pour it over them in a colander to warm them through.

BLISSFUL BUFFALO CHEESE WITH A BRANDY WINE TOMATO SALAD

This is a mozzarella made by Mike Hargreaves in Devon. The dish below is more of an assembly of ingredients than a recipe. The tomatoes must be heavy with juice for the dish to have a point.
SERVES 2

2 slices of stale crusty bread
good quality extra virgin olive oil
2 brandy wine or 4 ripe vine tomatoes, washed
200 g Blissful Buffalo mozzarella
1 small red onion, sliced into rings
fresh basil leaves, gently torn in pieces, not chopped
Malden sea salt and fresh milled black pepper

Pre-heat the oven to 180°C. Drizzle the bread with the olive oil, season with sea salt and black pepper and bake until golden and crisp. Allow to cool a little then crumble into bite-sized bits. Cut the green core from the tomatoes and dice into rough cubes. Dice the cheese, then gently toss them with the onion, basil and crispy bread bits. Spoon onto plates, season with some sea salt and black pepper and drizzle with oil, then leave for a minute to let the salt work before you eat.

SUMMER FRUITS WITH BERRY COMPOTE

There is something about summer fruits I find much more alluring than other fruits. I don't have to worry about getting my five portions of fruit a day when there's plenty of raspberries, strawberries and cherries around; in fact sometimes I almost overdose. I remember Fran, one of my apprentices, once bringing in some wild strawberries and loganberries from her garden and sharing them out with her infectious enthusiasm – such are the joys summer fruits bring to a kitchen. Although some look at wild strawberries as weeds, chefs view them as a mystical fruit seldom seen.

A very versatile food item to have in the fridge in summer is a good berry compote. You can have it in yoghurt for breakfast, or enhance clotted cream or ice-cream in a dessert or a refreshing smoothie. For this recipe a selection of cheap mixed berries is first cooked down with some sugar to release their hidden flavours before marinading them with the raw berries.

BERRY COMPOTE
SERVES 6–8

800 g mixed berries, preferably jam fruit going cheap and currants and a few cherries
200 g sugar
half a vanilla bean

In a round-bottomed bowl lightly bruise the mixed berries, sprinkle over the sugar and gently mix then cover tightly with cling film and place over a gently simmering pan for one hour. Strain through a cloth: without forcing any sediment, let it drip gently with a light weight on top to help push the juice through. Add the vanilla bean and reduce the juice to a syrup then remove from the heat and chill. This will give you a wonderful jammy fruit syrup which will enhance the flavour of the fresh fruits.

Golden rasperry Leo is sweeter but blots (softens) quicker than standard varieties.

Summer berry compote is a great example of how best to use perfect ingredients at just the right time.

1 punnet of blackcurrants
1 punnet of redcurrants
1 punnet of outdoor strawberries, if possible, if not the best you can get
1 punnet of raspberries
15–20 cherries

Wash, top and tail your currants and roll them in your Berry Compote first to allow the sweetness to counteract their sharpness and leave to stand for 30 minutes. Then hull and quarter the strawberries and half and stone the cherries. Add to the currants and gently mix well and allow to stand for another 30 minutes. Finally, fold in the raspberries so as not to break them up and, without further ado, serve in chilled bowls with Cornish clotted cream or Guernsey cream.

Potato and Goat's Cheese Blinis with Summer Fruits
SERVES 6

500 g Desiree or Maris Piper potatoes, scrubbed
1 heaped tbsp plain flour
1 egg
1 heaped tbsp soft goat's cheese such as Vulscombe or Woolsery
1 egg yolk
butter for cooking

Simmer the potatoes in their skins until they are tender through to the centre then, wearing rubber gloves, peel them hot into a food mill or a sieve and pass the potato through. Add in the flour and then the egg and mix well then fold in the goat's cheese and the egg yolk until you have a smooth thick batter. Keep in a warm place so it doesn't set.

Heat a little butter in a pan you know won't stick on a medium heat and spoon in little dollops of the batter. Let it colour a little then turn and colour the other side. Drain on kitchen paper while you fry the rest. Make sure you wipe out the pan each time and don't use too much butter or the blinis will absorb it and go greasy. To serve, spoon over some Berry Compote (see recipe above) with a little extra soft cheese.

COOK'S TIP
You could also use this recipe with smoked salmon and a little of the soft cheese on the side: just add a pinch of salt and pepper to the recipe.

What is Clotted Cream?

Somerset cream teas; Devon cream teas; Cornish cream teas: it would appear that residents and tourists alike in the West Country are fond of a cream tea. A hot fluffy scone, some with fruit, some without; homemade jam with its natural fruit flavours and slightly runny texture and then the crème de la crème – a wedge of silky, shiny clotted cream, almost yellow in colour and thick enough to hold its shape, creating a near perfect combination with each person adding as much or as little of each as they desire to suit their taste.

In the past clotting cream was another way of preserving cream. Generally associated with Devon, it's also long established in Cornwall, mainly because both have mild climates and rich grazing pastures with breeds of cattle that produce milk with a high butter fat content – up to 60 per cent butter fat is required to make clotted cream. The technique used to make the cream hasn't really changed over hundreds of years. It's a process of slow heating at low temperature (around 82°C) in a bain marie (double boiler) and cooking for around 2 hours until its honey-comb crust has formed. High-quality butter can also be made from this, although it's quite rare now, only being made by small-scale producers. Clotted cream has a protected designation of origin nowadays and no other region outside of the West Country can or is producing either the cream or the butter. And it's not just for cream teas: it's fantastic with summer fruits, hot mince pies, Christmas pudding or with stewed rhubarb or apple pie. Just try not to get too fond of it as I don't imagine it has many health-promoting properties.

Scones

Always split the dough and mix some with fruit and some without. The ones without fruit are better with jam and clotted cream; the ones with fruit are better buttered, preferably with a good rich Devon or Cornish butter.

Makes 15 x 100 g scones

Scones with clotted cream and jam make the classic West Country cream tea.

1500 g strong plain flour, sifted, plus extra for dusting
250 g unsalted butter, diced into small cubes
300 g sultanas
1 tsp salt
200 g sugar
3 tbsp baking powder
900 ml whole milk at room temperature, plus extra for brushing

Pre-heat the oven to 200°C. Crumb the flour and butter together then add all the other dried ingredients and mix well. Pour in the milk and bring the mixture together. Knead to a dough on a floured surface. Roll into a round shape about 4 cm thick then cut out rounds with a round-fluted cutter and turn onto a baking tray with the side that was touching the work surface facing up as this is the smoothest surface and will help the scones to rise more evenly. Brush with milk and bake until they rise golden. They give a slightly hollow sound when tapped; this is how you tell if the dough is cooked through and full of air.

Ice-Cream

There are quite a few companies in the West Country, and all over Britain for that matter, who are making really good quality ice-cream. When I first set about choosing recipes I thought at first that there was no point doing the ice-cream recipe as hardly anybody has an ice-cream machine at home and opening your freezer door every 15–20 minutes to stir it until frozen could end up with your freezer no longer freezing. However, it would seem that, along with bread-makers and pasta machines, ice-cream machines for the home have become popular wedding and Christmas presents over the last few years. So, due to popular demand this is the recipe for a basic but very good vanilla ice-cream that can be flavoured with whatever you fancy, but make sure you heat it to above 80°C: assuming you don't have a thermometer, it should be too hot to drop your finger in but not boiling so it curdles.

MAKES JUST OVER 1 LITRE

600 ml whole milk
300 ml double cream
75 g glucose (from a cake decorating shop)
1 split vanilla pod
6 egg yolks
150 g caster sugar

Boil the milk, cream, glucose and vanilla. Whisk the egg yolks and sugar until creamed together then slowly pour into a sterile container, cool to room temperature and refrigerator until needed. Just churn as much as you want; the mix will keep for 4 days in the fridge if covered.

Chilled Soups

I've found over my years cooking in Somerset that chilled soups seem to go down much better here than they do up north. Perhaps it's a climate thing, I don't know, but nevertheless chilled soups are the order of the day during the summer months. Originally a soup like gazpacho in the big hotels would be like a dustbin for salad trimmings. Chefs were constantly cutting things into cubes, diamonds or other unusual shapes, thus creating a lot of excess bits and these, along with the stale bread, went into the gazpacho bucket in the hors d'oeuvres fridge to be turned into the soup every day. These days, as food has become more rustic, it is also less wasteful. I also don't imagine people at home would create enough waste to require a gazpacho bucket!

Gazpacho

SERVES 4

4 good fresh ripe tomatoes, washed and
chopped
2 cloves of garlic, smashed
1 red pepper, deseeded and chopped
1 yellow pepper, deseeded and chopped
quarter of a cucumber, diced
2 slices of stale bread, diced (helps to thicken
but not essential)
1 tsp paprika
1 tsp celery salt
500 ml mild olive oil
salt and fresh pepper to taste
a little Tabasco and lemon juice to taste

Blend everything except the oil in a blender
or smoothie-maker then slowly add the oil
and adjust the seasoning. Strain through a
fine sieve and chill. Serve in chilled bowls
with an ice cube in it so the oil doesn't
warm.

Spring Onion and Crème Fraîche Soup

SERVES 4

4 bunches of spring onions, finely chopped
4 slices of white bread, diced into small cubes
1 heaped tbsp crème fraîche
salt and white pepper

Put the onion into a pan, boil the kettle and
pour over boiling water to just cover the
onion. Boil with a lid on a high heat for 3
minutes then pour into a blender with the
bread and blend for 3 minutes. Add the crème
fraîche and season to taste then pour into an
ice-cold bowl and chill down immediately.
Serve when cold.

Soft Herb and Yoghurt Soup

SERVES 4

500 ml whole milk
1 clove of garlic, chopped
10 slices of white bread, crust removed
a good sprig each of basil, tarragon, chervil and
chives
2 tbsp plain yoghurt
splash of good olive oil
salt and white pepper

Warm the milk and add the garlic. Allow to simmer on a very low heat for 2 minutes. Add the
white bread and stir until it thickens like bread
sauce. Add the herbs and stir well and simmer
for 30 seconds. Blend in a food processor for 3
minutes. Add the yoghurt, olive oil and seasoning then strain and chill. If the soup is a little too
thick when chilled then whisk in some cold milk.

Jam with Lamb

Jellies and fruit condiments have always worked
well with roast meats, cold meats, pâtés and
cheeses and I've found them to be very popular
in the South West. I think that probably comes
from the abundance of fruit we get here during
a good summer. We've got more redcurrants
than we know what to do with, so I always make
one big batch into syrup for sorbets and the rest
into jellies ready for the autumn game season.
But roe bucks are being culled on the Blackdown
Hills and forests and private estates all through
summer so by the time the grouse has been hung
for a week or so after the first shoots on 12
August, I've never got any redcurrant jelly left,
because it's been used with the roe bucks.
So all through summer, autumn and winter I
find myself making various different jellies and
fruit cheeses in preparation for the months

Jams and jellies are a great way of making summer produce last all year.

ahead but I invariably find they have all gone within a few months of making them. With any jelly or fruit preserve made with summer berries and currants, freshness is really important to retain the fruit pectin content and to catch the real zing of its flavours, but I still tend to use pre-mixed jam sugars so I always get a good set. If you don't mind them a bit softer then plain sugar will be OK if the fruit is straight from the garden. If you are using jam sugar, give the bag a good shake so the pectin is not all at the bottom of the bag.

REDCURRANT JELLY

The general rule of thumb for very sharp fruits such as redcurrants is equal quantity of sugar to liquid obtained after boiling the fruit, so if you have 1 litre of liquid you will need 1 kg of sugar, which may sound a lot but it is needed to balance the flavours. Take however many redcurrants you can get hold of, preferably at least 1 kg, and wash them in cold water but don't bother to destalk and pick them as we'll strain them later. Then in a very clean sturdy pan add the currants and just enough water to cover them. Fit the lid and bring to a boil and simmer on a low heat, covered, so it doesn't reduce. Strain through a muslin cloth or a jelly bag and a clean tea towel and squeeze out all the juice. Measure the liquid then match the amount with your sugar, and simmer them together until you have a deep red colour and a good fruity flavour. Spoon a little into a saucer and chill in the fridge to check if it sets. If not then reduce a little more and test again. When it's ready store in scrupulously clean jars with a little brandy or strong spirit brushed on top to keep away bacteria. Remember you can always use the jelly to make Cumberland sauce or to sweeten meat stocks or even in trifles.

REDCURRANT CRUSHED ICE

Wash 1 kg of currants and place in a pan with enough water to cover them. Simmer with a lid for 20 minutes. Strain through a muslin cloth and measure the liquid. If you have 1 litre of liquid you will need 780 g of sugar (or three quarters) so it's a little sharper than a jelly. Then simmer together until its colour is slightly deeper. Allow to cool and pour into a shallow tray about 1 cm deep but don't over fill (the rest of the liquid will keep for weeks in the fridge if you're only making a little). Put the tray in the freezer and every 30 minutes or so scrape with a fork until you have a tray of crushed ice. It's better than any chemically flavoured slushy thing any day.

A FOOLISH BLACKCURRANT

So called because its kind of a fruit fool and kind of not. Blackcurrant is one of my favourite flavours. I use it in jams and sorbets, but you've got to get in there quick before the juice companies buy the whole lot every year as it's such a highly popular flavour for fruit drinks and medicinal sweets.

SERVES 4

500 g blackcurrants
400 g sugar
small fresh vanilla pod or a drop of essence
100 ml water
500 ml double cream
1 tbsp icing sugar
little scrape of fresh vanilla beans or drop of essence
about 8 wholemeal digestive biscuits, crushed

Place the blackcurrants, sugar, piece of fresh vanilla pod and water in a very clean sturdy pan and simmer on a medium heat, stirring often until you get a good strong blackcurrant flavour

Garlic bulbs strung and hung to dry.

and deep colour. Then strain through a fine sieve and chill.

Whip the double cream to stiff peaks with the icing sugar and vanilla seeds. In four glasses layer up the whipped cream, blackcurrant coulis and crushed biscuits until you have a nice stripy effect up the side of the glass.

Garlic

Although garlic is viewed as a very non-English allium its popularity has grown since it was used in excess in the 1960s, 1970s and 1980s in the dreaded garlic mushroom which was, more often than not, seasoned with powdered garlic salt, which should only really be used in force-meats and pâtés. These days, however, garlic is commonplace in our cooking and used to enhance the flavours of many dishes and is grown quite widely in England. John Rowswell in Barrington, who claims the title of Britain's only banana shallot grower and seed producer, favours the giant variety, Elephant garlic, which although massive in appearance is much more mellow in flavour. I like to bake it whole and spread it on crusty toast. Just plonk them on the table, scoop the soft flesh out with your knives and spread it on!

Baked Elephant Garlic
SERVES AT LEAST 4 PEOPLE AS A GOOD APPETISER

2 whole bulbs of Elephant Garlic
honey
olive oil
sea salt

Pre-heat the oven to 180°C. Hold the bulb on its side. With a firm grip and a sharp knife cut about 3 cm off the stalk end of the bulb (not the root), this should reveal some of the flesh inside. Make two little tin foil parcels and place a bulb in each, drizzle over some honey, olive oil and sea salt, seal the parcels shut, and bake for 40 minutes until the flesh is soft and scoopable. It's also quite nice to serve as a side dish with a roast or a steak.

AUTUMN

Autumn is without doubt my favourite time of the year. The nights are still quite light and the scenery seems to change a little every day, the beautiful colours of the leaves make a quiet walk on a sunny morning quite inspirational and thoughts turn to different flavours and cooking methods. Fairytale fungi spring up in the woods overnight and the first pheasants start to bumble across the country roads in front of your car – all things that flash by but leave imprints in your mind when planning your meals. The sense of pride when the first apples arrive heaving with scent and juice for you to admire for a moment before you take the biggest bite you can, and the juice that drips from the fruit, is so good I have to grab any passing person to enthuse them to try one, just to see their reaction!

Terra Madra

In the autumn of 2006 I was lucky enough to be invited by the Slow Food Movement to represent the South West of England at the Terra Madra in Turin as one of the cooks from around the world who feel strongly about food, provenance, quality and ethically produced goods. Although there was a huge imbalance of intellectual foodies and laymen cooks it was still amazing to see cooks from 105 countries, plus hundreds of university lecturers from even more countries, not to mention the thousands of people just there to observe and absorb.

One of the important things talked about was cherishing regional products and making sure that foods that don't travel well stay where they are and foods that do travel are exported or imported fairly and that no one person alone gets fat from the profits, which are all principles with which any half decent person would have to agree. Italians know better than anybody about not letting those special ingredients of their regions, especially the Piedmont region, leave without making sure they have staked their claim for the best ingredients. As I walked through the stands at the Salon de Gusto, which is the huge food show attached to the Terra Madra, where products from all over Italy and a sprinkling from around the world are laid out in miles of stalls to be sampled, there were literally hundreds of cured meat stands with each one claiming to be a cut above the rest due to something special in their region, and the same with the cheese-makers too. Although Britain was represented with some choice meats and real ales and the usual tourist-pleasing preserves and biscuits with the ever present Scottish smokers and Colchester oysters, I didn't feel we had done ourselves justice. If you go to a restaurant trade show in Britain (which I do not recommend) you'll see more foods from abroad than from our own country. In fact, there's barely a thought put to the fact that Britain even has regionally produced food; only at farmers' markets and agricultural shows do you get that sense of pride. I can't tell you what a great feeling it is to show a new French waiter a selection of 15–20 unpasteurised artisan cheeses to rival any in the world. The look of disbelief and the spell of humbled silence as he views the board always gives me a great sense of pleasure. Luckily in the South West we have the Taste of the West that campaigns to promote the region's products, headed by great cooks such as Michael Caines. I hope in the future we can hold huge food shows with space for each region and a sprinkling of stands for the rest of the world and although we don't really have regional culinary practices compared with Spain, France and Italy, we do have the ingredients, a newly formed enthusiasm for food and cooking and an incredible mix of cultures which can be drawn upon to bring inspiration. I told one of the UK's Slow Food co-ordinators that although there was lots to be seen and tried at the Salon de Gusto food fair, I'd have rather gone to the Bath and West any day of the week and the Sturminster Newton cheese festival doesn't require a passport!

Cured Meats and Salamis

Ever since I've been lucky enough to be in a kitchen that has personal contact and an ongoing relationship with its producers, by which I mean farmers, growers, butchers and the like, I only really have one quibble and that is they expect all cooks to be solely responsible for creating a market for joints that they find harder to sell, especially if you're dealing directly with a farmer. It is much easier for them and less pressure financially to sell a kitchen half or a

The West Country now produces a wide range of cured meats, air-dried hams and salamis.

whole carcase, especially when it comes to pork. Unlike a butcher who can turn the legs into ham and all the trimmings into sausages and faggots, the farmer does not have the staff or the resources do this, and expects the cook to only offer pork until it's all gone. I do wish they could perhaps take a more diverse look at their product and step outside the British box and start to think more about other methods of pre-serving and extending their profits instead of just freezing the meat – think of the Parma hams and Prosciuttos, salamis and Coppa, and even Bresaola and Biltong for beef. All these products, if they are of a high standard, command a high price and good profits and something I hope in the future farmers will adapt to just as our cheese-makers have. Saying this, there are already some leading by example, such as Denhay with their excellent cured and air-dried hams, as well as their bacons and normal British

offerings. I'm sure the air-dried ham is now one of their most marketable products.

I've often wondered why as a country we've never been as creative at curing meats as other countries such as Spain, France and Italy. Although we have great hams and bacons, we never really seemed to get our heads around other dried hams and speckled salamis even when they have become very popular in the UK. In fact Parma ham has been on British menus for donkey's years so I have never been able to understand why we haven't taken a leaf from their book and started to manufacture these products ourselves rather than importing, espe-cially when you consider a lot of the pork they use comes from British breeding stock.

Over the years I have tried with mixed success at making my own but nothing as consistent as I'd like. Just recently I was browsing a little deli in Bath Place when I saw some rather traditional-

Jean Cole and Martin Edwards only two years into their business and having great success with a great product.

looking air-dried sausages. I asked to try a slice and was immediately impressed with the strong authentic taste untainted by chemicals. When I asked where they were from the enthusiastic owner of the deli said Deli Cornwall. At first I thought maybe she had got them from another delicatessen in Cornwall, but in further conversation I realised she meant they were made in a place called Deli Farm in Delabole, Cornwall. So I bought some salamis and rushed off to work. I later phoned the makers themselves to find out more. Jean Cole and Martin Edwards started this sideline to their business in 2005 out of pure interest in the curing process and driven by the talk of competition. They managed to get hold of a lactic culture, a bacteria they needed to get the flavour, and the right kind of mould. They then converted a shipping crate into a thermostatically controlled environment for the process of air-drying. Using a mixture of hands-on traditional techniques with modern methods of temperature control they have created some fantastic salamis and Coppa hams, which are a lot more natural than some that get imported to our supermarkets. When they're not messing around with lactic cultures they are making eco-electricity via their wind farm.

Another producer of very fine air-dried Prosciutto-type ham is Denhay. As well as producing an excellent dry, sweet cured bacon and other dairy products their ham is tender and succulent and easily rivals the continental producers of these kinds of hams. They are based in the Marshwood Vale, 3 miles from the sea just inland from Lyme Bay and have been making the air-dried hams since 1989 and the dry cured bacons since 1995.

Plums

Towards the end of summer, apart from a few hybrid varieties, which can often be a little diluted in flavour, most of our soft fruits and currants have gone on. So when the early plums, such as damsons, greengages and St Augustus come they help us to bridge the gap into autumn. Because there are so many varieties it is quite a good season going on to Victorias and then the gigantic late autumn Edward plums.

I use plums in all manner of ways to get the most out of the season – chutneys for savoury dishes, dried plums with cheese and in salads, roast plums with slow-roast duck or pork, poached plums with cream. Plums have endless uses in a busy kitchen but the favourite is always the crumble. Kevin Knapper, my pastry chef at the Castle and himself a Yeovil boy, appreciates how popular fruit puddings are in the West Country. However, even a crumble, if done in a lacklustre fashion can be so disappointing. The fruit needs to be good and ripe and sweet so you don't need to add too much sugar, and the crumble must be crunchy on top with an even ratio of fruit to crumble. With stone fruits it's also good to leave the stone in as the fruit retains its flavour better.

Plum Crumble
serves 6 to 8

175 g plain flour
115 butter
90 g Demerara sugar
55 g porridge oats
1 kg plums
4 tbsp brown sugar (taste the fruit first to gauge the amount of sugar to be used)
2 inch-deep pie or flan dish

Pre-heat the oven to 170°C. Crumb the flour with the butter and Demerara sugar until it has the texture of soft breadcrumbs. If you have a food processor it's much quicker but it's much more aesthetic if you do it by hand. Mix in the porridge oats by hand so as not to break them up. Tip onto a non-stick oven tray and toast in the oven until light golden in colour and crunchy to taste. Allow to cool on the tray before use. (You can store it for three or four days in a sealed tub.)

Turn the heat up to 200°C. Fill the bottom of the pie dish with the plums so there is no space and sprinkle over the brown sugar. Cover with foil and bake until the plums soften and start to omit their juices then remove from the oven.

Turn the oven down to 180°C. Sprinkle the crumble over the plums until the fruit is evenly and completely covered then bake until the surface is crisp and the juices are bubbling up the side of the dish, approximately 20 minutes. At work and at home the jury is still out on whether cream, custard or ice-cream is the best accomplice to a crumble. I myself prefer custard, my wife goes for cream and ice-cream together, and Kevin would have all three!

Custard
serves 6 to 8

125 caster sugar
5 egg yolks
500 ml double cream

Mix the sugar and egg yolks together. Bring the cream to the boil, pour over the egg yolks and sugar, return back to the pan to cook out the eggs. Pass and chill.

Crumble is now a speciality across the Channel where it's been borrowed by the French to accompany their Crème Anglais.

Plum Chutney

1500 g stoned and halved plums (preferably the smaller, early varieties such as St Augustus or even damson plums)
780 g brown sugar
20 ml sherry vinegar
½ cinnamon stick
3 cardamom pods
fresh grated nutmeg

Mix all the ingredients in a bowl then tip into a sturdy pan and cook on a low heat with the lid on for 10 minutes to allow the plum juices to seep out and dissolve the sugar. Remove the lid, turn the heat to medium, and allow to reduce, stirring with a wooden spoon on regular occasions until it takes on a deep pinky-brown colour and a jam-like consistency. Remove from heat and spoon into sterilised containers.
As a condiment this is great with cured meats, pâtés and salamis, and firm cheeses, and it improves after a few days of being made.

Candied Plums

Candying fruit requires a bit of love and patience as it is not an everyday task for even a keen cook, but I'm including this recipe for anybody who gets a glut of plums when they have run out of things to do with them and have got to the stage of leaving them for the wasps. Candied plums make great coffee table sweets and even though this method preserves them you won't find they are around for very long.

1 kg firm plums, washed, halved and stoned
900 g granulated sugar
1 litre water
1 vanilla pod, split, or a splash of essence
caster sugar or melted plain chocolate, for coating

Dissolve around 750 g of the granulated sugar in the water and bring to the boil with the vanilla pod. Add the plums and then turn the heat off and leave to cool. When the mixture is at about room temperature carefully spoon the plums onto a wire rack over a tray lined with grease-proof paper. Cover with greaseproof paper and leave overnight. Put the plums back into the cold syrup and bring up to a simmer on a low heat. Leave to simmer for a few minutes then transfer the plums back to the rack and cover with greaseproof paper. Add 150 g of sugar to the syrup, dissolve and turn off the heat. Leave the plums for another 24 hours and repeat the same process one more time but without adding any extra sugar. By the morning of the third day they should be firm and slightly opaque. Then roll them in caster sugar or drop them in melted chocolate and store on greaseproof paper in sealed tubs.

Plum Sauce

This is a great accompaniment to roast duck and pork, especially if you're the sort of person who likes apple sauce.

250 g ripe plums, taste tested for sweetness or sharpness
100 g Demerara sugar, less for sweet plums and more for sharp
50 g unsalted butter

Pre-heat the oven to 180°C. Put the whole plums in a roasting dish, sprinkle with the sugar and cover with foil and bake for around 30 minutes until they are plump and soft. Then push them through a sieve until only the stones and skins remain. Put the purée in a pan and reduce to apple sauce consistency. Add the butter, taste for sweetness and adjust if necessary.

MULBERRY SORBET

Not many people use mulberries these days and they are not widely recognised in England. I think perhaps texturally people don't like them and they're not a pretty fruit even though they come from a beautiful tree. They are also very messy, and if you eat too many you'd better be near a loo! Although you don't get them in the shops almost every picture box village will have a secret tree hidden somewhere, usually the old vicarage. If you find one and the owner will let you take a good quantity, this recipe, although impractical for those who don't possess an ice-cream maker, can be done: I've had to include it because I've just made the sorbet for Mr Chapman the Castle's owner and it was so lovely I didn't want to miss it out.

MAKES 1 LITRE

250 g sugar
250 ml water
500 g mulberries

Dissolve the sugar in the water, simmer for 10 minutes and set aside to cool. Blend the mulberries in a processor and pass through a sieve. Then, using an equal amount of fruit pulp to syrup, i.e. 500 ml syrup to 500 ml mulberry pulp, mix together and, if you have a sorbet maker, churn until set. If you don't it's a bit more laborious and the result will be a little bit crystally but equal in flavour. Just pour the mix into a bowl then put that bowl in a bowl of ice and stir until very cold. Transfer the bowl into the freezer and every 20 minutes whisk until set – but it's going to take some time.

SALAD OF EDWARD PLUM, OX BLOOD LETTUCE, APPLE, WALNUT AND EXMOOR BLUE

It's always a bit sad when Mervyn brings the first apples (usually the variety called Scrumptious) and some of the first Bramleys start to make an appearance. As much as I love a good apple, and believe me they're good, it is still the marker for the end of summer fruits and at work we're frantically bottling plums to stretch out the fruit season. One very special variety that comes with the first apples is the Edward plum, a giant almost black-skinned plum with yellow flesh dotted with honey-like sugar deposits. It has to be picked and sold when totally ripe and at its optimum sweetness, which doesn't make it ideal to cook with, but an amazing eating plum as it's best enjoyed as nature intended. I've never seen this plum anywhere else in the country and I always feel privileged that within this area we have such amazing and individual products.

SERVES 2

2 Edward plums or 3 Victoria plums
1 Scrumptious or Cox's Pippin apple
10 walnuts, blanched in boiling water from the kettle and lightly toasted (this removes any bitter aftertaste), and crumbled
2 tbsp walnut oil
100 g Exmoor blue cheese
good handful of washed ox blood lettuce or chard leaves
1 tbsp sherry vinegar
sea salt and black pepper
watercress, optional

Cut the plums into thin wedges and the same with the apple and put into a salad bowl. Sprinkle over the crumbled walnut, the walnut oil and vinegar, and season. Gently toss together then

A classic combination of fruit, nuts and cheese makes an easy seasonal salad.

arrange onto two plates. Crumble over some Exmoor blue. A few sprigs of watercress also adds some iron and a peppery edge to the salad.

Apple and Blackberry Pie

I like to blend an eating apple with a cooker for apple pie so you have a balanced sweetness without having to add too much sugar and masking the fruit flavours. Sweet varieties, such as Scrumptious and Cox, mixed with Bramley gives a good result. As with crumble there seems to be a north/south divide on the cream or ice-cream or custard decision.

SERVES 6

500 g flour, sifted, plus extra for flouring
300 g butter, diced
125 g caster sugar, plus extra
3 whole eggs
400 g eating apples, such as Scrumptious or Cox, peeled and diced
400 g Bramley apples, peeled and diced
200 g blackberries
4 tbsp caster sugar

25–30 cm pie dish

Rub the flour, butter and sugar to a breadcrumbs consistency. Make a well in the middle, add the eggs and slowly knead together to a soft dough. Then, on floured, greaseproof paper, while the dough is soft, roll it out into a 2 cm thick square so that when it's chilled it's easy to roll. Refrigerate the dough until it is firm, then flour your work surface and roll out to about 5 mm thick. Roll the pastry around the pin and roll over your pie dish and mould into the corners filling any gaps and sprinkle a little sugar across the surface of the pastry. Cut away the excess and remould into a dough and chill while you prepare the filling.

Pre-heat the oven to 160–180°C. You'll need equal amounts of cooking apple to sweet apple – enough to fill the pie to the brim when peeled and diced – then sprinkle over the granulated sugar. Roll out your leftover pastry until its circumference will cover the pie and then roll it over your pin and roll over the pie and pinch around the edge to create a seal. Make a couple of cuts with scissors to allow steam to escape. Bake until the pastry is nice and crisp and the filling is bubbling, normally around 40 minutes. Allow to cool slightly before serving because boiling fruit and sugar is a real shock if it's dribbled down your chin. For a change from custard or ice-cream, serve with Crème Chantilly, see page 73.

Apple and Blackberry Jelly

1 kg Bramley apples, chopped
400–450 g blackberries, washed (must be very fresh)
1.5 litres water
1 kg jam sugar

Simmer the fruit in the water until it has dissolved then strain through a jelly bag or clean tea towel with a weight on and leave to press for 20 minutes. Measure the liquid: if there is a lot more than 1 litre, return to a pan and reduce until you have a litre. Add the jam sugar and simmer until syrupy and test for setting on a saucer in the fridge.

Apple Sauce

Apple sauce is a staple of the table during autumn and winter, especially with pork and duck. As with the apple pie, I like to use a blend of cooking and eating apples to balance the sweet and sharp flavours so you don't have to add too much sugar. I also blend the sauce in a food processor to make it smooth, but if you prefer it chunky just don't blend it.

Bramleys are ideal for adding acidity to any apple dish.

1 Bramley apple, peeled, cored and chopped
1 Cox's Pippin or any other sweeter apple,
peeled, cored and chopped
50 g unsalted butter
1–2 tbsp caster sugar to taste

Put half the butter in a pan with the apple and a
little sugar, covered with a lid, over a low heat
and allow the moisture to seep from the apples.
Remove the lid, turn up the heat a little and stir
until all the apple has broken down. Blend while
hot until smooth, add the remaining butter and
sugar to taste.

> **COOK'S TIPS**
> This freezes well so if you have a glut of apples
> you can make more and freeze in batches.
> Refrain from adding spices like cinnamon, as
> they become very scented when mixed with
> the fruit and sugar and overpower the sauce.

Apple Charlotte

Charlottes are fantastic old-fashioned and simple
puddings. Like bread-and-butter and cabinet
pudding they were a way of utilising leftover
bread. These days it would seem white bread has
gone out of fashion: it bloats you, makes you fat,
give you headaches – which is absolute rubbish.
Bread is a very refined form of carbohydrate and
needs to be used to fuel hard work and play –
more park life and less pork life – but the result is
that bread pudding is no longer a household regular, and you will probably have to buy a small
white loaf just to make this delicious pud. I'm
sure even your slender non bread-eating friends
will want to try it, although they might decline
the dollop of clotted cream I would serve with it.
SERVES 4

12 slices white bread, crusts off, 8 slices cut into
discs and 4 slices cut in half
250 g butter, melted
2 large Bramleys, peeled, cored and diced
sugar to taste
4 180 ml dariol moulds or ovenproof dishes

Pre-heat the oven to 180–200°C. Lightly toss the
apple in 50 g of the melted butter on a low heat.
Season with a little sugar to taste as it softens
then remove from the heat and allow to cool.
Dip each slice of bread into the remaining butter
squeezing away the excess between two fingers
and then line each of the moulds with the discs
in the bottom first then two halves around the
sides. Fill with the apple filling and put the last
discs on top. As you put each piece of bread in,
press and pinch them together so they don't fall
apart after cooking. Cover with buttered tin foil
and bake until bubbling and the bread is nice
and crispy. Allow the puddings to cool and settle
for 5–10 minutes before serving or chill and
reheat before serving.

> **COOK'S TIP**
> The same pudding is just as good using plums
> instead of apples or with a few brambles
> added when filling the moulds.

Quinces and Medlars

These are real autumn treasures. A box of freshly
picked plump yellow quinces will fill a kitchen
with their sweet pear aroma. Although I have
included jelly and cheese methods, people tell
me they always end up with loads of jelly they
can't even give away as just four or five quinces
will give you a fair amount, so I have also
included a few recipes using the jelly and the

fruit. Mr and Mrs Covey, regular customers at the Castle for many years, bring me their Langaller quinces which are absolutely wonderful, and then later on the fruit from their medlar tree, an unfortunate-looking fruit from such a pretty tree. In France its name translates to 'dog's bum fruit' in slang and if you've ever seen a medlar this description could be quite off-putting. You also have to wait until the fruit is blotted – gone soft and brown, almost rotten – before use. This aside, the appearance of the fruit does in no way impair its flavour and fragrance when cooked.

Quince Trifle

Although most people's experience of trifle is soggy sponge cake, cheap jam, tinned fruit and powdered custard topped with whipped cream and decorated with hundreds and thousands, its history goes beyond its bastardisation in the 1960s, '70s and '80s. Before these times macaroons would have been soaked in a liqueur and covered in egg custard, then fruit and jam and lastly whipped cream. This is a method I much prefer and although I have included a macaroon recipe, buying plain ones is perfectly acceptable, but don't replace the egg custard with powdered as it's not as light, and fresh vanilla pods are readily available now and have a much better flavour than essence.

SERVES 6

1 quince or medlar, cored, peeled and quartered
350 ml water
juice of ½ lemon
250 g caster sugar
12 macaroons (see recipe below)
Somerset brandy or an apple digestive such as Kingston Black
500 ml double cream

Quince Jelly (see recipe on page 115)
icing sugar, to taste

FOR THE EGG CUSTARD
800 ml whole milk
½ vanilla pod, split lengthways
6 egg yolks
60 g caster sugar
80 g plain flour

To make the egg custard, bring the milk and vanilla pod to a simmer. Whisk together the yolks, sugar and flour and slowly pour over the milk. Whisk together then return to the pan and stir over a low heat until nicely thickened. Remove from the heat. Immerse the quince or medlar into the water with the lemon juice and caster sugar. Bring to a gentle simmer until the fruit has softened enough for a blunt butter knife to penetrate then remove from the heat and allow to cool. To assemble the trifle, lay the macaroons in the bottom of your dish or dishes (individual glasses look sweet) then drizzle over some Somerset brandy or apple digestive to moisten the biscuits. Pour over the custard and allow to cool and set. Slice the poached quince, mix it with some Quince Jelly and spread it liberally over the custard's surface then whip the double cream with a splash of apple brandy and icing sugar to taste and spread or pipe over the fruit. Chill for an hour or so before eating.

COOK'S TIPS
If you've made a big bath of jelly and the quinces have gone out of season, just use some poached pears instead or diced dessert apple mixed through the jelly.
This trifle is fine prepared a day in advance.

Medlars are a brilliant late autumn fruit. Don't be put off by their appearance as it's the flavour that counts.

Serve quince or any other trifle in individual whisky tumblers to show the beautiful layers.

Macaroons

This recipe makes a lot, but they keep well in sealed dry containers.

10 egg whites
625 g caster sugar
625 g icing sugar
325 g ground almonds

Pre-heat the oven to 180°C. Whisk the eggs slowly adding the caster sugar until stiff peaks form. Then fold in the ground almonds and icing sugar and pipe onto trays, or paper if the mix is quite loose because the eggs are older. Bake them immediately for 5 minutes then turn off the oven and leave them for 20 minutes. Pull them out of the oven and allow to cool fully before storing on paper towels in a sealed container. If the mix is quite stiff and holds its shape when piped, because the eggs are fresh, you will need to leave them to sit for 5 minutes or so before you bake.

Quince Jelly

1 kg quinces or however many you have acquired (you will need to adjust the quantity of sugar to liquid)
jam sugar

Wash and cut the quinces into rough pieces. If you are using medlars you will need to let them go brown and soft (blotted) first. Cover the fruit with water and simmer until the fruit has softened completely and is falling apart. Strain through a jelly bag or cloth with a weight on top to squeeze out the excess juice and leave for an hour or so, then measure your remaining liquid. Add 500 g of jam sugar to 600 ml of liquid. Boil gently until the syrup is deep red and then test

for setting on a saucer in the fridge or at jam on a jam (sugar) thermometer. Preserve in a sterilised container to use as a condiment with strong meats or for desserts.

Quince Cheese

As with damson, apple or any fruit cheese, extracting the liquid is the important factor in helping them set so try not to add too much water at the beginning as this just takes longer to reduce. The quince should be aromatic and ripe. The end result can be sugared and eaten as a sweet treat like fruit pastilles or grazed with cured meats and cheeses.

1.5 kg quinces, washed and chopped
just enough water to cover
juice of ½ lemon
jam sugar
caster sugar

Simmer the fruit in the water and lemon juice for about 30–40 minutes until the fruit is pulping. Pass through a food mill and measure it, then add the jam sugar at a 8:10 ratio, e.g. 1 kg fruit purée to 800 g jam sugar. Slowly reduce them together on a low heat until almost all the liquid has gone and the mix starts plopping like a mud geezer, then line a deepish tray with non-stick paper and pour in the mix. Put in a warm place like the airing cupboard to carry on drying out for a couple of days or so. To store, either cut into small pieces and roll in caster sugar or wrap in greaseproof paper, and store in a sealed container.

Medlar Jelly

As many medlars as you've been given or harvested and left to blott (go soft and brown)
jam sugar

Cut these squidgy medlars in quarters and put into a spacious pot, cover with water and simmer until they have disintegrated then strain through a cloth or a jelly bag. Reduce the liquid by a quarter then measure and add 400 g jam sugar to every 500 ml of liquid. Like other jellies, simmer until at jam on a jam (sugar) thermometer or until a sample on a saucer will set in the fridge. The jelly should be ruby red, and you'll be surprised as medlars make one of the best jellies you'll ever try.

> COOK'S TIP
> As well as an accompaniment to game and strong meats, medlar jelly is great with the pub classic deep-fried Somerset brie. Although not my cup of tea, deep-fried cheese is still a favourite for many and works well with any fruit jelly.

Salads – Not Just for Summer

The word salad has become a pretty versatile description on menus covering a broad spectrum of dishes. The word derives from the Latin term *sal* meaning salt and over hundreds of years it travelled across Europe to France as *salade* and then to England around medieval times as a *sallet* or salad, which would have been made up of a mixture of basic green leaves dressed with salt and vinegars. Progressively over the years more and more items were added such as fruit or cold meats and herbs. Because they are mostly made up of all cold ingredients or cold mixed with warm, we tend to associate them with spring and summer. But I always feel that this is a shame because a lot of lettuce leaves thrive, especially in the south's warmer climate, all through winter. I do not just mean your hardy cut and grow leaves

such as mizuma, rocket and mustard leaves, but also the softer more gentle and less spicy lettuce such as cocarde, red sails, unico and black seeded Simpson, which all do well through the winter outside or under poly-tunnels. Also during the winter months we tend to eat more roasts so there's always some cold meat to use up. A nicely dressed salad is a light, healthy way to use up these bits and bobs, whether it's a tin of Cornish pilchards or just some ham and cheese with good fresh crunchy lettuce in a sandwich. So don't rule out the salad option just because it's cold outside.

VENISON SALAD
SERVES 2

150 g piece of venison loin
1 ripe William or Comice pear
2 plums
50 g celeriac, peeled and grated
1 tbsp port
1 tbsp hazelnuts, toasted and crushed
1 tbsp pumpkin seeds, toasted
a selection of young leaves such as mizuma, mibuma, chard
2 tbsp pumpkin oil
salt

Season the venison with salt and seal in hot beef fat or oil and carefully turn to colour evenly. When it is nicely coloured, turn off the heat, dab away the fat with paper towels and leave the meat in the pan turning every minute or so to allow the residual heat to continue the cooking. Cut the pear and the plums in half lengthways and remove the cores/stones then cut into small wedges. Put them in a bowl with the grated celeriac and splash over the port. Add the nuts, seeds and leaves and toss together with the pumpkin oil. Thinly carve the meat, it should be nice and rare, and toss it through the salad with any juices from the pan being added to it. Serve straightaway so the leaves don't wilt.

> COOK'S TIP
> You could also use pigeon breast for this salad; just allow less cooking time if the breasts are off the bone or more if on the bone.

Rosehips

Come October rosehips fill our hedgerows weaving amongst the sloe berries and black-thorn and generally going unnoticed by most. Not so long ago rosehip syrup was an important source of vitamin C especially in the armed forces during the Second World War and for children and convalescents. It is really simple to make and it's great on ice-cream, and if you want to set it so it's spreadable for breakfast you just use sugar with added pectin instead of plain sugar when you make the syrup.

You need to wait until they are bright red or orange before you pick them; if they are still green don't bother. I tend to take two bags with me so I can pick between the plump ripe sloe berries and the best of the rosehips, usually making a few trips over a couple of weeks in Hatch. I freeze each batch of sloes and hips – this acts like a frost, which helps to sweeten them. I'm sure there are more scientific reasons to do with sugars and carbohydrates but nevertheless it seems to work and by doing so I can make one big batch rather than two or three smaller ones.

ROSEHIP SYRUP

500 g rosehips, washed, topped and tailed

750 ml water
400–500 g caster sugar

Simmer the hips in the water until soft – this usually takes around 1–1½ hours. If you have a little food mill pass the liquid through to squeeze out all the pulp but leave the seeds and hairs behind. If you don't have a mill just push the mix through a fine sieve, which will give you the same end product but with a little more effort. Bring back to a simmer and gradually add 100 g of sugar at a time and taste and keep adding sugar until you're happy with the sweetness. Simmer gently for a further 10 minutes and remove from the heat. Chill and store: if you're using jam sugar you'll need to test to see if it's set on a little plate in the fridge.

SLOE PRESERVE

500 g sloes, washed and pricked
2 Bramley apples, chopped
750 ml water
¼ vanilla pod (optional)
500 g jam sugar (with added pectin)

Simmer the sloes and apples in the water with the vanilla pod until the berries have completely broken down. Strain through muslin or a very clean tea towel and squeeze out all the juice and measure it. You need approximately equal amounts of jam sugar to liquid, i.e. 500 ml of liquid needs 500 g jam sugar. Simmer until dark and glossy and test for setting on a saucer in the fridge or at jam if you have a jam (sugar) thermometer.

SLOE GIN

Sloe gin – the favoured tipple at point-to-points up on cold hills in the rain, eating sausage rolls

and forgetting to watch the races while sat on somebody's car boot. Fantastic! So it would seem everyone in the West Country has got their own recipe. Mine's pinched from some friends in the village – Geoff and Pam. I just add a little bit of vanilla to make it smoother.

250–300 g sloes, washed, topped and pricked (do this before freezing, if you're freezing)
250 g sugar
¼ vanilla pod (optional)
1 bottle of cheap gin
1 bottle of cheap red wine

Roll the berries, sugar and vanilla together gently until the sugar has dissolved then tip into a jar and cover with all the gin. Clip on the lid and leave to steep for around three months. Carefully decant the liquid into a bottle using a funnel leaving the sediment and berries behind. Pour over the red wine and add a little more sugar. I leave it for a couple of days to infuse and then decant. It will give you a nice fruity and fortified wine for a colder evening after supper with some dark chocolate.

Crab Apple and Mint Jelly

Crab apples, like medlars, can get over cooked, but they are a useful tool to set mint jelly for lamb, or chilli jelly for game, and again they are something you can collect for free.

1 kg crab apples, washed and stalks removed
bunch of mint stalks and leaves, separated
jam sugar at a ratio of 9:10 sugar to liquid

Smash up the apples in a food processor or with a rolling pin. Add the mint stalks and cover with water. Simmer until the fruit is soft and strain through a cloth. Measure the liquid and add the sugar and boil until clear. Check the setting point on a plate in the fridge or at jam on a jam (sugar) thermometer then add the chopped mint leaves and store in a sterilised jar.

> COOK'S TIP
> If you want to make chilli jelly omit the mint and add fresh chopped chillis when you add the sugar.

Roasting a Loin of Pork with Good Crackling (and Not Terminally Dry Meat)

Pork can be a real treat but I think that more than any other meat it can also be a bore and this is generally due to using the wrong breeds and the wrong cuts for the wrong jobs. Pork for general cooking needs a good fat to meat ratio (not too lean or it will be dry) and for this you tend to find Duroc, Saddlebacks, Middle White and Gloucester Old Spot carry a good layer of fat. They also have a lot of hair and as it is not always appetising to see stubble in your crackling farmers tend to cross them with a less hairy and more commercially viable Large White, which then gives you a good fat to meat ratio, less hair to deal with – and he gets a heavier pig to sell. When choosing the right cuts of pork for the right job it is pretty straightforward as most of the pig lends itself better to long slow cooking at low temperatures such as the shoulder, belly, neck and leg. The only pieces you would cook quickly would be the tenderloin (the fillet) or loin chops, but these still need to be cooked through – not just for killing tapeworms and for the benefit of squeamish people who don't like bloody meat – because it can taste a little metallic and leave an aftertaste if not cooked through.

This doesn't mean grilling for hours, just either pan fry, grill or bake until the juices come to the surface and start to congeal then allow to rest on a rack for 5 minutes so it won't be so tough. When roasting a loin of pork you need to go somewhere in between. It needs to be cooked right through but it can be too lean for slow cooking so becomes dry; you need to start the cooking process fairly slowly then raise the temperature to crisp the skin in the last quarter of the cooking time. You also need to be looking for outdoor reared pork for better crackling, as the skin is dryer and crisps better.

1.5 kg loin of pork on the bone with the skin scored
4 onions, peeled and halved
300 g pork trimmings
500 ml water
2 cloves of garlic
salt and flour to thicken the gravy if necessary
sea salt

Pre-heat the oven to 200°C. Lay the onions on a roasting tray as a trivet to stop the joint burning. Lightly oil the skin and sprinkle with salt (the oil will help the salt stick). Add water to the tray to a depth of 2 cm. Lay a piece of greaseproof paper on the skin of the pork and lay the joint bone side down on top of the onions. Then cover the whole lot with a tight layer of tin foil. The greaseproof paper will stop the foil from sticking and the water will essentially steam the meat and keep it moist. Place in the oven for 1 hour to steam then remove the foil and continue to roast for another hour at 220°C to allow the skin to crisp up, checking every so often that the oven is not too hot and burning the crackling. As the joint goes in the oven, brown off the trimmings with a little oil in a sturdy pot. When they are evenly coloured and crispy remove from the heat and dab the fat away with paper towels. Return to the heat and cover with the water, add the garlic and a sprinkle of sea salt and simmer gently while the pork cooks. It should reduce to about 250 ml.

To make sure the meat is cooked through, push a skewer into the centre and when removed the juices should run clean and the point of the skewer should be hot to the touch. Put the joint on a rack to rest and dab away the fat in the tray with paper towels. Strain the stock into the tray making sure any sediment in the tray dissolves into the gravy then tip everything back into the stock pan and simmer for a few minutes and season to taste. If you want the gravy thick then mix 10 g of soft butter with 10 g of flour and whisk into the gravy and strain. If you don't thicken it, just force the onions through the sieve when you pass the gravy to give it some body, then whisk in a knob of butter.

Lizzie and Rob Walrond

The Walronds have farmed their 100-acre plot called Glebe Farm in Pitney in Langport for 200 years with three generations still involved on the farm today. They converted to full organic status in 2001 and are licensed growers and processors with the Soil Association. They have a wonderful small farm shop voted best in Somerset, which sells theirs and like-minded farmers' wares. They have a small herd of Saddleback sows, a flock of ewes, laying hens and beef cattle, all of which are fed on their own barley. Having worked with their produce for about five years now I'm always really impressed with how sincere they are about what they do and how they do it, involving local schools to help educate children on where their food comes from, doing special open days for the benefit of the farming community and have stood by Friends of the Earth to lobby against GM crops. Their philosophy of food travelling 100 yards not 1,000 miles is exactly what I'm always harping on about. Good people doing a good and hard job deserve all the harping we can give them!

Corn on the Cob

Whole buttered corn on the cob: a real treat as a simple lunch, a great accompaniment to roast pork or slow roast duck. Over the years, outside of rural farming communities where it is still a treat, corn on the cob has acquired an unfortunate reputation as a low-grade ingredient favoured by profiteers as a cheap imported frozen or canned, available-all-year-round ingredient. But like all the ingredients we are covering if you can get good corn grown for human consumption from a local grower and not from some vast expanse overseas, it is a special product and one I look forward to every year. Unfortunately my usual suppliers, Robert and Lizzie Walrond at Glebe Farm in Pitney, who sell organic pigs, sheep, eggs and all sorts of wonderful things, haven't been able to grow any to cob this year because the badgers have had them all and that's when I realised how much I'd missed cob off the menu. Instead I've had to source it from anybody in Somerset who's avoided the badgers, just to get my fill.

Buttered Corn on the Cob
SERVES 2

2 large firm bright yellow cobs, husks removed
1 tbsp Malden salt
lots of decent butter

Boil the corn in deep water with the salt for

around 20–30 minutes and serve daubed in butter. If serving it with a main meal stick a meat fork in the top and carve away the corn from the cob and roll in butter

Buttered Sweet Corn Soup

This soup requires the corn to be very very fresh; otherwise it is too hard and won't cook down to thicken the soup. The calorific value is high so if you're watching your weight I suggest you go for a run afterwards!
SERVES 6

3 corn on the cob, cut in half
2 litres water
150 g butter
good pinch of sea salt and the same of sugar

Poach the corn in the water for 30 minutes then spoon out the cobs and cut the corn away from the husks using a fork and a sharp knife. Discard the husks and put the corn back in the water, add the butter and simmer for 30 minutes. Blend for 4 minutes and pass through a fine sieve or cloth, adjust the seasoning and serve or chill.

Broccoli Florets with Soft Boiled Egg and Lemon, Almond and Rosemary Butter

This is a lovely healthy light lunch and you can easily replace the butter with a nut or mild olive or rapeseed oil . This is again an ensemble of ingredients rather than a recipe to follow with precision.
SERVES 2

3 free-range eggs
2 large very fresh heads of broccoli, with the florets cut away from the stalk. Cut a cross in any stalk remaining on the florets so they cook evenly

75 g unsalted butter
2 tbsp sliced almonds
sprig of rosemary, washed
zest and juice of ½ lemon
Malden sea salt and black pepper

Put a tissue in the bottom of the pan so the eggs don't crack then fill with water, bring to the boil and drop the eggs in gently on a spoon and boil for 4 minutes. Remove from the pan and allow to cool for 5 minutes then peel gently. When the eggs are peeled drop the broccoli into boiling salted water and separately melt the butter on a fairly high heat and add the almonds and rosemary. After about 2 minutes the water will start to turn green as the chlorophyll escapes the broccoli so drain straight away into a colander. Your butter should not burn but go lightly brown and clear and the almonds should colour slightly. Pick out the rosemary with tongs and grate in the zest and squeeze in the juice of the lemon. Turn off the heat, put the broccoli in individual bowls or plates, quarter the eggs and divide them between the bowls and then spoon over the almonds and butter. Season with fresh milled black pepper and a little Malden salt.

Pears

The window for getting perfect eating pears is pretty short. They are either too hard or the next minute they are blotting and fermenting. To catch one at perfect ripeness for eating is just a day almost. Sucking the juice through your teeth while the excess runs down your chin is quite a rare experience with English pears, although they do seem to fair better in the warmer climate of the south. You've got to catch them before the wasps do, especially with the Conference variety, which seem to be the most popular to grow. This is a shame as to my mind they are the most useless of pears. That said, they are good to eat if perfectly ripe.

The best way to enjoy pears, rather than sitting patiently waiting for the right moment, is to poach them when they are still a little firm. They lend themselves to this method of preserving very well. Some people like to add all sorts of spices and aromatics to the process but I find too much cinnamon and the like can ruin the flavour. Just a little star anise, which has an aniseed taste that brings out the flavour of the pear is enough as we don't want something that tastes like a cough sweet or pot pourri.

POACHED PEARS
SERVES 4

4 firm Comice or William pears
enough water to cover
an 8:10 ratio of sugar to water, e.g. 800 g sugar to 1 litre water
½ vanilla pod
½ star anise
50 ml pear Eau de Vie (optional), or if you can get a miniature of a pear liqueur rather than buying a whole bottle

Peel the pears and scoop out the core from the bottom with a teaspoon or melon baller. Bring all the other ingredients to a simmer and when the sugar has fully dissolved plunge in the pears. Simmer on a low heat covered with greaseproof paper and a saucer so they don't bob on the surface or cook unevenly. This will take 30 minutes for hard pears and 10 minutes for soft pears. Turn off the heat and leave to stand and cool. They will finish cooking in the residual heat as the liquid cools. Store in a sterilised, sealed container.

I love to serve this with a creamy rice pudding (see recipe below). It's actually more like a sweet risotto because of the cooking method and although it doesn't get the brown skin that people remember from their mother's rice pudding it is just as fulfilling especially when served with the poached fruit. To add texture just sprinkle sugar on the top and grill it like a crème brulée.

Rice Pudding
ENOUGH FOR 4 WITH SOME LEFT OVER FOR EATING COLD!

500 ml whole milk
250 ml double cream
30 g unsalted butter
½ vanilla pod
90 g pudding rice, washed
3 egg yolks
70 g sugar
brown sugar, to serve

Bring the milk, cream, butter and vanilla pod to a boil and pour over the rice. Then over a simmering pan of water stir the rice mix fairly constantly until the rice has absorbed the dairy and the grains have softened. Mix the egg yolks with the sugar and cream them well. Fold into the rice mix and stir until thickened. Spoon into bowls, sprinkle brown sugar on top and melt under the grill. Serve the poached pears either hot or cold laid on the side of the rice.

Damson Cheese

Fruit cheeses, like quince, apple or indeed damson, are a great preserve to have with cured meats and cheeses but also make great after dinner fruit pastilles just rolled in a little sugar or dipped in chocolate. Fruit cheeses themselves are a pretty laborious task but for produce such as damsons, which people are usually giving away because they don't know what to do with them, it's rewarding to be able to make something a little bit special from an ingredient that's not necessarily that versatile. A handy piece of equipment to pass out all the bits and save time is a Moulin or a food mill, but if you don't have one a sieve will do.

damsons, washed
a splash of red wine
jam sugar
granulated sugar

Put your damsons in a large, heavy-duty pan with a splash of red wine. Cover with a lid and sit over a low heat until the damsons have totally softened and the juice has turned purple. Pass through your Moulin or sieve to remove the skin and stones. Return the pulp to the pan and slowly reduce stirring on a low heat at regular intervals. But be warned, wear an apron as it is messy and stains. Keep stirring until the liquid has evaporated and you have a thick purple mass. Slowly add jam sugar until you have the required sweetness and cook until all the sugar has dissolved. Then in a deep tray lined with greaseproof paper, pour in the cheese. Cover with greaseproof paper and put in a warm place such as your airing cupboard. Allow to slowly set: it should be firm to the touch, which can sometimes take days. When ready, cut into squares and individually wrap in greaseproof paper. If you're making pastilles cut into small squares and roll in granulated sugar.

Mushrooms

One of the things cooks like to do come the beginning of autumn is to make the addition of wild mushrooms to menus to give them an autumnal feel, which it does as most people associate fungi with this season, although in reality wild fungi are around from early summer through to winter. The St George's mushroom, so called for being around at the time of St George's Day, and, if its fairly damp, summer girolles and other fancy varieties do very well and I'm constantly hearing tales from foody folks about their secret patch of ceps or clouds of orange chanterelles in mossy hedgerows. But truth be told, unless you know your *Boletus luridus* from your *Boletus edulis* or your *Cantharellus cibarius* from your *Calocera viscosa* then don't pick them.

The only wild mushrooms I would say to go for are good old-fashioned field mushrooms. They make beautiful soup and are perfect on toast or grilled for breakfast. Also giant puffball mushrooms are pretty easy to recognise as they look like footballs lolloping on the grass. They have no stem, cap or gills but like any mushrooms they must not be picked when still damp from rain or dew as they will be no use in the kitchen and go limp and soggy very quickly. They should be firm and dry to touch. There are other puffballs but stick to the giant as it is easily recognised because the flesh of the puffball is quite porous (spongy). It's great to use to mop up pan juices after frying a steak. Just pull out the steak to rest and gently fry the mushroom in the same pan and fat so it soaks up all the flavours. They are also great gently sautéed and folded through a risotto and a darn sight easier to recognise than a *Lactarius deliciosus*.

A lady called Sacha Swartz, who lives in Thornfalcon just outside Taunton, randomly brings us giant puffballs from her orchard as well as squashes and other vegetables and damsons, so without any effort on my part she helps me keep my menu on the seasonal track

as all I have to do is wait for her to arrive with the mushrooms, put them on the menu and cook them. Over the past few years I've found that as more and more people turn up randomly with different and individual ingredients, the simpler and more respectful of the ingredient the cooking becomes; mushrooms are a great example of something that doesn't need to be messed around with.

Puffball Mushroom on Toast

Rapeseed, grape seed or sunflower oil for cooking
Mushrooms, diced into rough cubes, about 3 cm
1 clove of garlic, crushed
little fresh parsley, chopped
drizzle of double cream, optional
salt and pepper

Pre-heat a pan, add a drizzle of oil and gently sauté the mushrooms. As they start to colour add the garlic and allow it to soften and the mushrooms to colour a little more. Then add the parsley and toss together. Add a drizzle of double cream and toss together over the heat until the mushrooms are coated with the reduced cream. Taste and add seasoning if required then spoon onto toasted brown bread.

Grilled Rabbit with Field Mushrooms, Toasted Hazelnuts, Sunflower Seeds and Honeyed Parsnips

This dish is a kind of warm autumn salad. It is healthy, cheap and gives a great sense of seasonality. If you are not the sort of person who eats animals that are popular as family pets then grilled chicken fillets will do the job.

To obtain the loin fillets for this recipe, buy two whole fresh-skinned rabbits. Remove the loin fillets from the saddle by running a sharp knife along the line at the side of the backbone, gently down to the rib cage and along the ribs using your fingers to help hold the meat from the bone as the knife works. Then with the tip of the knife release the loin fillet at either end. From the two rabbits you will get four finger-shaped loin fillets. Then chop the legs off and reserve for pies, pâtés and potting, chop up the carcase for stock or freeze for later use. Keep the liver, kidney and heart for pâté. Your butcher will do all of this for you if you don't want to.

SERVES 2 AS A MAIN COURSE

2 young parsnips
3 or 4 good-sized field mushrooms, sliced
local honey
1 clove of garlic, crushed
4 rabbit loin fillets
sherry vinegar
Marsala wine
2 tbsp hazelnut oil
oak leaf lettuce, baby gem or cocarde, trimmed, washed and spun
1 tbsp sunflower seeds, lightly toasted under the grill
2 tbsp hazelnuts, lightly toasted under the grill then crunched a little
salt and pepper

Pre-heat the oven to 180°C. Peel, half and core the parsnips. Cut into 4 cm long rustic shards and blanch in salted boiling water until soft to the touch – about 2–3 minutes maximum – then drain and keep to one side. If your mushrooms are large, peel them before you slice them. Heat up a griddle pan or heavy frying pan for the rabbit and a frying pan for the mushrooms and a small roasting tray in the oven for the parsnips. Add a spoonful of honey to the tray and roll the parsnips in it then bake

in the oven for 8–10 minutes until golden. Gently sauté the mushrooms in a little olive oil with the crushed garlic. At the same time lightly oil the rabbit loins, season and lay on to the griddle pan and gently griddle until they have got good charred crisscross marks all around, tossing the mushrooms at the same time. Season the mushrooms just as they finish cooking so they don't bleed out their juices and if the loins are coloured evenly they should be perfectly cooked.

Divide the mushrooms onto two plates then slice the loins and divide them. Put the mushroom pan back on the heat and add a small splash of vinegar and Marsala and the hazelnut oil and remove from the heat. Lay the parsnips and some leaves over the mushrooms and rabbit then sprinkle over the nuts and seeds and drizzle over the dressing from the pan.

Salad of Ceps, Parsnip, Celeriac, Chestnuts and Hazelnuts with Ox Blood Lettuce

I put together this combination of ingredients for a dinner party in October and the reason I used ceps, other than the fact they are the king of mushrooms, is that a guy called Addy turned up at the restaurant with 3 kg he'd just picked on the Quantocks from a site he would only share at pain of death, as he says he's been picking mushrooms there for twelve years. Lucky chap! The ceps were perfect, firm, no worms, and we were desperate to use them as freshly picked as possible: so Mr Chapman got them as a starter for his dinner party, which was described on his menu as an autumn affair! As ceps are a very glamorous ingredient and not easy to acquire for home use you can substitute them with Paris Brown mushrooms: it still makes a great combination salad.

**SERVES 4 AS A STARTER OR 2 AS A MAIN
COURSE**

2 medium or 4 smallish ceps or 10 Paris Brown,
caps brushed clean
4 tbsp hazelnut oil
¼ small celeriac
1 smallish parsnip, washed and peeled (only use
small, young parsnips for this salad)
2 tbsp sherry vinegar
10 chestnuts, cooked, peeled and chopped
100 g hazelnuts, toasted and smashed
200 g ox blood lettuce or red chard or radicchio,
depending on what you can get
Salt, black pepper and fresh nutmeg to season

Wipe clean the cap of the ceps and peel the stalk
(if using Paris Browns there is no need to peel
the stalk). Take the mushrooms and any trimmings, finely chop and warm them in the
hazelnut oil. Leave to infuse while you prepare
the salad.
Shred the celeriac and parsnip on a cheese grater
or, if you have one, the fine-tooth slicing blade
of a Japanese mandolin making sure to use the
guard provided. Mix them together with a little
salt, pepper and fresh grated nutmeg and mix
well. Add 1 tablespoon of the sherry vinegar and
set aside to marinate for a few minutes. Slice the
mushrooms as thinly as possible and season in
exactly the same way as the vegetables but in a
separate bowl. Mix the chopped chestnuts and
hazelnuts with the shredded vegetables and
salad leaves and strain over half the remaining
cep infused hazelnut oil and mix well. Pour the
other half of the oil over the mushrooms and
then fold them all together gently using your
fingertips and serve immediately.
To add depth of flavour you could use a finely
grated hard cheese like Spenwood.

COOK'S TIP
As an extra touch for the dinner we added
a reduction of Madeira, which is basically a
bottle of cooking Madeira reduced to a syrup
and drizzled over. This added an extra richness to the salad when drizzled over but it is
not essential as at home most of the reduction
would probably sit in the fridge for months
to come. If you do go the extra yard and use
this reduction, to use up the excess it is
excellent in rice or pasta salads.

Young Squash with Button Mushrooms and Corn

Squashes and pumpkins have become very popular over the past few years. They are easy to
grow, they look great on the land, in the shops
and on the plate. The most popular is butternut
squash with its flesh like a firm pumpkin but for
this dish I prefer the softer ones picked young,
smaller than a tennis ball. You can leave the
skins and seeds in when they're small so they are
easier to prepare and digest.

SERVES 4

1 uchee kee squash, 1 onion squash, 1 yellow
petit pan, 1 green petit pan, all washed, topped
and tailed and cut into 'orange segment' wedges
10 button mushrooms, washed, stalk removed
but not sliced
1 red onion, sliced finely
2 cloves of garlic, smashed and chopped
1 corn on the cob boiled in water with a little
salt for around 30 minutes then allowed to cool
and kernels cut from the husk
Pumpkin oil is great for this dish for obvious
reasons but if you don't want to buy it just for
this, then olive oil will be fine
salt and black pepper

Pre-heat the oven to 180°C. Heat a little of the oil in a frying pan and sauté the sliced squash and the mushrooms until golden in colour. You'll need to do this in smallish batches so you don't over fill the pan. As each batch colours, season with salt and black pepper and add some of the red onion and garlic and sauté together until the onion softens. As each batch is done tip onto an oven tray. Sprinkle over the sweet corn kernels, then heat through in the oven for 5 minutes. It is then ready to eat as a vegetarian meal or as an accompaniment to roast pork or chicken.

Rabbit, Wood Pigeon and Bacon Pie

Some people like the liquid in their pie thin. others prefer it thick. For this filling I have slightly thickened the stock, but if that doesn't float your boat then don't use the flour and butter and leave it thin: it won't affect the flavour either way.

MAKES A PIE FOR 2 HUNGRY PEOPLE

FOR THE FILLING

front and back legs of a large wild rabbit (save the loins for a sauté dish as they will be wasted in a pie but keep liver, heart and kidneys)
1 plucked wood pigeon, wash out the bird so it doesn't make the stock bitter
100 g unsliced streaky bacon from a good butcher
2 onions, peeled and quartered
4 cloves of garlic, peeled and split
1 bay leaf
fresh parsley and tarragon, shred the parsley fine but just pick the tarragon so as not to make it overpowering
25 g butter
25 g flour, plus extra for dusting
lard
egg yolk, beaten
black pepper and a little fresh nutmeg

FOR THE HOT WATER PASTRY

75 ml milk
75 ml water
90 g lard
350 g plain flour
½ tsp salt

Heat a little lard in a casserole dish, dust the meat with a little seasoned flour and brown in the hot oil using tongs so you can easily control it in the hot fat. Turn off the heat and using paper towels and the tongs mop away the excess fat. Add the onion, garlic and bay leaf and the stalks from the parsley and cover completely with water. Season with black pepper but no salt as we have bacon. Cover with a lid, turn on a gentle heat and poach until the meat is falling from the bone with ease, about 2½ hours. Warm up the milk, water and lard until the lard has completely melted then slowly work the liquid into the flour and salt until you have a dough. Because it is warm the dough will be very soft and too difficult to work with. Allow it to come down to room temperature so you can roll it out.

Pre-heat the oven to 200°C. To finish the filling, strain away all the liquid from the meat into a pan and bring back to a boil. Melt the butter in another pan and beat in the flour on a low heat until bubbling with the consistency of wet sand, then slowly add the stock, stirring all the time so no lumps form until all the stock is in or you have a silky consistency that coats the spoon. Allow to gently simmer for a further 10 minutes then flake all the meat from the bone and flake up the bacon. Discard all the bones and stalks but not the onions or any meat that has fallen off during cooking and make sure you don't waste any juice. Then add all the meat and onions into the thickened sauce with chopped

Rabbit, wood pigeon and bacon pie is old-fashioned soul food.

parsley and picked tarragon. Grate in a little fresh nutmeg and taste for seasoning then pour into your pie dish.

Roll out your pastry on floured greaseproof paper to about 5 mm thick. Brush the edges of the dish with water and lay over the pastry and peel off the paper and pinch the pastry around the edge to seal it. Cut a steam hole in the centre and finish the pastry with egg yolk and bake until the pastry is crisp and golden brown. Serve with creamed potato and turnip, greens, or sprouting.

Steamed Line-Caught Sea Bass with Purple Sprouting , Pumpkin Purée, Seeds, Oil and a Marsala Syrup

Sea bass, especially the non-farmed variety, is an expensive fish and if you go for nice thick 100–125 g portions cut from the centre of the fillet, you're looking at £5–7 a portion, so it's a special occasion fish. If you want a much cheaper alternative, you could use Gurnard fillets, but make sure your monger pin bones them properly as they can be tricky to bone if you don't know the fish.

SERVES 4

4 x 100 g fillets or centre cuts of sea bass, scaled and pin boned
as much purple sprouting as you like but try and pick out smaller florets as they are more tender, and cut a deep cross into the stalk for even cooking
2 tbsp pumpkin seeds, toasted lightly
olive oil

FOR THE PUMPKIN PURÉE
200 g wedge of pumpkin (Crown Prince has a good nutty flavour) or alternatively butternut squash, de-seeded
pumpkin oil

50 g unsalted butter
sea salt, fresh black pepper and nutmeg

FOR THE MARSALA SYRUP
250 ml Marsala wine
1 tbsp brown sugar

If you make the purée and syrup in advance you won't be so rushed when finishing the dish. Pre-heat the oven to 180°C. Reduce the Marsala wine down with the brown sugar over a medium heat until it coats the back of a spoon like caramel. Set aside to cool to room temperature. Season the pumpkin with sea salt, black pepper and fresh grated nutmeg. Drizzle with pumpkin oil, wrap in foil and bake for about 45 minutes or until you can skewer with ease. Remove the pumpkin from the foil, peel away the skin and put the flesh in a blender with the butter and a little pumpkin oil and blend to a smooth purée. Pour into a pan and cover with greaseproof paper so it doesn't skin over.

Sprinkle each fillet with a little salt and drizzle with olive oil and wrap individually in cling film as this helps to keep them moist after cooking. Pre-heat a steamer, set a timer for 9 minutes, and drop in the fish. Meanwhile gently warm through the purée with a little more butter. When the timer is up carefully remove the fish, being mindful of the steam, and replace them with the purple sprouting for 3 minutes while the fish rests. Drain the sprouting and divide between four plates, unwrap the fish and allow it to drain for a second. Spoon some purée onto the plates, sprinkle on some seeds and oil and a drizzle of the Marsala syrup and rest the fish on the purple sprouting and serve. A less pressured alternative would be to put everything on the table and let everybody help themselves!

Steamed line-caught sea bass with purple sprouting, pumpkin purée, seeds, oil and a Marsala syrup.

Shepherd's Pie

I love cooking with mince – the sound it makes when all the juices are evaporating and crackling in the fat and the way the smell keeps changing as the cooking progresses. Shepherd's pie and cottage pie are great British classics that need no modernising. When in season I like to peel and par-boil good new potatoes such as Charlotte and finish cooking them in the mince so they soak up the fat on the surface. (While writing this I had to go and buy some mince because I was drooling on my pad!) Later on in the year when potatoes are old, slicing or mashing them for the topping works just as well.

Obviously, as this is shepherd's pie, lamb mince is the meat of choice. Ask your butcher for mince that's not too lean but not too fatty either; minced neck fillet, 'scrag end', is excellent and cheaper than shoulder. You'll also need about 500 g of any bit of cheap non-fatty lamb bone or trimmings that he will give you that's as close to free as possible; neck bones are ideal. For cottage pie it is all the same method except you use beef instead of lamb.

serves 4

500 g cheap non-fatty lamb bone or trimmings
2 onions, one peeled and halved, the other peeled and finely chopped
2 sticks celery, washed, one roughly chopped, the other finely chopped
500 g lamb mince
1 large carrot, peeled and finely chopped
4 large button mushrooms, washed and finely sliced
1 clove garlic, chopped
salt and peppercorns
bay leaf (optional)
sprig of rosemary (optional)
little fresh nutmeg

4–5 medium-sized potatoes, scrubbed
few cubes of butter

Pre-heat the oven to 200°C. Brown off the bone and trimmings in the oven for 20–30 minutes adding the onion halves towards the end to colour lightly. Soak away any rendered fat with paper towels and swill the tray with water until all the sediment is diluted into the water then transfer to a pot and cover with more water, chopped celery, a little pinch of salt and 3 or 4 peppercorns. Allow to simmer for an hour or so and then strain.

Put the mince in a sturdy pot and cover with a lid. Heat over a low heat to let the juices run from the meat so you can then reduce them until they coat the bottom of the pan with a nutty coating and the fat is rendered and start-ing to crackle. Add the finely chopped onion, carrot, mushrooms and celery and stir well. As the vegetables start to colour, if there appears to be a lot of fat, dab a little away with paper towel, but not all, then add the garlic and slowly start to add the stock, stirring so as to dissolve the sediment on the bottom of the pan back into the stock.

When the mince is covered with stock if you like your food a little more fragrant add a bay leaf and a sprig of rosemary; if not leave plain. Simmer as slowly as possible for about 20 min-utes, adding more stock if it reduces down too much. Then remove the herbs, season to taste and add a little fresh nutmeg. Pour the mix into your pie dish and leave in a cool place to set a little while you make the topping.

Pre-heat the oven to 180°C. Cook the potatoes at a low simmer in salted water in their skins until a butter knife will pass through with ease. While they are still hot, wearing rubber gloves, peel away the skin and crumble the potato into a food mill. Season with fresh pepper, add a few little cubes of butter and mix it with a fork while in the mill then slowly mill the potato on top of the mince until it is covered and to your desired thickness. Pat down with a fork and bake until the juice is bubbling through the cracks. Serve with a classic combination of mashed swede and carrot and buttered cabbage.

Ox Tongue

I have found ox tongue to be surprisingly popular in the West Country. I've served it in London and up north and it was never as popular as it seems to be here. Unfortunately there does not appear to be many butchers around anymore that brine tongues for sale. Now most will cook it themselves and sell it as cold meat. However, I'm sure if you're a regular your butcher will brine one for you, or if you are a bit of a diehard you can ask for the tongue raw and uncured and brine it yourself. Because it is such a tough muscle it can take about two weeks to cure fully, but if cooking is a hobby, curing meat yourself is like alchemy and very rewarding at the end. If, as I imagine, there are a few of you who don't happen to own a tongue press at home, to press the tongue after cooking just curl it into a pudding bowl lined with cling film, fold the excess film over the tongue and press down with plates and a heavy book. But if you happen to see a press in a cook shop, even if you will only use it once, they make a great decorative piece of clutter for any country kitchen.

I recommend you brine three tongues together then freeze two and cook one so you don't have the long wait for them to cure.

FOR 3 TONGUES

FOR THE BRINE
3 litres water

1 kg sea salt
500 g sugar
50 g saltpetre (a nitrate used in curing)

3 ox tongues
1 onion, peeled and halved
1 carrot, peeled and halved
1 leek, washed and halved
4 cloves of garlic, split
10 black peppercorns
2 bay leaves
sprig of thyme

Boil all the brine ingredients together until all the salts and sugars have dissolved then allow to cool. Whatever container you are going to use make sure it is very clean and sterilised then cover the tongues in the brine with a weight on top, to ensure they don't bob on the surface, and that they cure evenly. Leave in the fridge for 2–3 weeks.

Soak in fresh water throughout the day changing the water every now and again. Freeze two of the tongues and put the other in a pot with the onion, carrot, leek, garlic, peppercorns, bay leaves and thyme. Cover with cold water and simmer for around 3 hours on a low heat with a lid (do not boil it or it will be dry). When the tongue is cooked it will fall off a fork with ease. Remove the tongue from the pot and rinse under the cold tap to make it easier to handle then peel away the knobbly outer skin and press in the fridge over night. Strain and reduce the liquor down to about a cup full and use this jelly as an accompaniment to the cold tongue (see below) or whisk in butter and maybe some fresh herbs like tarragon or parsley to serve with hot tongue, mash and greens or fried with eggs and chips.

Tongue Salad

Slice the tongue as thinly as possible and line the surface of your plates with the meat as if it's a carpaccio then brush the meat with its own jelly and a drizzle of diluted horseradish cream. Sprinkle on a peppery leaf such as watercress or rocket. Grate or slice a carrot into very thin strips, dress with some of the tongue jelly and sprinkle over the plate and for a crunch either serve croutons or some diced celery or both!

Sausages

Sausages. What a great word! Sausages. They're probably my favourite food, and are one of the last remaining food products for which there are regional differences throughout Britain. But it seemed to me there wasn't a West Country variety: no Somerset with its own special seasoning or a Devon or Dorset, which seemed strange, as we have such fantastic pork and beef, and so many great sausage-makers.

My butcher, Steve Baker, makes excellent sausages, as do many others around the region. I've tried some excellent sausages from Bonners in Ilminster and from Glebe Farm shop in Pitney, made with their own pork, but none come with a title of provenance. I was at the Castle at least two years before I stumbled across my first titled West Country sausage at a barbecue up in the hills. The Blackdown Banger, I was told, was the name of these sausages I was about to enjoy, and enjoy them I did. They were coarsely minced with a high meat content and not too much cereal so you could really taste the meat and seasoning; not too spicy, very simple and flavoursome. This was without doubt the best sausage I'd ever had, and I've had some petty good sausages, coming from York where there are many great pork butchers. So I was over the moon to have finally found a breakfast sausage that I could serve with confidence, pride and provenance. The Blackdown Banger, I was told, came from a farm called Beech Hayes, itself situated in the Blackdown Hills and the farmers, Nick and Ruth Strange, had turned to selling their own meats as a finished produce, like many other farmers, to keep their business viable.

They use the butcher at Wallace's of Hemyock, a venison farm and shop, to make the sausages for them and then sell them themselves at farmers' markets, hotels, pubs and restaurants. If you happen to be at a farmers' market in Somerset, Devon or Dorset and see a stall for Beech Hayes farm, buy some and stock up your freezer – you won't be disappointed. Or if you get chance or happen to be in Churchinford between 10 a.m. and noon on the first Saturday of the month, there is a small farmers' market that Ruth and Nick set up that is really cheery with lots of local produce.

When cooking sausages it is fairly well documented in modern cookbooks that you do not prick the skins before cooking and this is absolutely correct. It is common sense really: if you prick them, all the fats and juices will run out. The pan should not be too hot as to scorch the skin and cause it to split, and use just enough fat or oil so it doesn't stick, or it will make the sausage greasy. Start on a medium heat in very little lard and turn regularly with tongs to get an even colour. Then lower the heat and allow them to fry very gently turning at odd intervals so they cook through evenly. You'll know when they've cooked because the juices will run clear and the smell of the molten fats and cooked meat juices and seasoning will have filled the room. Hot, fresh-cooked sausages with a runny egg and hot tea to wash it down has to be my favourite way to start the day.

Sausages with Onion Gravy

SERVES 2

250 g cheap pork dice
1 onion, chopped
4–6 sausages
1 medium onion, sliced along the lines of the
onion, not across them, as this bruises the onion
fresh thyme and bay leaf or sage and rosemary
(optional)
salt and black pepper

To make a pork stock for the gravy, brown off the
pork dice until golden. Add the chopped onion
and allow to colour a little then dab away the
excess fat with paper towels. Cover with water and
a pinch of salt and simmer for 20–30 minutes.
Start to colour your sausages on a medium heat in
a little lard turning to get an even colour. Add the
sliced onion and allow to colour slightly then turn
the heat to a lower setting and let the onions cook
down, turning the sausages regularly. When the
onions have no bite and have caramelised and the
sausage is cooked through remove the sausages
and keep in a very low oven. Ladle a little of the
pork stock onto the onions, turn the heat up and
reduce. As each ladle of stock is reduced then add
another and keep going until you have a shiny
sauce that coats a spoon. Season with salt and
black pepper and pour over your sausages.
If you want to make them more fragrant and less
oniony add a little fresh thyme and bay leaf or
sage and rosemary to the sauce as you reduce it.

Toad in the Hole

SERVES 2

3 eggs, beaten
250 g strong plain flour
500 ml whole milk
4 sausages

3 or 4 rashers of streaky bacon, diced into small
pieces
salt and white pepper

Pre-heat the oven to 200°C. Mix the eggs with the
flour then mix in the milk. Season with salt and
white pepper and strain so there are no lumps.
Gently colour the sausages on a medium heat in a
little lard, turning regularly to get an even colour.
Add the streaky bacon and allow to colour slightly.
Transfer to an ovenproof dish, pour over the
batter to almost cover the sausages and then bake
until the batter is risen and golden and has a hollow sound when tapped – about 20 minutes.

Poached Whole Duck

SERVES 4

1 small/medium duck (about 2 kg) with neck
and giblets
good splash of white wine
750 ml water
bay leaf, sprigs of thyme and rosemary in leek
leaves and tied with string
6 baby onions
6 cloves of garlic, peeled
8 baby or small turnips, peeled and halved
2 bunches of carrots, peeled
1 small swede, peeled and roughly diced
8 Pink Fir Apple potatoes, peeled and halved
lengthways
duck fat
salt

Take the wings, chopped neck, gizzards, heart
and kidney and brown well in duck fat. Drain
away the fat with paper towels and add a good
splash of white wine and the water. Bring to the
boil and skim away any scum and then simmer
for about an hour.

Meanwhile rub a little oil all over the duck then a little salt and sprinkle a little salt into the bird's cavity along with the herb bundle and place in a pot big enough to hold the duck and the vegetables. Brown the duck in duck fat upside down then using tongs and a meat fork manoeuvre and brown the sides. Remove the duck from the pan and brown the onions and garlic. When they are lightly coloured drain the fat into a separate container and return the duck to the pot. Strain over the stock so the duck is almost, but not quite, covered. You may need to add extra water. Cover with a lid and leave to simmer very gently with barely any bubbling for around $2\frac{1}{2}$ hours. Add the other vegetables and potatoes and cover again for about 30 minutes. Serve at the table straight from the pot, although be warned it does get messy to serve.

If you wanted to make the dish less savoury you could add a little cider and some orange zest, or more savoury with a little smoked bacon and a sprinkle of dried chilli.

Kingston Black

Julian Temperly has been experimenting and creating ciders, brandies, digestives, Eau de Vie and other apple products for nearly twenty years. In fact in 2006 he released Britain's first 15-year-old cider brandy good enough to give any vintage calvados a run for its money. His farm and orchards are at Burrow Hill near Kingsbury Episcopi in Somerset where he uses two former calvados stills known as Josephine and Fifi to help create his magic. Over the past few years he has won many prestigious awards for his products and, with his passion and vision, has become an inspiration to other cider makers. His orchards are like fine vineyards to him and the blend of apples imperative, using, as he does, a mix of sweet, bitter and sharp varieties to get the right balance. Most ciders contain up to eleven different varieties so getting the blend right takes a great wealth of experience. Kingston Black, being his prince of apples, takes pride of place on the labels of his Kingston Black digestive, and the Pomona. Both of these are delicious drunk as aperitifs as well as digestives. Their personalities change according to whether they are served chilled or at room temperature but both are equally as good and excellent with a good mature hard cheese like Montgomery's cheddar or Keen's. I use them often in the kitchen in autumn and early winter as I find the flavour they bring to a dish gives a sense of seasonality, which in turns becomes very comforting to eat.

Celeriac and Kingston Black Soup

I used to make this soup using Madeira before I moved to the West Country where I discovered Kingston Black. It is a great autumn warming soup but does require some love and attention for the required result. I recommend purchasing the celeriac from a farmers' market or a greengrocer. It should have a fresh earthy smell; the older it is the less aroma it will have.

SERVES 4

1 celeriac
2 large potatoes
175 ml Kingston Black
1 litre whole milk
100 g butter
salt, white pepper and fresh nutmeg

Use a fairly large pan with a thick bottom, or use a Le Creuset, so the heat is distributed evenly and caramelises rather than burns. Peel and finely dice the celeriac and potato but keep them separate. In a little oil, just enough to cover the surface of your pan, cook the celeriac on a low

Kingston Black sabayon with a fruit and nut crunch is a West Country take on Italian Zabaglione.

heat. Use a lid to help draw liquid from the cele-riac, then stir attentively until all the liquid is reduced to caramelise on the bottom of the pan and the celeriac is browning – you may need to add a little extra oil during the process so it doesn't burn. Add 100 ml of the alcohol and rub away the colour from the bottom of the pan with a wooden spoon. Pour over the milk, add the potato and allow this to simmer until the potato is breaking down to the touch of the spoon. Drain the mix in a colander and retain the liquid. Blend the celeriac and potato together with the butter and slowly add the retained liquid until you get your desired consistency. Season with the salt, white pepper and nutmeg and add the last little bit of Kingston Black to reaffirm its presence.

If you like some texture to your soup you could crush in some walnuts or pecans instead of croutons as their flavour lends itself well to celeriac and apple.

Kingston Black Sabayon with a Fruit and Nut Crunch
serves 2 to 3

for the muesli
2 slices of dried pear, finely chopped
2 slices of dried apple, finely chopped
1 tbsp dried cranberries
1 tbsp toasted nibbed almonds
1 tbsp toasted crushed hazelnuts
2 tbsp toasted jumbo oats

for the sabayon
3 egg yolks
50 ml Kingston Black
50 ml water
50 g sugar
50 ml apple purée (sieved apple sauce)

Mix all the muesli ingredients together. Dissolve the sugar in the water and allow to cool a little. Place all the sabayon ingredients together in a high-sided bowl and whisk well over a pan of simmering water, whisking continually until it foams up and thickens as the egg cooks. You will need to whisk vigorously so it doesn't curdle. Once it has thickened, just spoon it straight over the nuts and dried fruit and serve immediately.

Creamed Potato and Mashed Potato

It wasn't until recently, I'm ashamed to admit, and like most professional cooks I hasten to add, that I thought creamed potato and mash on menus were interpreted as one and the same thing. But a lady in the restaurant pointed out this is not the case. Mash, and I tend to agree with her (well now she's pointed it out anyway), should be fairly dry but for the addition of butter and therefore lends itself to absorbing stewing liquors and meat juices, unlike creamed potato which, because of its fat content, tends to amalgamate itself with the juices rather than soak them up.

If you're eating it with mince, a dry mash eats much better but for most other things a nice, fluffy, smooth, creamed potato is favoured.

For both you should have the right potatoes simmered slowly in plenty of water so they cook evenly and prevent lumps. Scrub but don't peel the potatoes as this helps retain flavour and keep the starch fluffy. I usually use either Yukon Gold, Maris Piper or Desiree potatoes. A food mill is essentially for eliminating lumps and quicker than sieving for mash; just add a little butter and seasoning for mash, but for creamed add warm whole milk and butter, beating really well and adding the liquid slowly to get to the desired creaminess. Some prefer to use double cream but I find it masks the potato flavour and it also makes for quite expensive mash!

Baker's Potato with Belly of Lamb

This is a kind of hybrid between the French boulangiere, translated as baker's potato, and Lancashire hot pot. As we are using lamb from the West Country and I'm cooking in the West Country, it would not be too cheeky to call it a Somerset Hot Pot.

SERVES 4

> COOK'S TIP
> This dish is lovely with mashed butternut squash and sweet potatoes for a sweeter nutty flavour.

2 lamb bellies with ribs attached
2 onions, 1 halved and 1 thinly sliced
1 sprig of rosemary (not too much)
6 small or 4 large Maris Piper or Desiree potatoes, peeled
salt and pepper

Pre-heat the oven to 175°C. Cut the bellies in half and brown off each one in hot fat, season-ing well. Make sure not to burn the bottom of the pan on too high a heat. When they are all browned mop away the fat from the pan with paper towels and swill out the pan so as not to waste any flavour. Pour it into an oven dish with the bellies and onion halves, the rosemary and cover with water. Seal the pan with tin foil and a lid so no steam can escape and braise for 2 hours until the meat is falling apart.

Turn the oven up to 200°C. In a dish big enough for 6 portions slice some potatoes about 5 cm thick and line the bottom of the dish with them. Season and sprinkle over some sliced onion and flaked lamb and repeat the process until the dish is well filled. Pour over some of the cooking liquor, cover with foil and bake until the potato is soft.

Baked Egg with Elmhirst Cheese and Bacon

The Italians do a similar dish to this with white truffle as the partner for the egg but at around £1,000 per kg and non-existent in England we change this versatile dish to suit ourselves. I love the slightly bitter bite the Elmhirst adds to the dish but if you don't like your yolk runny I wouldn't bother as mixing the rich runny yolk into the dish as you eat it is part of its pleasure.

SERVES 4

4 slices of dry cured streaky bacon, cut into small pieces
1 slice of bread, crusts removed and finely diced
4 20–35 g slices of Elmhirst, cut into small pieces
4 organic or free-range eggs

FOR A BÉCHAMEL SAUCE
30 g unsalted butter
30 g plain flour
500 ml whole milk
1 small onion, peeled, scored and studded with
1 clove
bay leaf
1 slice of bacon
fresh nutmeg
salt and fresh black pepper

4 soufflé moulds

Melt the butter on a medium heat and when bubbling evenly stir in the flour with a wooden spoon until it's plopping like hot sand. Slowly add the milk a little at a time until you have a

custard-like consistency. Add the onion, bay leaf and bacon and a little grated nutmeg. Turn the heat down to its very lowest setting, season to taste, cover with greaseproof paper and allow to cook gently for 30 minutes. Strain through a sieve and cover again so it doesn't skin over. If the béchamel has gone too cold and set before you want to use it, re-heat with a little water until its warm enough again.

Pre-heat the oven to 200°C. Fry the streaky bacon until crisp and drain on a cloth. Pour a little of the sauce into the individual soufflé-type moulds. Sprinkle the bread and bacon over and half fill with the sauce. Add the pieces of cheese to the sauce in each dish. Take one egg at a time and separate the white into the dish with the sauce and keep the yolk in the shell in the box being careful not to burst it. Gently stir the white into the sauce and tap the dish on the surface so it sinks in. Repeat until all the moulds are done and bake them for 10 minutes.

Gently pour each of the yolks from the shell-halves into the centre of each dish and using a cloth so as not to burn your hands tap each dish on the work surface until the yolk has sunk. Leave to stand for about 3 minutes and serve with bread soldiers.

LEEK, POTATO, BACON AND CHEESE BAKE

This can be eaten as the main dish with a salad or as an accompaniment to a roast chicken, or with chicken wings and thighs.

SERVES 6

12 slices of dry cured smoked bacon
8 potatoes, peeled and sliced as thin as you can by hand
1 large leek, trimmed, washed and sliced
200 g good quality but pasteurised cheddar (unpasteurised cheese tends to split because of the extra fat from the bacon) or, even better, Jersey Shield or Ogle Shield, grated
fresh black pepper

Pre-heat the oven to 200°C. Lay out the bacon between 2 sheets of greaseproof paper and roll them with a rolling pin to make them thinner. Line a non-stick (or line with greaseproof paper first) ovenproof frying pan with the bacon so there is an overlap over the side. Create a layer of sliced potato, sprinkle over some leek and cheese and a little black pepper. Cover with another layer of sliced potato, leek and cheese and repeat the process until the pan is full and the filling is a little higher than the rim then pull over the overlapping bacon to cover it. Lay a sheet of greaseproof paper over the top, along with an ovenproof plate or tin foil and bake for around 40 minutes. Test with a fork in the centre to see if it is cooked; if not leave the plate and greaseproof off and continue to bake.

When it is soft to the fork, cover with a plate larger than the pan and turn upside down to free the cake from the pan.

VULSCOMBE GOAT'S CHEESE CREAMS WITH PICKLED BEETS

Vulscombe is a full-fat soft creamy goat's cheese made by Graham Townsend. It has a lovely smooth texture with a nice sharp taste.

SERVES 4

4 beets, scrubbed
sugar
cider vinegar
175 ml double cream
100 g goat's cheese
salt and fresh black pepper

To pickle the beetroot, simmer very gently until soft to a fork, then peel while hot wearing rubber gloves so it doesn't burn or stain your hands. It's also sensible to wear an apron so you don't ruin your clothes. Slice fairly thickly then dissolve 1 tablespoon of sugar to 250 ml cider vinegar and pour over the sliced beets and leave to cool. If you want to preserve them make sure the jar is sterile and the lid is tight.

Simmer the double cream with salt and black pepper to taste. Whisk in the goat's cheese and allow to simmer for 1 minute. Pour into a deep tray and refrigerate to set.

To assemble, arrange the beetroot on plates and scoop out the cream on top. Serve with some Melba toast or crusty toasted bread.

COOK'S TIP
Instead of the pickled beets you could serve this with fresh sliced plums or halved cherries, or a nice ripe pear sliced with some walnuts.

WINTER

Boo, I hear you say as the cold months of winter arrive. Dark nights, log fires and wellie boots are the staples of the days, but for cooking there is still plenty of pleasure to be had. Although winter is not as fruitful as other months there is still plenty to choose from with added spice here and there for different aromas and extra warmth. Slower cooking techniques need more time set aside but fill the kitchen with richer, deeper aromas and give a fulfilling result. Herbs such as rosemary, thyme and bay seem to be so much more fragrant this time of year and after a cold grey, rainy day a piping hot soup can heal, and a sticky, hearty pudding can comfort the soul.

TREACLE TART

Treacle tart is always in my favourite top three winter puddings. I baked and shared one with friends on Guy Fawke's Night and we gorged ourselves that much we nearly missed the bonfire, so be warned how rich and filling it is. Like many of the best dishes and puddings this is the sort of thing that requires a good long walk before or after, to relieve you of the guilt.

SERVES 8

300 ml double cream
3 eggs
zest and juice of 1 lemon
zest and juice of 1 small orange
900 ml golden syrup
250 g breadcrumbs

FOR THE PASTRY
200 g soft flour
50 g lard, cut into small dice
50 g butter, cut into small dice
4 tbsp water

flan ring approximately 20 cm across and 4 cm deep

To make the pastry, sift the flour and rub in the fat with your fingertips until you get a sandy texture. Make a well in the centre and add the water. Knead together to form a dough. Roll out a little and refrigerate for an hour before using. (The pastry is best made the day or just the night before. After 24 hours it will oxidise and turn grey.)

Pre-heat the oven to 150°C. Whisk together the cream, eggs, fruit zest and juice (don't worry if the mixture splits) then slowly beat that into the golden syrup. Fold in the breadcrumbs and mix really well.

On a lightly floured surface, roll out the pastry approximately to the thickness of a pound coin. Then roll the pastry around the rolling pin and roll it over your flan ring and gently manoeuvre it down into the ring and into the edges. Trim off the rough edges leaving about ½ cm overlap to allow for shrinkage. Pour the filling into your pastry case and bake (turn the temperature down a little if your oven is hot) for about an hour or until it has lost its wobble and is firm to the touch.

> COOK'S TIP
> When rolling out your pastry, as you want to change the angle you are rolling, roll the pastry around the pin, turn the pin and roll it off before continuing with the rolling. Don't just roll the pin forwards then sideways as this will given an uneven surface. Doing it as described means you'll only roll the pin forward because you've turned the pastry around.

PECAN PIE

This is an alternative tart, which is made in a similar fashion. I also like to change the pie by replacing pecans with walnuts, hazelnuts, macadamias and sultanas and chopped dates for a different effect but they cook exactly the same.

SERVES 8

800 ml golden syrup
100 g unsalted butter
6 eggs
25 g corn flour
200 g pecan nuts, chopped
1 quantity of pastry (see Treacle Tart)

flan ring approximately 20 cm across and 4 cm deep

Using a short crust pastry rather than the usual sweet crust adds balance and crispness to an otherwise very sweet pudding.

Pre-heat the oven to 150°C. Melt the golden syrup gently with butter then allow to cool slightly. Mix in the eggs, corn flour and then the pecan nuts. Prepare the pastry as for the Treacle Tart. Pour the filling into your pastry case and bake until firm.

Winter Condiments

If you like to make your own preserves then you have probably got a cupboard full of jellies and pickles for use through winter. I feel that comfort condiments are always appreciated during the cold months, and especially so in rural areas. Bread sauce and the like are never as nice re-hydrated from packets and are easy to make. When I was at the Savoy, where they always had a trolley for the roast of the day and the appropriate game for the season, the accompaniments were more European than British, so when I moved to the West Country it was a little while before I realised the benefits of offering your diners the sort of sauces and jellies that have remained popular outside of big cities.

BREAD SAUCE

1 small or ½ onion, peeled and finely chopped
½ clove of garlic, crushed, or ½ tsp garlic salt
25 g unsalted butter
6 slices stale white bread, crusts off and chopped small
bay leaf
whole milk
fresh grated nutmeg, fresh milled white pepper, salt to taste

Sweat the onion and garlic slowly in the butter until translucent. Add the bread, bay leaf, and enough milk to just cover the bread and no more. Season and stir on a very low heat until the bread has absorbed the liquid. Adjust the seasoning and blend until smooth in a food processor. If you're not using it straight away you may need to dilute it with a little hot milk to reheat.

ONION SAUCE

400 g white onion, finely diced
1 clove of garlic, crushed
1 little strip of bacon or rind
bay leaf
50 ml whole milk
25 g butter
25 g flour
salt and white pepper

Poach the onion, garlic, bacon and bay leaf in the milk on a very low heat for about 1 hour until the onion has softened completely. Melt the butter in a separate pan and stir in the flour until it's bubbling evenly. Then slowly pour over the milk and onion mix to make a thickened sauce. Remove the bay leaf and bacon. Pour into a food processor and blend until smooth and season to taste.

> COOK'S TIP
> You can leave both these sauces lumpy if you like, but after years in a professional kitchen I have developed a phobia for lumpy sauces.

ORANGE SAUCE
(for serving hot with poultry or with cold meats)

zest and juice of 2 oranges
zest and juice of 1 lemon
4 tbsp Grand Marnier, or any orange or mandarin liqueur
2 tsp English mustard
1 small pinch of chilli flakes

250 g Redcurrant or Quince Jelly (see recipes on pages 95 and 115 respectively)
salt and black pepper

On a medium heat, mix the juices, zest, liqueur, mustard and chilli flakes and reduce by half. Whisk in the jelly and simmer until it's well infused. Season to taste, strain through a sieve and store in the refrigerator. Be careful when reheating that, because of the jelly, it doesn't catch and burn: use a non-stick milk pan or a bowl over hot water.

Cumberland Sauce

4 oranges
2 lemons
400 g Redcurrant or Quince Jelly (see recipes on pages 95 and 115 respectively)
200 ml port
pinch of chilli flakes
pinch of ginger
2 tbsp sugar
1 tbsp French mustard
50 ml cider vinegar
salt and black pepper

Zest the fruit with a zester, or peel and cut into very thin strips, making sure there is no pith or it will make the sauce bitter. Blanch the zest in boiling water for 10 seconds and refresh in cold water; this also removes bitterness.
Melt the jelly on a low heat with the strained citrus juice, port, chilli and ginger. Dissolve the sugar and mustard into the vinegar. Mix with the jelly, port and juice and simmer for 10 minutes then add the peel and cook until the mix becomes syrupy. This will take a little longer if it's homemade jelly, as manufactured jellies are usually set firmer to start with. Test the jelly on a plate in the fridge to check it's not too runny then pour into sterilised containers and store in the fridge after it has cooled.

Christmas Salad

I love the idea of a salad for all seasons and Christmas should be no exception. For this salad I use flavour and texture combinations that remind me of the different traditions of Christmas food.
SERVES 4

2 English flat leaf lettuces, washed and outer leaves removed
1 large or 2 small smoked duck breasts, sliced very thinly
1 orange, split into segments
1 tangerine, split into segments
1 tbsp dried cranberries
1 tbsp toasted broken hazelnuts
1 tbsp toasted broken almonds
8 pre-cooked chestnuts, chopped up fine
seeds from ½ pomegranate

FOR THE DRESSING
4 tbsp hazelnut oil
juice of ½ small mandarin
2 tsp dark brown sugar
tiny pinch of ground cinnamon
freshly grated nutmeg
fresh black pepper

Whisk together the dressing ingredients to your desired acidity. Lay the lettuce leaves flat on the plates and share out the sliced duck between them and the orange and mandarin segments. Drizzle over a little dressing. Mix the cranberries with a little dressing and sprinkle them over. Finish by warming the hazelnuts, almonds and chestnuts in a dry pan and sprinkling over each plate, followed by the pomegranate seeds.

A Useful Joint

One of the most useful joints for multi-tasking during busy months, when you're up to your neck at work and at home, is a joint of ham. In a professional kitchen and at home it has endless possibilities, whether as the main meal with parsley sauce (see recipe below) and mash and veggies, in a salad, or with fried egg and chips or hash browns and poached eggs. Sometimes when I'm late after a long service at the restaurant I'm more than happy to have ham, cheese and pickle with a few spring onions for supper. Then there's the multitude of combinations for sandwiches, and the stock in which you cooked the joint can be used for pea and ham soup, lentil soup or broth. So for a bit of effort at the weekend you get a range of meals for the week, which has to be better than time-saving ready-meals or take-aways, and cheaper as well.

At home it's totally impractical to try and cook a whole 'D' cut gammon because you don't have large enough equipment, so realistically go for a 2 kg, bone off or on. Off is easier to carve but on the bone keeps more moist; either way make sure your butcher has tied it good and tight with proper string, not that rubbish netting, so it holds its shape and moisture and doesn't break up.

Like any meat, you get good and bad gammon but if your butcher already has a good reputation for the quality and regionality of his produce I imagine he's pretty proud of his hams. Most large gammons are cured in brine, a salt solution; very few still dry cure gammon and those that do use specialist nitrates that will turn pork belly into streaky bacon in a week, but they'll let you believe it takes months, because they can still call it dry cure and charge the price that slow curing warrants. On the other hand the product is generally very good, even if the curing nitrates and other antioxidants do sound a little suspect. The worst kind of gammon is of pork that is intensively farmed and pumped full of chemicals in life and then injected with saline and chemicals in death. They inject the brine to speed up the process even more and the meat will probably end up in thinly sliced squares in flat packets on supermarket shelves. If you are not sure whether your pan is big enough for the job take it with you to the butcher so you can eye up a joint that will fit! The joint will need to be soaked for 12–24 hours, changing the water three or four times on the way; this reduces the salt content. For cooking times start with cold water, bring to the boil then drain, this will again reduce the salt content and removes some of the scum that comes from the proteins, so you'll get a purer, less salty stock. Cover again with cold water and bring to a simmer with a few onions, carrots, celery, bay leaves, thyme and white peppercorns and allow 1 hour of simmering per kilogram and leave to cool in the liquid so the residual heat finishes the cooking. If you want to honey roast the ham, drain it well and carve off the outer skin leaving a layer of white fat. Make a thick paste of honey and brown sugar with freshly grated nutmeg and a sprinkle of garlic salt. Score the fat and rub over the paste so it coats the whole surface then stud with a few cloves. Pre-heat an oven to about 180°C and bake the ham on a rack so it doesn't burn on the bottom and baste it every 5–10 minutes until it is golden and shiny. Leave to cool at room temperature and refrigerate as soon as it has lost its heat. Stock can be frozen in plastic freezer bags or cups for later use (see below).

Parsley Sauce

50 g butter
50 g flour

180 ml hot milk
ham stock (see A Useful Joint)
1 onion, peeled
bunch of parsley, stalks split
salt, white pepper and nutmeg
fresh chopped parsley, to serve

Melt the butter on a low heat and when it's bubbling evenly stir in the flour until it's bubbling like hot sand then slowly add the milk and stir to a smooth paste. Slowly stir in ham stock until the sauce coats a spoon like silk. Add the onion and parsley and season with salt, white pepper and freshly grated nutmeg. Cover with greaseproof paper and allow to cook out very slowly for about 30 minutes then strain through a fine sieve. If you're using it straightaway then add plenty of fresh chopped parsley but if you're going to reheat it, add the parsley later. If you fancy a change, use fresh picked tarragon instead of parsley.

Ham and Egg Pie
This sort of pie can have whatever topping you like. If you prefer potato topping it will save you making pastry, and if you're really busy you could buy puff pastry. This recipe uses potato topping.
SERVES 2

4 medium-sized, all-purpose potatoes, scrubbed
as much ham as you want, diced
3 eggs
25 g butter
25 g flour
250 ml ham stock, heated (see A Useful Joint)
1 tsp English mustard
fresh parsley, chopped
picked tarragon
breadcrumbs (optional)
salt and pepper

Put the potatoes on to simmer over a gentle heat. Boil the eggs for 5 minutes and allow to cool down naturally, so they finish cooking with residual heat. Melt the butter until evenly bubbling and stir in the flour. Mix well on a low heat and slowly add hot ham stock until you have a sauce that coats a spoon. Whisk in the English mustard, some fresh chopped parsley and tarragon.
Pre-heat the oven to 180°C. Peel and quarter the eggs and lay into a pie dish. Scatter over the ham then pour over enough sauce to cover. Drain the potatoes, and wearing rubber gloves, peel away the skin. Break them into a food mill and season with salt and pepper. Pass through the food mill directly on top of the pie and pat down with a fork. Bake until the sauce is bubbling at the sides and the top has crisped. If you want a really crisp finish sprinkle some breadcrumbs on the top before placing in the oven.

Split Pea and Ham Soup
This is a very filling soup and a meal in itself if eaten with buttered crusty bread.
SERVES 4

250 g dried split green peas
1 tsp of bicarbonate of soda
500 ml water
500 ml ham stock
salt and white pepper

To open the pores of the pulse and help to rehydrate, soak the peas in the water and bicarbonate for 6–8 hours in the fridge. Drain well and rinse, cover with ham stock and simmer until it resembles mushy peas, diluting with more ham stock as it thickens. Season to taste and blend for 2 minutes until smooth. Check the seasoning and sprinkle with all the crumbly bits and trimmings of your ham, or dice a bit up and stir it in.

Game

Although rabbits and pigeons are available all year, as is farmed venison, and stalkers will shoot roe bucks even in the summer months, the game season is marked by the first bird shoots, which begin in the north with grouse on the Glorious Twelfth (12 August), followed by partridge and mallard from September to February and pheasant from October to February, which is why people generally associate game with autumn and winter.

Grouse and woodcock have a strong game flavour that may be a little overpowering for some. Pheasant gets a raw deal because it has so often been eaten by people in their younger days and they have been put off by it being too dry or tough. I have made the same mistake myself in the past and you only learn through experience. If you're roasting a pheasant you need a younger bird and preferably a hen. You can tell if its young by its feet, they won't be as tough and worn as on an older bird. The hen birds tend to be plumper and carry more fat and are usually recognised by their plumage, which is speckled brown, unlike the males, which have bright vibrant colours. Game birds, like other meats and poultry, need to be hung, but not until maggots are festering, as some would have you believe. I think this is a countryman's tale to keep all the game for themselves! I find deeper fleshed birds, such as grouse, woodcock, partridge, teal and mallards, usually need a little longer than the pale-fleshed birds, such as red-leg partridge, which to those in the know is the lesser in comparison to the English grey partridge but breeds better and is favoured for shoots and has forced out the grey. For those who don't count themselves as connoisseurs, the red leg is still a fine bird to eat. Pheasants are generally over hung and become dry. The rules I use are: for younger birds, 3–5 days if it's a warm autumn, 6–8 days if it's cold; for older birds 2 days more. The darker fleshed birds would be hung for 5–6 days if warm and 8–10 days if cooler. The tail feathers are a good gauge as they should pull out with ease. If you buy or acquire birds direct from shoots then you will obviously have to pluck them after hanging (hang them in a cool outhouse or shed by their necks). This is an arduous task, but if you try to avoid it by skinning the bird it will only be good for casseroles and even then tends to go dry without the skin to protect it.

To pluck them, set up a stool outside with a bucket of warm water, to wash excess feathers from your hands, and a large black bag for the feathers. Hold the bird head side down in the mouth of the bag and pull the feathers in small clumps towards the head and into the bag. Don't pluck the wings, feet or head as you will chop those off later. When the bird is plucked, remove the entrails by cutting a small slit in the cavity between the legs and, using a freezer bag if you are squeamish, poke two fingers into the cavity and draw out the intestines. The heart and kidneys should remain attached inside the bird's frame; leave them there until you need them. 'Having fun?' I doubt anybody ever imagined it to be enjoyable, but preparing and cooking game is a labour of love for people who care passionately about food and cooking and treat it like a hobby rather than the cook who enjoys good food and cooking but prefers quick, everyday functional cooking. Although, that said, all good butchers will sell fully prepared birds at an increased price, so you can just skip the messy bits and get straight to the cooking.

Cooking times vary between the birds with some eating better a little pink and some cooked through, so I have included some basic roasting times for game birds cooked in a modern oven and rested properly.

Trussed and larded hen pheasants. The lard helps to preserve moisture.

Roast pheasant with roasted winter vegetables.

GROUSE

Pre-heat the oven to 220°C. Season the bird inside and out. Stuff the cavity with chopped red onion, bay leaves and orange zest – if you're new to grouse this will help tame its strong game smell. Prick the legs together with a cocktail stick so the thighs don't over cook. Heat some oil in a frying pan and brown the bird using tongs to help you control it in the hot fat. When it's evenly coloured turn off the heat and put the bird in a roasting tray. Place in the hot oven for 10 minutes. Remove and wrap in tin foil upside down so the juices stay in the breasts and rest for 5–10 minutes, this should give you a nice medium rare bird.

RED-LEG PARTRIDGE

The red leg is bigger than the English grey and not as highly priced but it will be more palatable for people who don't go for really strong flavours. Pre-heat the oven to 220°C. Stuff the cavity with thyme, garlic, shallots and diced butter. Prick the legs together with cocktail sticks and brown the bird in hot oil like the grouse. Scrunch up some tin foil to create a trivet on which to rest the bird and place in a roasting tray. Lean the bird on the foil so the legs point up and as the butter melts it will moisten the breast meat. Roast the bird for 10 minutes and rest in foil upside down, just like the grouse.

GREY PARTRIDGE, WOODCOCK AND SNIPE

These are more difficult to obtain from any-where but a top-notch game merchant. Purists like to roast them with the entrails intact and they have them spread on toast! These take less time in the oven, just 8 minutes on the highest oven setting after browning, but then resting a little longer, maybe 10–15 minutes. The snipe won't even need to go in the oven, just rest with a lid on after browning.

HEN PHEASANTS

To prevent the pheasant going dry, the bird must be stuffed with a good fatty pork stuffing and the breasts either wrapped in slices of pork fat or ask the butcher to lard the breasts (using a special needle to poke fingers of pork fat into the breast meat to prevent the meat from drying out). Pre-heat the oven to 180°C. Put the pheasant in a roasting tray with water to a depth of about 1 cm. Cover the whole tray with tin foil and seal well around the edge so steam doesn't escape: this again will help prevent the bird from drying out. After 30 minutes remove the foil and continue roasting for a further 10 minutes on high to colour the skin, then turn off the heat and rest in the oven for 10 minutes.

DEER

Deer have been thriving in the West Country over the past few years thanks to less pesticides being used and warmer climates creating an easier environment for them to feed and breed. Over the past few hundred years different varieties have been brought into the West Country as pets and have escaped or been released into the wild, so that landowners have to deal with Muntjacs and Sika as well as red, fallow and roe. Pete Samways, who I'm lucky enough to do business with, stalks deer on the Quantocks, and culls at Hestercombe and other National Trust estates where numbers are in need of control. Because they cull the roe bucks through the summer as well, it means that venison is available almost all year. If you're not lucky enough to know a game dealer, your butcher no doubt will, and there are plenty of good venison farmers, such as Wallace's of Hemyock who do mail order but also have a farm shop. If it's not meat you've tried before then it will be worth the effort just to break away from the norm and try a new flavour. The saddle and haunch are ideal for roasting and serving pink and moist but the haunch also lends itself, like the shoulder, to slow cooking and braising. For this recipe I have used the term venison to broadly cover whatever deer you get.

Braised Venison with Crown Prince Pumpkin and Chestnuts

About a quarter of a good-sized Crown Prince will probably be enough but as they vary in size considerably just take a view on how much you need. If you can't get a Crown Prince, which is a greeny blue pumpkin with bright orange flesh and a nutty flavour, use a butternut squash instead.

SERVES 4

500–600 g haunch of venison, cut into large dice
150 g smoked streaky bacon, diced
2 bay leaves
sprig of thyme
8 juniper berries
½ bottle Côte du Rhône
2 red onions, peeled and quartered
4 cloves of garlic, split
2 carrots, peeled and quartered
½ litre Beef Stock (see recipe below) or tinned beef consommé
beef fat for browning
flour for dusting
enough pumpkin for 4
pumpkin, rapeseed or light olive oil
Malden salt, black pepper and nutmeg
demerara sugar
12–16 cooked, peeled chestnuts (see page 155)
fresh chopped parsley, to serve

Put the venison, bacon, bay leaves, thyme and juniper berries in the red wine and cover in the fridge for 24 hours.

Pre-heat the over to 180°C. Remove the meat from the marinade and pat dry; set the marinade aside. Lightly dust the meat in flour then brown the pieces in beef fat until evenly coloured. Add the onions, garlic and carrots and allow to colour slightly. Dab away any excess fat with paper towels. Pour in the marinade, stir well and pour over the beef stock. Cover with a lid and braise in the oven for about 2 hours. Remove the lid to allow the sauce to reduce and the meat to carry on cooking until falling apart, about another hour or so.

Peel and cut the pumpkin into nice big chunks and place them in the centre of some tin foil. Season with some sea salt, fresh milled pepper, grated nutmeg and sugar and drizzle over some oil. Seal the foil up to create a bag in which the pumpkin will bake. Bake in the oven at 180°C until you can push a skewer through with ease. To serve, remove any hard herbs from your liquor and taste for seasoning. Crumble in the chestnuts and, if you like, some fresh chopped parsley to lighten the richness. Ladle into bowls with your baked pumpkin and perhaps some boiled curly kale or turnip greens.

Beef Stock

1 kg beef rib meat (cut from between the rib bones)
150 g mushrooms, diced
150 g tomatoes, diced
1 small leek, chopped
2 carrots, diced
2 red onions, chopped

Brown the beef rib until all the fat is rendered off and nicely coloured. Put the meat in a large pot, mop away the fat from the tray with paper towels and swill with boiling water. Pour the liquid over the meat. Top the pan up with water to cover the bone, add the mushrooms, tomato, leek, carrots and red onion and bring to a simmer on the lowest heat possible for about 4 hours. Strain the liquid and reduce until it will lightly coat the back of a spoon. Strain again and chill or freeze in plastic cups for future use. You can make the addition of tomato purée to help thicken the stock, but I find it makes all the sauces taste the same, that's also why I don't include herbs in the base stock.

Pork Chop with Pumpkin and Sage
serves 2

2 120–140 g pork chops
½ pumpkin, de-seeded, skinned and sliced
1 red onion, peeled and cut in eighths
2 cloves of garlic, peeled and split
4 Pink Fir Apple potatoes, boiled in salted water, peeled and split in half lengthways
8 leaves of fresh sage, or rosemary if you prefer
butter
sea salt and black pepper

Pre-heat the oven to 200°C. Heat a little oil in a sturdy frying pan on a medium heat and brown the pork chops on both sides so they are nicely coloured. Turn off the heat and drain away any excess fat with paper towels. Leave the chops in the pan to rest. Lay the pumpkin, onion, garlic, potatoes and sage on a baking tray and drizzle with olive oil and a sprinkle of salt and pepper and bake until the pumpkin is soft and lightly coloured. Add the chops to the tray to heat through for five minutes. There should be a little juice and sediment left in the pan from the chops. Add a splash of water and a knob of butter and mix with the juices using a spatula to make a little gravy. Although it won't make

much, the flavour will be pure. Share the pumpkin and potatoes, onion and any oils and juices from the tray onto your plates with the chops on top and the pan juices around the edge.

Baking and Peeling Fresh Chestnuts

Although you can buy perfectly acceptable chestnuts that have been prepared and vacuum packed, it is still a nice thing to do around Hallowe'en time: the smell that fills the house cannot be imitated. The problem that most people have is peeling the tough little blighters without burning their fingers; even for cooks who handle hot stuff constantly, chestnuts can literally be a real pain. The knack is how you score them. I've seen chefs deep fry them, boil them – all sorts of methods to ease the removal of their armoured plating – but in reality just go and watch the chestnut vendors on the street corners peel them without any fuss with their black leathery fingers and you'll see that they haven't scored the point of the chestnut with a modelling knife, they score around the circumference before they roast them. Be very careful when you do this, as you don't want to split your thumb. Cradle each nut in a thick cloth as you score it then boil them in salted water until the two halves of the shell separate (stir them every few minutes so they blanch evenly). Then just pull away the shell with a cloth and rub off any excess skin. Don't cook them all the way through or the chestnut will crumble when you try to peel it: the skin comes away much easier if the chestnuts are still hard. You can finish cooking the peeled chestnuts on a tray in the oven until they are soft to the touch.

Sweet Mincemeat

October or early November is usually the time when we make our mincemeat so we can let it steep for a good while: some even make theirs in September when they bake their Christmas cake but I'm generally not that organised. Like all recipes for fillings this one tends to make quite a lot, but as far as I'm concerned the more mince pies the merrier.

250 g finely chopped dried apples and pears
1 kg apples, peeled, cored and finely chopped or grated
500 g beef or vegetarian suet (I prefer beef)
500 g raisins
500 g sultanas
500 g currants
500 g dark brown sugar
½ nutmeg, grated
150 g toasted nibbed almonds
good glug of Somerset apple brandy
good glug of Kingston Black digestive

Mix all the ingredients together really well.

Mince Pies

I like to top mince pies with crumble mix to give an extra crunch and they are great with clotted cream.

MAKES 30

1 quantity of Sweet Mincemeat (see recipe above)

FOR THE PASTRY LINING
100 g lard, diced

100 g butter, diced
400 g plain flour
½ tsp salt
2 eggs

FOR THE CRUMBLE TOPPING
150 g plain flour
115 g butter
90 g Demerara sugar
50 g jumbo porridge oats
50 g ground almonds

To make the dough, rub the fat into the flour and salt and then knead in the eggs to form a dough. The dough can be refrigerated for up to 4 days. To make the crumble topping, pre-heat the oven to 180°C. Crumb the flour and butter together then mix with all the other ingredients and bake until lightly coloured and the oats are crunchy. Set aside to cool and store in an airtight container.

To assemble the mince pies, roll out your pastry nice and thin on a lightly floured surface. Cut out the bases with a cutter and line the tartlet trays. Fill the moulds halfway with the Sweet Mincemeat, top with crumble and bake for 15–20 minutes.

Dark Chocolate Christmas Fondant with Almond Milk Ice-Cream

We made this as an alternative to Christmas pudding and the end result was well received – so well in fact that I thought I should include it here. It is basically a hybrid of a chocolate fondant, all runny in the middle with Christmas pudding spices and fruits. Although the recipe makes a lot, it freezes really well. Make sure you have good quality dark chocolate (around 70 per cent cocoa).

MAKES 10

Home-made mincemeat is a natural alternative to the much sweeter shop bought varieties

FOR THE FRUIT MIX

100 g sultanas

100 g raisins

100 g chopped candied peel

100 g almonds

100 g chopped dates

glug of rum and brandy

good pinch of ground mace, nutmeg, ginger and cinnamon

FOR THE CHOCOLATE MIX

500 g chocolate

500 g butter

10 eggs

10 egg yolks

250 g caster sugar

300 g plain flour

4 pudding moulds

Combine all the fruit mix ingredients really well and allow to sit overnight.

Pre-heat the oven to 200°C. Melt the chocolate and butter together in a bowl over gently simmering water and set aside to cool a little. Whisk the eggs, egg yolks and caster sugar together. Whisk the chocolate into the creamed sugar and eggs then gently sift in the flour and fold together. Fold in the fruit mix. Butter and flour the pudding moulds and fill with the chocolate fondant. Freeze what you don't need and chill the chocolate fondants in the refrigerator if not required straightaway. Bake for 11 minutes so the outside is crisp and spongy and the centre molten liquid.

TRADITIONAL CHRISTMAS PUDDING

Making Christmas pudding is a laborious affair. This recipe will make two large puddings or three medium ones, so to save expense and workload I would say it's quite sensible to get a

couple of friends involved to lighten the load and split the cost, though I suggest you put the brandy away as soon as you've used it so things don't get too merry!

FOR THE MARINATED FRUIT

juice of 1 orange

zest of 1 lemon

100 g mixed peel

300 g currants

200 g sultanas

400 g raisins

200 g chopped whole almonds

200 g chopped dates

good slosh of Guinness and Somerset apple brandy

FOR THE PUDDING

175 g fresh breadcrumbs

175 g plain flour

175 g caster sugar

250 g dark brown sugar

1 tsp salt

1 tsp ground mace, cinnamon, nutmeg and ginger

4 eggs

a little milk to help it mix

300 g beef suet

75 g black treacle

125 g grated fresh carrot

250 g grated fresh apple

2 large pudding bowls, or 3 medium ones

Combine all the ingredients for the marinated fruit and marinate for 2–3 days.

Mix together the breadcrumbs, flour, sugars, salt and spices then beat in the eggs and the marinated fruit and a little milk. Fold in the suet, treacles, carrot and apple and mix until evenly distributed. Grease your pudding bowls, fill them with your mix, cover with greaseproof and tin foil. Pre-heat the over to 175°C. Place the pudding in a roasting tray lined with a cloth and fill the tray with water to a depth of about 2 in. Bake for about 2 hours or until a skewer comes out clean.

Brandy Butter

Not as popular as it used to be, but traditionalists will have nothing but with their pudding.

250 g good unsalted butter at room temperature
2 tbsp icing sugar
Somerset apple brandy to taste

Beat the butter and sugar to form a white paste then slowly beat in the brandy. Roll into logs, wrap in cling film and chill until needed.

Brandy Sauce

The old-fashioned way to make brandy or rum sauce is to thicken milk with corn flour and season with icing sugar and brandy to make a kind of powdered custard, but a nice egg custard with vanilla and brandy is much nicer.

500 ml double cream
100 ml milk
½ vanilla pod
125 g caster sugar
5 egg yolks (save the whites for meringues)
brandy or run to taste

Set a pan of water to boil. In a separate pan, bring the cream and milk to a simmer with the vanilla pod. Cream the egg yolks with the sugar. Pour the hot cream over the egg mix then pour into a bowl and whisk over the boiling water until the custard really coats the spoon. Add brandy or rum to taste.

Roast Potatoes

During my first few years in the West Country I took up a rather strange sport, which usually took place on Sundays between me and my mother-in-law Margaret. This sport was competitive potato roasting – only the crispiest would triumph! Motivated by Margaret's almost legendary reputation and goaded by my wife's taunts that although crispy my roasties weren't fluffy enough in the middle, I felt compelled to match, if not to better Margaret's roasties and restore my culinary status.

One Sunday while on a surveillance mission during a family lunch at Margaret's I noted that we both plumped for the same potato varieties such as Maris Piper, Desiree, or Yukon Golds, the current favourite (which gives me extra points as it was me who introduced this variety to John Rowswell in Barrington after reading of their popularity in America and Canada; this is now his mainstay potato).

I then noticed that she, as I, boils the potatoes that are cut in even-sized shapes until they are just about to collapse, then gently drains them in a colander and gives them a ruffle to fluff up the starch on the surface for optimum crispy effect. The fluffed-up potatoes are then rolled in hot oil about 2 cm deep and placed in a hot oven at around 200°C, which is the same for me. So we use the same spuds, use exactly the same technique, and we both have electric ovens, as by this time Margaret's marvellous old Aga had lost the gusto to crisp them up. While roasting, she turned the potatoes occasionally but not so frequently as to break them up (also if basted too often the oven's temperature will drop) and then as usual the potatoes were served to a rapture of applause for their golden crispy coating and the white fluffy interior.

So, humbled by another marvellous Sunday

lunch, the next day at work I brought the subject up for debate with the other cooks. One of the young guys shuffled around to my bench and under his breath asked what kind of fat she was using, like it was some sort of industrial espionage. But he was right; this had to be the reason. Later, after interrogating my wife Victoria into giving me the secret of her mother's cooking oil, I realised the reason why my roasties, although starting out nice and crispy, were starting to go a little chewy by the time seconds came round. I use dripping, either lard or goose fat. As the roasties cool the fats that have been absorbed by the potato set, causing them to loose their fluffy interior. As Margaret uses sunflower oil, which doesn't set and isn't absorbed as much by the potatoes, they remain crisp and fluffy for longer. They are also a little kinder on your heart valves. However, spuds cooked in the meat fat do have a meatier flavour, which I prefer, so to stay in the competition I just make sure I have sunflower oil in the cupboard for when the in-laws are coming round.

Christmas Birds

Although roast chicken is just about everybody's favourite meal throughout the whole year, it is around Christmas time that the other birds gain a sudden popularity – turkey for Christmas Day, roast duck or goose on a wintry Sunday or even for an alternative Christmas Day lunch. For most, including myself, it has to be turkey on Christmas Day because it just feels right, and if you've got a crowd in, a large bird like turkey is more economical and easier to carve – and there's so much more room for stuffing! On the other hand, if there is only two or even four of you for Christmas Day, turkey can be a bit of a chore if you've got to carry on eating it for some time afterwards. As much as we all like meals

made with leftovers, there is a limit, so a smaller bird is more practical on these occasions. I like a duck if there's a group of three or four, or a pheasant for two, which I know is a game bird but it's white meat and pretty much as organic as you can get and also very cheep, if not free. The important thing with all poultry and game birds is to keep them moist and as Fanny Cradock said, 'turkey is essentially a dry bird', which is true but only if it's been overcooked for about an hour and a half! I agree that all white poultry needs the addition of fat to keep it moist, but in modern ovens with constant temperature you don't need to put the bird in on bonfire night for Christmas lunch. Nevertheless it is important to cook them through to the bone to eliminate any bacteria. For cooking times and methods for moistness I've started with the smallest bird and worked my way up.

Larded Pheasant

Pheasant is more generally used for casseroles. It is the drier of the birds, so requires plenty of moistening. Try to use a hen bird as they tend to carry more fat. Stuff the bird full with chopped streaky bacon mixed with bay leaves, diced unsalted butter, a couple of cloves of garlic and a diced shallot. This isn't a stuffing for eating, it's just for the moistening. Then with a larding needle and strips of pork fat poke little strips of fat through the plump area of the breasts; otherwise slice the fat and push it under the skin, and then wrap the legs in some fatty bacon. Pre-heat an oven to 190–200°C, place the bird in a snug roasting tray with a little water in the bottom and cover with greaseproof paper and tight-fitting tin foil to keep the steam in. Roast for 30 minutes then remove the foil and paper and put some sliced sweet potato and butternut squash in the tray and roast for a further 10 minutes until the vegetables have soaked up the juices and start to colour. Add thin strips of streaky bacon, small pre-cooked sprouts and a handful of cooked chestnuts and roast for another 5 minutes. Remove from the oven and rest the bird upside down in the tray so all the juices run into the breast meat. Serve with bread sauce and Cumberland sauce on the side.

Stuffed Roast Chicken

I can wax on for hours about how great a plain roast chicken is, but one thing I feel I need to point out very strongly is that you should know where your chicken has come from. If the bird doesn't have a clear label of provenance then buy it either straight from the farm or a farmers' market, or your butcher after giving him the third degree over where he gets them.

You are looking for firm plump flesh; it should be heavier than it looks with no deformities to the breastbone. The skin should be dry: a really good bird will have been dry plucked so expect some feather stubs still in the skin. To my mind, as in the rest of Europe, the bird should have its feet and head on which are an indication of freshness and how it has been reared. An outdoor bird's claws and spurs will be much more developed, so too its beak; the wings on an un-caged bird, even though they are clipped, will again be bigger and more developed.

A good example of a decent poultry farm would be Creedy Carver who work out of Merrifield Farm just outside Crediton, where Peter and Sue look after 80-odd acres of farmland. They rear barn and free-range chickens and ducklings as well as speciality rare breed chickens reared for extra flavour, old breeds such as Plymouth Rock, and Cornish Game feature in some of the hybrids. Whether in barns, outside or in arks, the birds are fed on natural feeds and matured at a leisurely pace, and as they're in small flocks there is less stress when the ducklings are out, they even have paddling pools to keep them happy. As a result they get tastier birds that seem to retain their moisture well and get nice crispy skin. Peter and Sue are a great example of farmers who have a sympathetic approach to the happiness of their birds and have great pride in what they do and in return we benefit from their products.

Now I can step off my righteous poultry soap box and write about the ins and outs of cooking them. Over the years I've read and tasted plenty of roast chicken recipes which suggest twists such as stuffing with whole lemons, garlic and thyme to add fragrance, and why not. But if you've gone out and bothered to get a decent chicken then I prefer not to mess with its own wonderful flavour too much with fruits and pungent aromatics. I use a simple stuffing of coarse minced pork belly, shoulder or neck, with a little diced and sweated onion, salt, black pepper, fresh nutmeg and a little pinch of garlic salt and stuff the cavities until no more will go in, probably about 250 g for a 1.5 kg chicken. Rub the skin all over with softened butter, season with just salt and cover with a damp cloth. Pour water to a depth of about 5 mm in the bottom of the roasting tray and cover tight with tin foil so no steam can escape then bake in a pre-heated oven at 190–200°C for 45 minutes. Turn down to 180°C and remove the foil and cloth and finish roasting for another 30–40 minutes until the skin is golden and the juices are running clear when skewered with a meat fork right to the bone at its thickest part. If you're high tech and have a digital meat thermometer, it should be 76° and rising deep into its centre. Lift the leg end of the bird up onto the side of the roasting tray so the juices run into the breast.

For the gravy the stock needs to be made in advance. Roast 10 chicken wings in a medium oven until golden then dab away the grease with paper towels. Scrape all the bits into a pot and swill out the tray with boiling water and pour over the wings and cover with 400 ml of water and simmer for 1 hour, then strain and reduce to 150 ml. When your chicken is cooked dab away any fat and while the bird is being carved boil the stock in the tray and stir with a wooden spoon or spatula so no flavour is wasted. Don't thicken the gravy or it will just sit on the meat rather than soak in and moisten.

Slow-Roast Duck

Although farmed, ducks can be slow cooked so the meat is falling from the bone. They can also be served with the meat still pink but I find cooking it pink never seems to render the fat down and the skin can remain a little chewy rather than crispy and melt in the mouth. So generally I go for the slow-cooked option as it seems more widely appreciated – only the tiny wild duck, teal, are best served medium rare. Other wild ducks such as mallard fair better gently poached and can be tough with a liver taste if served pink. Because farmed ducks are so fatty slow cooking does not render them dry, but when carving it is important to get a good ratio of the leg meat and the breast for each person as the leg is always more moist. Once again, like chicken, dry plucked will give a better, crispier finish so you may need to pull out a few feather stubs. Make sure it comes with its giblets and neck for the gravy and the liver, heart, kidney and gizzards for the stuffing.

For a medium-sized 3 kg bird allow 3 hours cooking and resting. Remove the neck and giblets and chop off the wings, trim any sinew from the gizzards and either mince or blend the liver, heart, kidney and gizzards together and mix with 250 g coarse minced neck of pork belly. Mix in one finely chopped onion that has been sweated down without colour, 1 teaspoon of garlic salt, fresh picked thyme leaves, sea salt and fresh black pepper.

If you prefer a sweeter stuffing add cooked chestnuts or almonds and some chopped dried apricots or prunes and dates. Then with or without the fruit and nuts you'll need 2 tablespoons of dried breadcrumbs to be mixed in to absorb some fat and stop the stuffing shrinking. Season the internal cavity of the duck and pack it full of the stuffing, then dampen the skin with a little water or oil to allow the salt to stick, and season the skin with salt. Place onto a cooking rack in a deep roasting dish and pour water to a depth of 2 cm in the bottom. Cover with greaseproof paper and tin foil very tightly so no steam can escape, then roast at 175°C for 2½ hours then remove the foil and baste the skin with some of its rendered fat, crank the oven up to 200°C and finish cooking for another 30 minutes to crisp up the skin.

While the bird is cooking you can make your stock for the gravy by chopping up the wings and the neck. Brown them gently in oil then dab away the rendered fat with paper towels, add a diced onion and a carrot, allow to colour a little then cover with 500 ml of water and gently simmer for about 2 hours, then leave to sit until the duck is cooked. Skim away the fat from the roasting tray and add the stock to the tray to collect all the flavours and season to taste but do not thicken, as once again if the sauce is thick it will just sit on the meat and do nothing to moisten it. All the fats skimmed from the tray should be kept for roasting the potatoes, which if you've pre-boiled and fluffed up you should have enough time to roast in the fresh fat while the duck rests for 20 minutes before you carve. Although the duck fat will make them a little more sticky than vegetable oil they will taste all the better for it.

Goose

A goose is much bigger and heavier than a duck but to cook it right through doesn't take longer than a duck because most of the weight and size is taken up by its frame. So don't be misled to how many you might feed from say a 5–6 kg goose. Although it might look huge, it will probably only do eight people, so it is a good job there's plenty of room for the stuffing. Rub the skin of the goose with a little water and salt the night before to allow the salt to work into the skin, and it may also help to make the stuffing the day before cooking to give you more time.

For the stuffing dice up 2 large or 3 small peeled Cox's apples and stew down in a little butter until soft as if you're going to make apple sauce. Allow to cool and mix with 500 g minced pork, neck or shoulder, 4 tablespoons of ground almonds, fresh picked thyme leaves, season with salt, black pepper and fresh grated nutmeg and stuff the goose good and full. Place on a rack in a deep roasting dish, cover the bird with a wet cloth and pour water to a depth of 2 cm into the dish. Cover with a tight lid or tight-fitting tin foil and bake for 3 hours at 175°C. Skim away any fat with a ladle and, as for the duck, reserve for roasting the potatoes. Then put back in the oven uncovered at 200°C until the skin is crisp and golden. Allow to rest for 30 minutes; in this time you can finish your roast potatoes and finish your gravy, just as for the duck.

Turkey

'It must be a bronze or Wellington bronze.' These were my instructions for my first Christmas at the Castle. So a bronze it was, and it was excellent, but if I am being completely honest, if your standard white turkey has been raised and fed properly and killed without too much stress it is just as good, although not quite as gamey in flavour, and does stay more moist. This year our Christmas Day birds came from Rosie Boycott's farm in Dillington, as did a lot of the veggies. The turkeys, as to be expected, were as fine a bird as any but I still think it is down to the rearing and the farmer than the colour of the feathers. I also wish turkey was more popular all year round because it is a good healthy meat with excellent yield and as versatile as you want it to be. As with stuffing and roasting any bird there are many variations of stuffing with fruits, nuts, herbs and spices, but I'm sticking with sage and onion. However, if this is too savoury, again, just take away the sage and breadcrumbs and add fruit and ground nuts. A good-sized family turkey will be around 6 kg, maybe a little less, maybe a little more. If you bought your turkey and froze it make sure you defrost it slowly in a cold place or even in the fridge. If it was wrapped in skin-tight coloured cellophane and you don't know where it came from then you should be ashamed of yourself.

For the stuffing sweat 2 finely diced onions with 4 crushed cloves of garlic and about 2 finely chopped sage leaves until the onion and garlic are soft. Allow to cool then mix with 150 g breadcrumbs, 400 g minced pork belly or neck, season with salt, black pepper and the grated zest of 1 lemon, just for a hint rather than a citrus expedience. Then, with the help of a piping bag or a roll of greaseproof paper, roll around the stuffing and squeeze it into the bird. Liberally spread butter all over the bird with extra in the thigh joint area. Season and cover with a damp cloth and pour water to a depth of 2 cm in the bottom of the tray and cover with foil. If you know anybody in the catering trade, get them to get you a proper roll of tin foil and cling film: those stupid little rolls designed to run out when you've only covered half the bird are useless for turkey and don't seal in the steam. Bake the turkey at 180°C for 2½–3 hours. Remove the foil and paper and finish cooking until the skin is golden and crisp, but the juices must be running clear. If they are pink and cloudy but the skin is coloured, lay the dampened cloth back on the bird and return to the oven until the juices are clear.

To save you time the gravy is best made in advance by using your giblets without the liver and kidneys and a few turkey necks. Brown off in a little oil in the oven then cover with about 1½ litres of water, a bay leaf, 1 sprig of thyme, 1 whole split onion, 2 peeled carrots and 1 washed and split leek and simmer very slowly for around 3 to 4 hours. Strain and reduce to about 500 ml. (When you strain the mix, push the vegetables through the mesh sieve into the stock as this will naturally thicken the gravy but not over-thicken it like cornflour or arrowroot would.) This can then be reheated on the day with the juices from the roasting tray.

The Day After Christmas Soup

This is chunky enough to be eaten as a main meal or as a light lunch after a Boxing Day walk down the beach at West Bay. As much as we call this The Day After Christmas Soup, in reality it's the waste management soup, and of course the same principles apply to any leftover poultry lunches. And the bigger the carcase the more soup you get.

SERVES 4

chicken or turkey carcase and any leftover meat such as sausages, bacon and ham
1 or 2 onions, peeled and chopped
3 or 4 cloves of garlic
bay leaf
few parsley stalks
75 g butter
75 g plain flour
fresh picked tarragon
nutmeg
pinch of chilli flakes
salt and black pepper

Any carvable meat left on the carcase, slice up and keep separate for cold meats. Then with a spoon or a fork scrape any meat away from the bone, turning the carcase over and make sure you're thorough so there is no waste. Crack open the carcase and scrape out any leftover stuffing and keep to one side with the meat. Put the carcase in a large pot with the onions, garlic, bay leaf and parsley stalks and cover with cold water. Bring to a simmer, skim off any scum and simmer for about 45 minutes to 1 hour, but no longer as it starts to taste of bone and takes on a nasty aftertaste. Turn off the heat and leave to stand while you make a roux. Melt the butter and stir in the flour until it's bubbling evenly then slowly ladle in the stock little by little until you have a desired thickness and allow this to cook on a very low heat for around 20 minutes. Tip in all the meat and stuffing leftovers, any leftover bacon and sausages chopped up and, if there are any, crumbs of ham. Season with fresh picked tarragon, freshly grated nutmeg, a little pinch of chilli flakes, fresh milled pepper and salt to taste.

The day after Christmas soup is a great way to avoid the inevitable turkey sandwiches.

Other Simple Soups to Warm Your Soul

BROCCOLI SOUP
SERVES 4

500 ml water
500 g broccoli, stalk sliced thin and florets
chopped roughly
salt and white pepper

It doesn't get much easier than this! Bring the water to the boil. Add a little salt and all the broccoli and boil for 3 minutes then pour straight into a blender and blend for 3 minutes. Add fresh white pepper to taste and serve straight away or cool down quickly over ice to keep it green. To add a few calories drop in a knob of unsalted butter in the last minute of blending or sprinkle over some blue cheese and walnuts.

SPINACH SOUP
SERVES 6

500 g potato, peeled and cut into small pieces so it cooks quicker
2 cloves of garlic, peeled and crushed
2 or 3 rashers of bacon
500 g baby spinach, washed thoroughly
salt and fresh nutmeg

Cover the potatoes, garlic and bacon with water and simmer until the potato is disintegrating. Then in a separate pan boil some water and drop in the spinach and boil for 30 seconds. Drain in a colander and add the spinach to the potato pan. Pull out the bacon with tongs and pour everything else into a blender and blend for 3 minutes. Season to taste with salt and fresh nutmeg and pass through a fine sieve for extra smoothness.

PARSNIP SOUP
A soup this simple requires the parsnips to be as fresh as possible otherwise they will lose their sweetness
SERVES 4

4 very fresh parsnips
whole milk
salt and nutmeg to season

Wash and peel the parsnip and roughly chop. Cover with the milk and simmer very gently until the parsnip is soft to a spoon. Place in a blender and blend for 3 minutes. Season to taste and pass through a fine sieve. Add some cumin and cayenne pepper if you want to spice it up a little.

SMOKY SWEDE SOUP
SERVES 4

2 small swedes or 1 large one, peeled and diced
8 rashers of dry cured smoky bacon
salt and white pepper

Cover the swede and bacon with water and simmer until the swede is very soft. Pull out the bacon with tongs and chop into small pieces and fry in a little oil until crispy. Meanwhile, blend the soup for 2 minutes and season to taste. Sprinkle over the crispy bacon.

SWEET POTATO SOUP
SERVES 4

4 small or 2 large sweet potatoes, peeled and chopped
2 cloves of garlic
1 tsp ground ginger
1 tbsp maple syrup

salt and black pepper
50 g butter (optional)

Put the sweet potatoes in a pan and add water to cover by about 2 cm over. Add the garlic, ginger and maple syrup and a little salt and pepper and simmer until the flesh is soft and pulpy. Add the butter, or if you want you could use hazelnut or walnut oil. Blend the soup for 2 minutes until smooth and season to taste.

COOK'S TIP
This is the first year John Rowswell has grown sweet potatoes and I have to say the difference in flavour from ones flown across the planet and stored for months was amazing – so much nicer and sweeter. I wasn't a great fan before but I'm a convert now. Just slice about 1 cm thick and bake at 200°C in a little nut or olive oil until soft; they are a really tasty way to add starch to a dish.

WATERCRESS SOUP

Although not typically a winter soup (watercress is good all year) it makes a lovely peppery soup for a cold day. To balance the soup it is better to use stock rather than just water.

SERVES 4

250 g potato, peeled and diced
2 bundles of watercress, stalks cut from the leaves
salt and pepper

FOR THE STOCK
12 chicken wings
750 ml cold water
1 onion, peeled and halved
2 cloves of garlic, split

Blanch the chicken wings in boiling water for 30 seconds then drain and cover with the cold water. Add the onion and garlic and simmer for 1 hour. Either pass and freeze or leave un-passed while you prepare the other ingredients.
Strain enough stock to cover the potato and watercress stalks and simmer until the potato is disintegrating. Add the watercress leaves, cover with a lid and boil for 1 minute. Pour into a blender and blend for 3 minutes. Season carefully to taste and serve piping hot.

Sprouts

Sprouts fall into the marmite category of food: you either love them or hate them. For me they are as good as any other vegetable as long as they are not too crunchy and not boiled until billiard green and disintegrating. Choose small 10-pence-sized sprouts or a little bigger for plain boiling and use the larger ones for shredding.

SPROUTS IN ROSEMARY AND GARLIC BUTTER

as many sprouts as you need
butter
2 cloves of garlic, crushed
2 sprigs of rosemary
fresh chopped parsley
salt

Trim away the outer leaves and score the stalk end of the sprouts to allow even cooking. Melt as much butter as you will need to coat the number of sprouts you have on a very low heat with the garlic and rosemary and allow to infuse. Meanwhile boil the sprouts in salted water until they have the texture you prefer and drain in a colander. Turn up the heat under the butter and just as it starts to bubble vigorously add the sprouts and sauté for a few seconds until they colour, but only a little so as not to burn the garlic. Add some chopped parsley to stop the butter burning, pick out the rosemary stalk and serve.

CREAMED SPROUTS AND BACON

as many large sprouts as you need
smoky bacon, cut into thin strips
double cream
fresh chopped parsley
salt

Peel the outer leaves of the large sprouts, cut them in half and then shred as if shredding a mini cabbage. Gently fry the bacon in its own fat. When the bacon starts to colour drop the shredded sprouts into boiling salted water and boil until they are bright green and have lost their bite. Drain in a colander. Add a glug of double cream to the bacon pan and bring to a rapid boil. Add some parsley and then the shredded sprouts and toss and stir together until the cream has coated everything. Check the seasoning and serve.

SPROUTS WITH TOASTED ALMOND BUTTER

small sprouts, peeled and scored at the stalk end
75 g butter
flaked almonds, toasted
salt, pepper and nutmeg

Boil the sprouts in seasoned boiling water until they are bright green and have lost their bite. Melt the butter in a frying pan on a low heat then add toasted flaked almonds and cook together until they start to colour a little and the butter has gone clear. Drain the sprouts and roll them in the hot butter and almonds, check the seasoning and add a little fresh nutmeg.

SPROUTS WITH CHILLI FLAKES AND GARLIC

large sprouts
75 g unsalted butter
2 cloves of garlic, chopped
1 tsp mild chilli flakes
1 shallot, finely chopped
salt and black pepper

Trim, halve and shred the sprouts like a mini cabbage. Melt the butter then add the garlic, chilli flakes and shallot and allow to simmer gently. Cook the sprouts in boiling, salted water until bright green with a pleasant bite. Drain well in a colander and add to the chilli, shallot and garlic butter. Season with salt and fresh milled black pepper. If you are serving these with a traditional lunch don't be tempted to add chopped coriander as it will ruin the lunch.

Preparing and Cooking Mussels

You can generally tell if the mussels you're buying are grown on ropes. This, is not the end of the seafood world, but they are just not as good in my mind, as their fished and foraged wilder competitors. You can tell the difference by the state of the shells: if they're rope grown the shells are much cleaner and barnacle free. One thing in the rope grown mussel's favour is they don't have the tough beards that the wild ones use to cling on to rocks, but they have shells that are usually more brittle and open quicker when cooking. So if you don't relish the task of scraping away barnacles and sea moss and tugging out the beards you will probably go for the cultivated option, but if taste is what you're after, and you don't mind the extra preparation time cleaning and cooking them, you'll be rewarded with the fresh smell and taste of the sea at home. I don't tend to worry about picking off the

As usual with any shellfish, make sure the shell is firmly closed or closes when handled to ensure freshness.

barnacles, I just rinse them under cold water to wash away the sand and grit. Pull away any beard that protrudes from the shell, which can be quite tough. I recently tried some wild mussels from North Cornwall sent from the Falmouth Bay Oysters company which had beautiful blue shells but pulling the beards out of these little hard knocks was not the easiest of tasks, so in the end we left the beards on and just pulled them out with our fingers before we ate them. A trick we use at work is to have the wine already cooked out and infused with garlic, onion and herbs so you don't get that uncooked acrid wine flavour in the juices that you get if you just pour raw wine into the pan with the mussels. The mussels cook quite quickly, which doesn't allow enough time for the wine to cook out.

The two camps of people who enjoy mussels cooked simply as marinière are the purists, who insist on no cream being added as this masks the flavour of the mussel juices, and the other 99.9 per cent who think this looks like grey dish water and demand a dollop of double cream, which does mask the flavour slightly but also dampens the sea saltiness of the juice.

Infused Wine for Mussels

1 bottle dry white wine
1 small onion, peeled and diced
8 cloves of garlic, split
sprig of parsley
bay leaf
8 peppercorns

Gently simmer all the ingredients for 30 minutes and leave to infuse. Keep refrigerated in a sealed jar until needed. This keeps for weeks in a fridge and can be used for other dishes and sauces.

Moules Marinière
SERVES 2

1 kg mussels
Infused Wine (see recipe above)
double cream (optional)
freshly chopped parsley (optional)

When cleaning the mussels, do not immerse them in water as this will kill them. If you're not cooking them straight away wrap them in paper and store at the bottom of the fridge.
If any of the mussels are fully open before you cook them, and don't shut when you tap them, discard them as they are dead and probably for a good reason! Heat up a large pot that has a tight-fitting lid. Let the pan heat for about 1 minute on a high heat then add your mussels and a glug of the infused wine and cover and cook for about 1 minute before checking. If they are not all fully open return the lid and keep cooking until they are. Spoon out the mussels with a slotted spoon and strain the juice to remove any grit. Return the juice to the pan and, if you wish, add your desired amount of double cream and parsley. Bring to a boil and reduce a little and pour over your mussels.

Mussels in a Tomato Sauce
SERVES 2

1 kg mussels
Infused Wine (see recipe)
fresh chopped basil
fresh chopped parsley

FOR THE TOMATO SAUCE
500 g ripe juicy tomatoes, like plum or vine, chopped
3 or 4 cloves of garlic, chopped

The long coastline of the West Country provides us with a great selection of fresh shellfish and seafood.

Whelks freshly landed in West Bay.

pinch of chilli flakes or ½ tsp harisa paste
sea salt and fresh black pepper

To make the sauce, heat up some olive oil in a frying pan and add the tomatoes, garlic and chilli and fry until they have broken down to a pulp, then season to taste and pass through a food mill.

Just as in the marinière recipe, heat up your pan and add your cleaned mussels and a little Infused Wine. Cook until they have all opened. Using the lid to keep the mussels in the pan strain the juice to remove any grit, then pour back over the mussels in the pan and add a couple of ladles of the tomato sauce and lots of fresh chopped basil and parsley and stir so the sauce gets in the shells with the mussels. Serve with lots of crusty bread.

Cabbage and Mussel Salad

I had this dish at Fergus Henderson's brilliant restaurant, St John, in Smithfield, London. I ordered it because in my mind I didn't think cabbage and mussels would work but I was wrong. It worked great and I found it a lovely little autumn and winter starter.

SERVES 4 AS A STARTER

40 decent mussels, scrubbed of debris
3 tbsp cider vinegar
1 clove of garlic, crushed
½ small white cabbage
1 flat tbsp wholegrain mustard
3 tbsp mild olive oil or rapeseed oil
1 tbsp fresh chopped parsley
salt and sugar for seasoning

Steam the mussels, vinegar and garlic together in a pan with a tight lid until they open. Drain the mussels and strain the vinegar stock so there

is no grit in it. Pick the mussels from the shells and refrigerate.

Shred the cabbage with a sharp knife as fine as you can and pick out any stalk. Season with a good pinch of salt and a little sugar.

Reduce the vinegar stock down until there's about 1 tablespoon then add the wholegrain mustard and the olive or rapeseed oil. Mix the dressing, cabbage and mussels together, add the parsley and serve.

Falmouth Bay Oysters

For centuries families in Cornwall have grafted a living from dredging oysters in the Carrack Roads and surrounding creeks of the River Fal with some of the oldest boats still working the sea. Some of these boats date back to 1860 and most were built in the boatyards around the river Fal. All are governed by ancient bylaws put in place to protect the natural ecology of the river beds and oyster stocks. Fishermen are prohibited from using engines and still use sail boats and hand-pulled dredges, which makes the industry one of the last in Europe where these methods are used. The oyster beds are marked with withies, which are long sticks that protrude from the water.

The fishermen in 20–30-foot gaff cutter rigs rely on the tides, winds, their skill and knowledge of the waters to enable them to dredge these native oysters.

Falmouth Bay Oysters work very closely with the fishermen and are dedicated to the protection and future of the marine community, which means these wild oysters come from one of the most environmentally protected areas in the world and are watched over by the Marine Stewardship Council.

Native oysters are to my reckoning a superior product to Pacific or rock oysters, which are generally cultivated by appearance. They are

Falmouth Bay native oysters are deemed by some to be superior to the rock oyster.

identifiable by their rounder flatter shell whereas the Pacific are more curved and contoured.
The oyster's shell must be tightly shut or closed
when handled to ensure it's not dead. Do not
immerse them in water, just rinse in cold water.
Place the oyster convex side down and hold in
place with a thick cloth. Using a pointed oyster
knife (they sell them, too), wriggle the knife
side to side until it slides in between the shells
then twist to break its clasp. Run the knife along
the inner top side of the shell to release the
muscle, cut the oyster away from its shell and
brush away any shell debris. Then either eat
them straightaway, or season with a little lemon
or Tabasco sauce first, or prepare a little red
wine vinegar with finely diced shallot to add
texture. I don't normally cook native oyster,
although you can, as I think it destroys their
fresh and natural flavour.

MULLED WINE

1 bottle Côte du Rhône
1 large measure of port
1 large measure of apple brandy
150 g brown sugar
1 mandarin, halved
1 orange, halved
1 small piece of cinnamon bark
½ vanilla pod (optional but excellent)
100 g frozen cranberries
50 g dried hibiscus flowers

Gently warm together the ingredients and allow
to simmer on the lowest heat possible for about
30 minutes. Serve straightaway. If you have really
big wine glasses I suggest you don't over fill
them as the fortification from the port, brandy
and sugar makes it pretty potent. Too many,

too early, and you'll be bouncing off the walls.

Non-Alcoholic Mulled Wine
(something for the designated driver)

250 ml cranberry juice
250 ml pomegranate juice
½ vanilla pod
½ piece of cinnamon bark
4 cloves
200 g brown sugar
1 mandarin, halved
1 orange, halved
1 apple, halved
1 pear, halved

Prepare in the same way as for the Mulled Wine.

Mutton

Mutton has long been forgotten in Britain since sheep's wool and wool grease lost its value with cheaper foreign imports pushing them out of the market. As a result, there has been no point in keeping a sheep two years until it becomes mutton and paying for all the necessary vet bills, feed and shearing. Lamb has become a much more popular meat and most people under 30 don't even know what mutton is, or hogget (a lamb over a year but not yet mutton). You only have to look at the number of recipes for mutton in Mrs Beeton's book published 100 to 120 years ago to see how popular it was, and it also shows just how much and how quickly world trade can alter our dietary habits.

But all this is about to change. It would seem that recently mutton is enjoying a bit of a comeback, commanding the same price as new season lamb, partly due to the Prince of Wales's mutton renaissance initiative. The country's new hunger for food knowledge has also been fed by the Slow Food Movement and newspaper supplements, which is exactly how Mr Chapman brought mutton to my attention. He was always leaving newspaper clippings on my desk about things he thought I ought to know and things he thought put across the right message for the Castle. So it was that about six years ago we started introducing mutton to our winter menus. It was always slow-cooked joints, as that is what it lends itself to best, and steamed puddings or slow poached with capers to cut the fat, hot pots and the like. All these are transformed by using mutton instead of lamb. Even a slow-roast leg cooked until it is hanging off the bone is one of the tastiest joints with onion sauce and mint jelly. But you have to double the cooking time: one shoulder we cooked late winter last year took 8 hours in a medium oven, which is about 5 hours more than it would take to slow roast a normal shoulder of lamb.

Mutton should be over a year old and up to 3 or 5 years. They say wethers (a castigated male) make the best mutton but I've never made the comparison. It should also be hung a little longer than lamb – two to three weeks preferably. During the spring and summer months steer away from mutton because of lambing, and during shearing the flesh and fat gets tainted by the wool grease and has an unpleasant aroma. If you want to try mutton and your butcher does not sell it, the best way to find out if there are any suppliers in your area is to contact the Mutton Renaissance organisation and they will be able to put you in contact with someone who does.

Steamed Mutton and Caper Pudding
It was my wife's grandmother, Aggy, who waxed lyrical about boiled mutton and capers, which evolved into a steamed pudding at work and

became one of my favourites to make. Individually puddings take a little, but not much more, preparation, but because we pre-braise the filling they steam much quicker and are easier to serve.

MAKES 4 PUDDINGS

FOR THE STOCK
500 g mutton or lamb trimmings
1 onion, chopped
1 leek, chopped
1 carrot, chopped
1 stick of celery, chopped
1 litre water

FOR THE PASTRY
375 g self-raising flour
just under 200 g of beef suet
1 tsp table salt
water at room temperature
1 egg yolk

FOR THE FILLING
500 g neck or shoulder of mutton, boneless weight, diced
1 onion, peeled and finely chopped
1 leek, trimmed and finely chopped
10 fillets salted anchovies
2 tbsp capers, drained and washed well
fresh chopped parsley (optional)
seasoned flour
fresh nutmeg and white pepper

4 individual pudding moulds or 4 small coffee cups (not espresso)

Brown the trimmings slowly, preferably in lard but oil if not, until dark brown and crispy. Add the onion, leek, carrot and celery, and allow to tenderise and colour a little. Tilt the pan and drain away excess fat with paper towels. Return the pan to the heat and cover with the water. Bring to a simmer and cook for 1 hour then leave on one side or refrigerate until needed. Only strain it if you're freezing the stock otherwise don't strain it until you need it.

Mix the dry ingredients together then slowly mix in water until you get a firm dough. The amount of water is different every time. I think this is probably due to the amount of flour in the suet being unevenly distributed but I may be wrong. Then knead in the egg yolk and chill a little until needed.

Pre-heat the oven to 170–180°C. Lightly flour the meat and brown it in a sturdy casserole dish, preferably in lard but oil if not. Use tongs so you get a good even colour and don't turn the heat up too high as the flour coating burns easily. When the meat is evenly coloured drain away the fat with paper towels, add the onion and leek to the pan and colour lightly. Cover with the stock and a lid and braise the meat in the oven until it is falling apart, about 2½ hours. Crush the anchovies, capers and parsley in a mortar or spice grinder or just chop together finely with a knife. Flake up the meat and mix with the capers, anchovy and parsley mix, season with nutmeg and white pepper and keep to one side.

Line the pudding moulds with butter and flour. Cut your pastry into snooker-ball-sized lumps. Roll each one out into ½ cm thick rounds. Mould the disc over the end of the rolling pin and then place the mould over the pastry. Remove the pin and make sure the pastry is snug in the mould. When each mould is lined chill for 5 minutes then fill them with the meat filling and spoon in some liquor. Then cut four pieces of pastry for the lids, rolling them to the same thickness, place over the rim of the mould and roll over with the pin to seal the

Steamed mutton and caper puddings.

edges and remove excess pastry. Cover the mould with buttered foil and steam in a pre-heated steamer for 20 minutes. If it makes life easier you can cool and refrigerate and reheat when convenient. They take about 15 minutes to reheat in a steamer.

Mutton and Caper Sauce
SERVES 4

600 g 'scrag end' (neck) or shoulder of mutton (add an extra 150 g if it is on the bone)
1 onion, peeled and roughly chopped
1 stick of celery, washed, peeled and roughly chopped
1 carrot, washed, peeled and roughly chopped
1 leek, washed, peeled and roughly chopped
bay leaf, sprig of thyme and sprig of rosemary, tied together in leek skin
1 shallot, finely chopped
2 tbsp capers, rinsed and chopped
1 tbsp chopped anchovies
fresh chopped parsley
seasoned plain flour

Roll the mutton in the flour and fry in lard until oaky brown. Add the vegetables and allow to colour slightly and then dab away excess fat with paper towels. Add the bundle of herbs, cover with water and simmer very gently for anything between 3 and 4 hours until the meat is falling off the bone. Drain the stock and keep the meat covered so it doesn't dry out. Reduce the stock down until there's only about 6 tablespoons left then add the shallot, capers, anchovies and lots of fresh chopped parsley. Portion the meat out and spoon over the sauce. I love to eat this with purple sprouting and plain mashed potato but it also eats well with Mediterranean vegetables dishes such as ratatouille.

Winter Roots

I remember a few years ago a so-called inspector from one of the many hotel and restaurant guidebooks came to inspect us in February and told us he thought we were using too many winter vegetables and that we should maybe consider more interesting varieties such as asparagus! Fool. Winter roots – carrots in their various sizes and colours, parsnips, turnips, swedes, celeriac, Jerusalem artichokes and beets – are all great vegetables in their own right and work equally well together as combinations and when coupled with greens such as kale, sprouting, and all the different cabbages. If I'm going to buy anything from the tropics in winter it will be mangos, pineapple, paw paws and pomegranates, not asparagus and green beans.
If you get your vegetables from a box scheme or farmers' market and they are covered in dirt don't wash them if you are not using them immediately as I find the soil helps keep them fresher tasting – so only wash just before use.

Jerusalem Artichoke Soup
(two methods: two totally different results)
SERVES 4

300 g Jerusalem artichoke, peeled and diced
200 g potato, peeled and diced
1 clove of garlic, peeled
whole milk
sea salt and white pepper

Place the artichoke and potato in a pan with the garlic and a little sea salt and white pepper and add just enough milk to cover. Simmer until both vegetables are soft enough to break when touched. Blend for 2 minutes, strain through a fine mesh sieve and season to taste. (You can use 100 per cent artichokes but it is quite a strong flavour.)

or

Caramelised Jerusalem Artichoke Soup

300 g Jerusalem artichoke, peeled and diced
1 onion, peeled and chopped
2 cloves of garlic, crushed
500 ml Madeira or sherry
200 g potato, peeled and diced
whole milk
freshly grated nutmeg
salt and fresh black pepper

Sweat the artichoke, onion and garlic in a little butter until they start to colour and catch on the bottom of the pan. Add the alcohol and rub the sediment from the bottom to help create a nutty flavour. Add the potato and enough milk to cover and simmer until the potato is breaking up. Add some freshly grated nutmeg, plenty of fresh milled black pepper and blend for 2 minutes so it is really smooth. Strain through a fine mesh sieve and add salt to taste.

Rosemary and Thyme Baked Roots
This is excellent with lamb and deer.
SERVES 6

selection of root vegetables – carrots, swede, turnip, celeriac
sprig of thyme
sprig of rosemary
sea salt and black pepper

Pre-heat the oven to 200°C. Peel, and core if required, and cut into fairly large chunks around 2–3 cm square but no particular shape, equal amounts of carrot, swede, turnip and celeriac. Lightly toss in a little duck fat or melted dripping and season with sea salt and fresh milled pepper.

Place in the centre of a large square of tin foil with a good sprig of thyme and the same of rosemary poked in the middle of the vegetables. Pull the sides of the foil up and pinch together to make a sealed bag. Place on a baking sheet and into the oven for around 20 minutes until they are soft to touch through the foil. It is quite nice to open the bag at the table, because the herb aromas escape with the cooking vapours.

Braised Oxtails and Creamed Potato
Oxtail is perfect for slow and moist cooking methods as it's a tough, sinewy cut that requires slow gentle cooking but it carries plenty of inner fat marbling to keep it moist. By cooking it on its cartilage it retains great flavour. It was a favourite of mine to cook when I worked with Jean Christophe Novelli where we braised it in an intense wine and stock reduction. The whole process, right from learning where the cartilages were so you could cut them into their segments with ease, to trimming and marinating, and then the browning and braising with different colours and smells changing right through the process, to the end result where the meat is only just clinging to the bone and the liquor had taken on a deep shine, was hugely satisfying. These days I omit the use of litres of wine and instead rely on the flavour of the meat itself to infuse the dish, and I will say this is a cook's dish as it requires a good stock, which in turn requires advance preparation and time.
You could use beef or veal stock that I've noticed is now available in supermarkets to lure the hobby cook away from making their own, and to offer alternatives to powdered stocks, but I still think it is not as fulfilling as knowing you made everything from scratch.
SERVES 4

1 oxtail, prepared and cut into pieces by your butcher
1 onion, peeled and diced
1 garlic bulb, halved
1 carrot, peeled and diced
1 leek, washed and sliced
1 stick of celery, washed and diced
salt and pepper

FOR THE STOCK

500 g beef skirt, diced
2 split pig's trotters
1 onion, peeled and diced
1 large carrot, peeled and diced
1 leek washed, trimmed and chopped
2 sticks of celery, washed and roughly chopped
1 tbsp tomato purée
2 bay leaves
1 sprig of thyme

To make the stock, heat some lard in a large pot and brown off the beef and trotters, a little at a time. When each batch is nicely coloured drain in a colander and repeat until all the meat is brown and the bottom of the pan has a good bronze coating on the bottom. Add the vegetables and sweat until they start to colour. Add the tomato purée and the drained meat and stir well. Fill the pan up with water, add the bay leaf and thyme and allow to simmer gently for the whole day, about 12 hours, before straining. This can then be frozen for later use or stored in the fridge for up to 4 days.
I don't recommend you butcher the oxtail your-self, unless you've been shown how to, cutting through oxtail cartilage requires a very sharp knife and the kind of pressure required to sever a finger. Instead ask your butcher to cut it for you.

Pre-heat the oven to 175°C. Roll the pieces in seasoned flour and heat up some lard in a sturdy pot and brown them in fairly deep fat using tongs to help get an even colour. Drain or mop away the fat, add the onion, garlic, carrot, leek and celery, and pour over enough stock to cover the meat. Cover with a tight lid or foil and braise for 1½ hours, then remove the lid or foil and continue cooking for a further hour adding more stock if the level of liquid falls below the meat. The meat is cooked when it is falling from the bones with ease. Then taste and adjust the seasoning as required. There are lots of things that go well with braised dishes such as dry mash or creamed potato, mashed swede and carrot, celeriac or cauliflower purées, braised cabbage, sprouting and greens to name a few, but my favourite is puréed potato with loads of dairy to make it smooth and shiny.

POTATO PURÉE
SERVES 6

6 medium sized Maris Piper or Desiree potatoes, peeled and diced
1 clove of garlic, peeled
whole milk
75 g unsalted butter
salt and white pepper

Poach the potato and garlic in just enough milk to cover until the potato is crumbling then drain away half the liquid. Transfer into a food mill with the butter and then pass through a sieve. Reheat and give it a good beating with a wooden spoon or spatula to make sure it is smooth and shiny then season to taste.

ROOT VEGETABLE BAKE
This a comforting side dish to many winter

meats such as slow-roast shoulder of lamb and crispy roast duck. Although there is certainly nothing wrong with honeyed parsnips or mashed swede and carrot, this should just add another string to your bow when it comes to winter vegetables. I'm sure if you're part of a vegetable box scheme, which many people are in the countryside – and towns and cities for that matter – you'll be getting plenty of root veggies through the winter months.

SERVES 8

2 turnips

1 swede

1 celeriac

2 sweet potatoes

3 large parsnips

3 onions

nutmeg, salt and pepper

FOR THE STOCK

250 g chicken wings

2 cloves of garlic, split

bay leaf

sprig of rosemary

sprig of thyme

To make the stock, blanch the chicken wings in boiling water for 1 minute then drain and recover in cold water. Simmer them together with the garlic, bay leaf, rosemary and thyme for 40 minutes then strain. If you are not using the stock straightaway you will need to reheat with some fresh herbs to replenish their flavours as they fade a little with time, especially if you're freezing it. Pre-heat the oven to 200°C. Peel all the vegetables and slice them as thinly as possible. Mix them all together with a little of your chicken stock, season with salt, pepper and nutmeg, and pack into a pie dish. Spoon over a little more

stock and cover the dish with greaseproof paper and tin foil so it steams itself. Bake for about 45 minutes until the vegetables are nice and soft and all their flavours have mingled.

SLOW-COOKED BRISKET OF BEEF WITH CONFIT OF WINTER ROOTS AND CREAMED POTATO

This is another slow-cooked winter warmer but the meat itself could easily be used as an alternative for a Sunday roast beef, especially if you've got guests who don't like their meat pink. Rather than give them a lean cut all dried out, enjoy a slow-cooked joint such as brisket or a rib roll, which is a flap of meat that wraps around the rib eye. Ask your butcher to cut away all the gristle and tie it in or roll it. If the joint is for lunch I recommend you get it in the oven for about 8 am as cooking time can vary by as much as an hour depending on how mature the beef is and what the fat-to-meat ratio is. So don't expect the timing to be the same every time.

SERVES 6

1 kg brisket, rolled

sea salt and black pepper

FOR THE GRAVY

400 g diced brisket for the gravy

2 onions, peeled and chopped

2 carrots, peeled and roughly chopped

2 sticks of celery, washed and chopped

1½ litres water

2 cloves of garlic, split

FOR THE CONFIT OF VEGETABLES

1 swede

2 large carrots

2 parsnips

2 cloves of garlic, split

2 bay leaves
sprig of thyme
1 litre of duck or goose fat
fresh nutmeg

FOR THE CREAMED POTATO
12 Maris Piper or Desiree potatoes, peeled and diced
150 ml whole milk
100 g unsalted butter

Pre-heat the oven to 150°C. Prepare the brisket by rubbing the outside with sea salt and fresh milled black pepper. Rub some lard on to tin foil then roll the beef in at least four layers of foil. Pinch the ends so it looks like a giant Christmas cracker, fold the ends over and make sure the seam of the foil is facing up so no fat or juices can escape. Place it on a wire rack on a tray in the oven and leave for about 4 hours. It should be soft to the squeeze. While the beef is cooking you can make the gravy, confit the vegetables and cream the potatoes. Roll the diced brisket in seasoned flour and in a fairly large pot brown the meat in some lard until it is dark and crispy. Add the onion, carrot and celery and allow to colour a little. Drain away the fat by tipping everything into a colander so you can keep the dripping, then pop the meat and vegetables back in the pan and cover with about 1½ litres of water. Add the garlic and herbs and simmer very gently while the beef cooks. When the beef is resting strain and season a little but not too much as it's going to be reduced. Reduce down until you're happy with the flavour, making sure to add all the juices from the tin foil.
Peel and cut the vegetables into chunky pieces. If the parsnips are large remove the core then season with salt, fresh black pepper and some freshly grated nutmeg and leave to let the salt work in for 10 minutes in a colander then transfer the vegetables to the pot. Add the garlic (you can retain and reuse the bay leaves and thyme from confit of vegetables), cover with duck or goose fat and simmer until they are nice and soft. Drain away all the fat through a colander. If you cook them in advance, put them in the freezer for 20 minutes so they don't over cook then reheat in a hot oven with a little of the fat.
Poach the potato in the milk until the potato is crumbling, then drain away half the liquid. Transfer into a food mill with the butter and pass through, then through a fine sieve and then reheat. Give it a good beating with a wooden spoon or spatula to make sure it is smooth and shiny, then season to taste.

Stew and Dumplings
Dumplings, with their fluffy texture from the beef or mutton suet, crispy on the surface and full of all the flavours of the fats that they have soaked up while bobbing on the surface of the stock, always reminds me of childhood meals. Mum was a dab hand at dumplings and always got the crispy/soggy ratio just right. I love the way, especially on a cold day, a dish of stew and dumplings seems to ready you for hard work or play, and winter vegetables seem to sweeten the broth. When you consider that the best cuts for stew are brisket and silverside, it also makes a very cheap meal. Although shin is also very good it's a little more expensive. If the silverside and brisket is salted then you'll have to soak it overnight but few butchers bother to salt it these days as not many people bother with cold pressed meats any more. This is a shame because if these sorts of cuts were more popular it would drive the price of the choicest cuts down.

Dumplings

MAKES ENOUGH FOR 4

125 g plain flour
60 g beef suet
1 flat tsp baking powder
pinch each of garlic salt, normal salt and fresh
parsley

Mix everything together and add water at room
temperature a little at a time until it forms a
dough. Roll into 10-pence-sized balls, as they
will swell during cooking. Keep them cool while
you make the stew.

Stew

SERVES 4

500 g trimmed brisket or silverside, cut into 50 g
chunks
8 baby onions, peeled
1 large carrot, peeled and sliced fairly thick
1 small swede, peeled and roughly diced
1 turnip, peeled and roughly diced
bay leaf
sprig of thyme

FOR THE BEEF STOCK

205 g diced rib meat
1 onion, peeled and chopped
1 carrot, peeled and chopped
500 ml water
2 cloves of garlic, split
6 peppercorns
bay leaf

To make the stock, roll the meat in seasoned
flour and brown gently in lard. Add the onion
and carrot and allow to colour gently, then turn
the heat right down and dab away the excess fat

with paper towels. Pour over the water and add
the garlic, peppercorns and bay leaf and simmer
for an hour or so and strain.

Roll the brisket in seasoned flour and brown
gently in a sturdy pot using tongs to get an even
colour. Add the baby onion and allow to colour
a little then pour over your beef stock and allow
to simmer very, very gently with a lid on for
around 1–1½ hours.

Pre-heat the oven to 220°C. Add the vegetables
and the dumplings and cover with a lid and
again gently simmer for around 15 minutes to
cook the vegetables and half steam/half poach
the dumplings. Remove the lid and add the bay
leaf and thyme and place the pot in the hot
oven. If there's a little fat floating on the surface
brush it over the dumplings, which will allow
the dumplings to crisp a little on the top.

> COOK'S TIP
> This dish needs to be eaten for lunch or dinner
> on a bleak day when lots of outdoor chores
> either need to be done or have been done.

Turbot with Golden Beetroots, Creamed Cauliflower and Crispy Bacon

This is another dish that lets very simple ingredients rule. If golden beetroot is not available
then I wouldn't bother to suggest using candy
striped beets instead. I'm sure if you look to
market gardens, farm shops and the like, you'll
get some good comparisons. Somerset Organic
Link is great for sourcing unusual fruit and vegetables, and there is always my grower John
Rowswell in Barrington.

People don't always associate the vegetables that
are good this time of year with fish dishes but if

Turbot with golden beetroots, creamed cauliflower and crispy bacon.

treated very simply they can make great light combinations.

SERVES 4

3 tennis ball-sized beetroots
2 potatoes
½ small cauliflower
whole milk
butter
12 thin slices of dry cured smoked bacon
4 100–130 g turbot fillets, cut from a larger fish so the flesh is nice and thick
little dry white wine
salt

Pre-heat the oven to 180°C. Scrub (but don't peel) the beetroots and completely cover with cold water. Add a little salt, cover with a lid, and bring to a simmer until you can push a butter knife through with ease, then remove from the heat.

While these are cooking, peel and chop the potatoes into small pieces and chop the cauliflower. Place together in the same pan, cover with the milk and simmer on a low heat for 30 minutes until the potato is soft to touch. Remove the potato and cauliflower with a slotted spoon into a blender and blend until smooth, slowly adding a little of the cooking milk to get a smooth consistency then add a knob of butter and season to taste.

Crisp the bacon in the oven and leave to dry out at 100°C.

Pan fry the turbot in a little olive oil until golden on both sides. If bubbles of white protein start to appear on the flesh, remove from the heat as it is over cooking. After removing the fish, splash a little dry white wine in the pan and a knob of butter.

Peel and slice the beetroot into about 1 cm thick rounds (wear rubber gloves if necessary) and mix them carefully in the pan with the wine and butter then spoon them onto plates. Place the fish on top and spoon around some creamed cauliflower. Slice the crispy bacon and lay that on top. Melt a little butter on the bacon tray to get the bacon flavour and drizzle around the dish.

Fish

Fish is a very broad subject but it seems that in Britain it's something we have only scratched the surface of and are stuck with what we believe to be our favourites, and I don't just mean battered fish or fish pie and fish cakes. I mean fish such as turbot, sea bass, halibut and Dover sole, all beautiful fish and very expensive, and rightly so when people risk their lives daily to catch them and also because the stocks take a hammering. Hence if you see a recipe using prime fish like the turbot dish I have featured, don't be afraid to ask your monger for a cheaper alternative such as brill or large plaice fillets, which, if fat enough, are also a good replacement for halibut. Dover soles have long been the most expensive of the small flat fish but if day boat fresh, lemon sole, dabs, witches and megrims are a delicious alternative for a plain grilling fish. Pollock and hake instead of cod and haddock for fish and chips, when really fresh, are good replacements. If a recipe states sea bass but there's some huss (dogfish or rock salmon) on the counter that is far cheaper, go for it. The same goes for mackerel and gurnard instead of red mullet and snapper. There are great debates throughout the food industry about fish stocks, especially popular fishes I have mentioned such as cod and halibut, so purchasing farmed versions of these fish seems at first to be a sensible option, but it has become clear that, just as on land, there are less ethical people who abuse this situation and cause

Matthew Oxham dragging the lobster pots back onto the boat.

damage to the environment. So it would seem that we are stuck between a rock and a hard place, but this is not so if you look hard enough. Just like great farmers on land, the fish farmers who take care not to harm the ocean are not great at publicising themselves, so don't dismiss all farmed fish. Also, don't be afraid of buying a fish you have never heard of (these tend to be cheaper, too). Just because it's not readily used in fish and chip shops or restaurants does not mean it's no good. Obviously when buying fish, freshness is what you are looking for – bright, shiny eyes and deep red gills. The fish should smell of the sea and should not have a fishy odour or, particularly with skate, one of ammonia –this smell is a sure sign of decay. Beware of supermarket fish counters, a fine mist of water is sprayed constantly over the fish and creates an illusion of freshness by keeping the fish looking shiny or wet, so ask to see the gills or even have a sniff!

The Castle Hotel has been buying fish from local mongers, Phil and Christy Bowditch, for many years and I didn't need to makes any changes, as the service I get is irreplaceable. A plentiful supply of fish as and when I need it all day, all week, so I never have to hold stock, and if I run out at lunch I just pop out and get more. To deal closely with suppliers like this is a real luxury for a restaurant. In the past Phil had his own trawlers as well as buying from day boats and markets. He has a huge depth of knowledge about the South West coast and fishing, which I draw upon regularly to keep the menu seasonally in check and to learn when fish are spawning. Towards the end of winter they are carrying a lot of roe so pound for pound you luck out on fish weight and after they spawn the flesh becomes transparent through lack of proteins and slimy with a jelly-like texture, especially in flat fish. But they don't all spawn at the same time so

there is always another fish to choose from, and the fisherman going out from Brixham will travel far as the North Channel and the Scottish Borders to fish; a good trawler man shouldn't even be bringing fish that have spawned ashore. Phil also gets us River Exe mussels that seem to flourish in the river water that's not as dense with salt as it is out at sea and I personally have yet to try a cultivated mussel as good as those on the River Exe.

The West Country as a whole has a lot to offer from its shores with the ancient methods such as those used by the mud horsemen in Bridgwater Bay bringing in brown shrimps and prawns, working the same shores as modern trawlers. It's the people of this region who hold onto these unusual and ancient methods that give us diversity in our products. Brixham, where pretty much all of the fish I use comes from, is still one of the busiest fishing ports in England, which is actually quite a sad statement to make considering it has only got about fourteen trawlers. Brixham itself is a beautiful little coastal town and well worth a visit just to see the boats all lined up in the harbour with the huge great rusty chunks of machinery that show years of toil and the great ropes that you can barely get your hand around let alone tie a knot in! Witness the weather-worn men climbing aboard these iron tubs with the young local lads all pale-faced following behind; it's quite humbling to think just how hard these men work to bring fish to our tables and cash to theirs. It makes you wonder why they actually do it, but they do, and I thank them for it, because you wouldn't get a lily-livered landlubber like me smashing through those waves in freezing temperatures, with sleep deprivation, and storms brewing on the horizon.

Gurnard is a less popular but cheaper fish that can be used instead of more expensive fish such as red mullet.

Seared Brixham Scallops with Puréed and Marinated Celeriac

The combination of celeriac and scallops works so well. The really sweet flavour of the scallops balances perfectly with the earthy, nutty flavour of the celeriac, which you prepare in two different ways to add texture to the dish.

SERVES 2 AS A MAIN OR 4 AS A STARTER

12 scallops
Malden sea salt

FOR THE CELERIAC PURÉE

150 g Maris Pipers or Desiree potatoes, peeled and diced
150 g celeriac, peeled and diced
1 clove of garlic, peeled
whole milk
butter
salt and fresh black pepper

FOR THE MARINATED CELERIAC

150 g celeriac
juice of 1 lemon
coriander seeds
1 tbsp light honey
rapeseed oil
fresh chopped parsley or chives
salt and fresh black pepper

To make the celeriac purée, put the potatoes, celeriac and garlic on a low heat with enough milk to cover. Simmer until the potato and celeriac are soft to touch then strain the mix in a colander over a bowl to retain the liquid. Blend the mix, adding a little of the liquid to get the purée to the desired consistency. Add a knob of butter and season to taste. If the purée is a little thin, just put it in a pan on a low heat, stirring continuously and allow some liquid to evaporate and the purée to thicken. Cover with grease-proof paper to prevent a skin forming and leave to one side.

For the marinated celeriac, ideally you need to dice the celeriac into 5 mm squares, but if dicing this much celeriac into little tiny cubes sounds daunting, just use a cheese grater instead. Finely dice or grate the celeriac on the larger setting of a grater and squeeze over the lemon juice. Sprinkle over a little salt and freshly milled black pepper. Mill 4 twists of coriander seeds in a pepper mill or crush 6 in a mortar, and sprinkle on. Drizzle over the honey and allow to marinate for 5 minutes. Add enough rapeseed oil to cover and when needed, finish with some fresh chopped parsley or chives.

Heat a frying pan on a medium heat then add a little oil and roll it around the surface of the pan. Lay in the scallops, round circle down and season with Malden sea salt and allow to colour. When nice and brown turn them over and allow the other side to brown. Turn off the heat and place the scallops onto some paper towels to drain away any excess oil.

Gently warm the marinated celeriac on a low heat and add fresh chopped parsley, place the scallops on plates and spoon around some purée and then drizzle over the marinated celeriac and its dressing.

Fresh Brixham Crab with Marinated Vegetables

Although in the restaurant we tend to go for large cock crabs, for home the smaller hen crabs will be much easier to tackle, and besides, you need a pretty big pot for a large cock crab. For two healthy portions you will want a crab each at about 500 g and make sure they are good and lively; you don't want them dead because the meat will have all but disappeared.

Seared Brixham scallops with puréed and marinated celeriac.

Fresh crab meat is a beautiful treat on its own or with simple leaves and with a slice of lemon but I like the textures that the marinated vegetables add to the dish, as well as the additional entertainment they bring to the plate.

SERVES 2

2 500 g hen crabs
few cloves of garlic
2 florets of Italian cauliflower (the green spirally one), washed
2 florets of plain white cauliflower, washed
2 florets of purple cauliflower (if you can get it), washed
1 carrot, peeled
¼ butternut squash, peeled
1 small stick of celery, washed and trimmed
1 lime
1 tbsp honey
fresh ground coriander seeds

rapeseed or avocado oil
2 spring onions, sliced
English lettuce, washed
Malden sea salt

Bring a large pot of salted water (it should almost taste of the sea) to a rolling boil. Put the crabs in, cover with a lid and simmer for 15 minutes. Drain the pan and rinse the crabs under cold water to stop the cooking process. Let the water run until they are cold enough to handle.

Then, as for any crustaceans, prepare yourself and the kitchen for a messy job. I find covering your work area with cling film is good for damage limitation. You then pull the claws and legs off, cover with a tea towel and crack the shells with the back of a sturdy knife. Pick out the meat with a crab pick or cocktail stick. If you are not eating the meat straightaway,

The unusual looking Romanesque cauliflower is now readily available and locally grown.

191

Fresh Brixham crab with marinated vegetables is a light and tasty salad for winter.

refrigerate as soon as possible; in fact if you can put the meat into an ice-cold bowl from the start, this is recommended as shellfish deteriorates quickly.

Pre-heat the oven to 180°C.

Cracking the body is the messiest part. Tap the head with the back of the knife to split it then pull apart to reveal the inner skeleton. Put the head shell and all the other parts of shell in a tray to roast for soup, leaving the brown meat in the head to flavour and thicken the soup. Split the skeleton into quarters with a large chopping knife and pick out any meat from the crevices with your pick until you are satisfied you are not wasting any. Put any remaining shells and bone in the tray for stock.

To make stock, dab the bones with a little tomato purée or put a few fresh tomatoes in the tray and dry out in the oven until there is no liquid left in the tray and it's starting to colour. Cover with water and pour the whole lot into a pan with a few cloves of garlic and simmer until the stock takes on a good crab flavour. Then freeze for later or reduce down and thicken with a roux or arrowroot and finish with cream. For soup you could add a bit of spice such as ginger or chilli to add an edge or a little orange zest and basil. The process is really about reducing wastage.

Break the cauliflowers into as small florets as you can with a sharp little knife then either finely dice or grate the other vegetables into a bowl. Zest over the lime and squeeze over its juice and add the honey and a little Malden salt and allow to dissolve. Add the crushed coriander seeds and mix well. Cover with your oil and and mix in the sliced spring onion.

Place your crab onto some fresh English lettuce leaves then drizzle over the marinated vegetables. If you want to garnish, just sprinkle over some cress.

COOK'S TIP
If you're doing this for a dinner party it serves 4 for a starter. You could try to get different coloured cauliflower such as purple, green and yellow to really make it colourful, or purple potato grated on a fine grater before marinating to add even more colour. You can even use a tiny melon baller to scoop out balls of squash to add another dimension to its presentation.

Apple Chutney

Apples are our most verstile fruit as they can be stored and used throughout autumn and winter.

1 kg Bramleys or rustic cooking apples at peeled and cored weight
500 g onions, peeled and finely chopped
2 lemons, halved lengthways. sliced into semicircles and deseeded
300 g raisins
500 ml cider vinegar
1 tsp salt
500 g brown sugar
1 tsp ground ginger
½ nutmeg, grated
1 tsp ground cinnamon
3 cardamom seeds

Put everything in a pan, except the sugar and the spices, with plenty of room so you don't spill when stirring. Allow the mixture to simmer until the apple has softened then add the sugar and spices and reduce down until the liquid has evaporated and the mix has thickened. Spoon the mix into sterile receptacles and store.

The same recipe can be used with hard pears or ripe quinces, each adding its own flavours to change the chutney's finish. All are good with cheeses as well as meats.

Sauce or Gravy, Gravy or Sauce?

A sauce to me is something involving either a reduction of wines and other alcohols with a stock that, if not over reduced, should give a clear, rich and only slightly gelatinous consistency or a flavoured reduction finished with either cream or butter. Other variations such veloutés and béchamels are liquids thickened with a butter/flour roux. A gravy on the other hand, which is a great word in itself and not one used enough as a menu item, is different in that its flavour shouldn't be altered with the addition of wines and cream. It should be an extension of the pan juices that you create during the roasting and frying of meats. As the juice from the meat cooks and rests, it forms the purest meat flavour you can get. The only issue then is to make the tiny amount of juice that you get stretch to everyone around the table, and the mistake made here is that people start chucking that half bottle of Merlot that's been open for weeks into the pot and boil it for 10 minutes, then thicken it with flour or cornflour. This is a misconception to say the least as most wine needs long slow simmering to concentrate the flavours of its fruits and sugars. It also dilutes the flavours of the juices, and because the wine isn't cooked it ends up tasting like thick warm wine and flour and not of the meat it came from and for which it is supposed to be the lubrication. The best way to extend the sauce, while your meat is cooking or even before you start, is to make a light stock using trimmings of the type of meat you're using, So, for example, if you're cooking two steaks you would make the stock 20 minutes before you cooked the steak by browning off a handful of stewing steak in lard until oak brown all over. Turn down the heat, soak away the fat with tongs and paper towels and swill the pan out with a cup of water and simmer together for 20 minutes. Then either refrigerate until needed or while your cooked steaks are resting, dab away the fat from the pan and pour in your stock and reduce by about three quarters then add a small knob of cold butter and stir it in and adjust the seasoning. This method can be used for lamb or pork chops, chicken breasts and any meat you are pan frying, even scallops if you use the coral to make the stock, and the same can apply to roast joints, except you will need to make more of the basic stock and reduce for longer. If you want to flavour with herbs, drop a sprig of thyme or rosemary in right at the end so the flavour remains fresh.

This basic meat gravy can be turned into sauces if you wish by adding a little alcohol or wine, just a splash before you add your stock and allow it to almost evaporate before adding the stock. For instance if you wanted a pepper sauce you would cook your steaks then add chopped shallot to the pan, 1 tablespoon of brandy and 1 of white wine and evaporate then add about 20 washed peppercorns and your stock and reduce by 80 per cent. Then add a splash of double cream and fresh milled black pepper, a knob of butter and reduce until it coats a spoon and season to taste.

If you were cooking chicken and you want to make a chasseur sauce you would cook your chicken, whether it be a roast or breast or legs, making the sauce in the same way. When the meal is cooked, dab away most of the fat then add sliced button mushrooms to the pan and fry gently until golden brown. Add chopped shallots and a pinch of salt and cook until softening slightly. Add a splash of dry white wine and evaporate, then your stock and reduce by 70 per cent. Then add fresh picked tarragon and a knob of cold butter.

These basic methods of making the sauce or gravy means the flavours remain fresh and are a lot less labour intensive than vast reductions that are not practical and also very costly in pounds as well as time.

FAGGOTS

When I first arrived at the Castle in late 1999 I was given my briefing of how, regardless of my Francophile cooking background, all menus at the Castle were to be British and the best of. So, as embarrassing as it may sound, I had to research the foods of the country I was born and raised in. Thankfully the hotel where I apprenticed in York was quite a traditional British hotel and restaurant, but in a Steak Dianne kind of way rather than food from British roots, and at the Savoy in winter steamed steak and kidney pudding was on the trolley once a week, but it was lost among the other modern European dishes.

The first dishes I introduced comprised classics such as suet puddings, pies and roasts, and it was during the BSE beef crisis that I decided to combine different traditional methods to kind of pooh-pooh what was happening, with a celebration of British beef combining roast fillet with an oxtail suet pudding and braised heart faggot and poached tongue in a beef tea. The best part of serving this dish was seeing which aspect people preferred: for some it's straight to the fillet; others prefer the suet pastry and sticky oxtail; and some of the older customers thought the beef tea brought back fond memories; but the bit most raved about was the faggot, especially from Mr Chapman. I find the kind of people who are fond of a kipper for breakfast and have a penchant for strong cheese prefer the faggots to all the other aspects on the plate. Although most traditional butchers can make good faggots, hygiene laws forbid them from cooking meats in the same shop they prepare their raw meats thus making the number of butchers who produce them dwindle as they don't have the facilities to separate the process. Also reheating faggots that have been pre-cooked means that the end product will never be as moist and tasty as when cooked fresh. If you don't mind a bit of blood, guts and labour and you want to make them at home, don't use a food processor if you don't have a mincer of any kind, hand or electric, as the texture will be all wrong and too firm. Instead, give your butcher the list of ingredients and he will mince them for you.

SERVES 4

300 g diced ox heart
100 g beef suet (freshly minced if possible)
100 g minced belly bacon
1 heaped tbsp breadcrumbs
½ nutmeg, grated
1 tsp garlic salt
1 tsp salt
black pepper
250 g caul fat in which to wrap the faggots
2 large or 3 small onions, peeled and thinly sliced
bay leaf

FOR THE BRAISING STOCK
200 g cheap beef trimmings
200 g cheap pork trimmings
2 onions, peeled and finely chopped
1 clove of garlic, crushed
bay leaf

Mix the ox heart, beef suet, mince, breadcrumbs, nutmeg, salts together thoroughly and season with 8 twists of black pepper. Separate the mixture into 6 balls and give them a firm squeeze so they are nice and compact. Wrap each ball in just one layer of caul fat (make sure the caul is very well rinsed). Leave to stand for at least 1 hour in the fridge. If you can leave them overnight all the better for the seasoning and bacon cure to work through the mixture.

To make the stock, roll meat in seasoned flour and brown well on a medium heat in lard or dripping then drain away the fat with paper towels and add the onion and garlic and allow to colour a little. Cover with water, add the bay leaf and simmer for an hour. Leave to stand until room temperature then strain.

Pre-heat the oven to 220°C. Using an ovenproof frying pan start to sweat the onions in a little lard. Meanwhile bake the faggots on a lightly greased tray in the oven for just 10 minutes as the onions colour. This will melt away excess fat from the faggots. Pull them out of the oven and drain away the melted fat. Lower the oven temperature to 180°C. Put the faggots on top of the onions and pour on enough stock to cover the onions but not the faggots and braise them in the oven for 10 minutes. Put the faggots in a serving dish and put the onions and stock on a high heat and add the rest of the stock and reduce until you have just enough to pour over the faggots to serve.

> COOK'S TIP
> If you can't get caul webbing from your butcher you could roll the faggots in herbs and breadcrumbs to keep the moisture in.

Warts and All

If you come from a background of regimented consistency where all baby vegetables had to be the same size, potatoes had to be blemish free and totally devoid of dirt, and (God forbid) if you ever saw a lettuce leaf with a hole or a slug, it would have gone straight back to the supplier, you get to the stage where, because of the standard you are working at, this becomes the norm. Now we realise that this kind of uniformity in products actually constrains cooks and deprives their customers of real flavours. For my first year in the West Country I was lucky enough to work with produce from the Victorian walled gardens at Hatch Court where Dr Robin Odges had re-established the vegetable garden and through connections with Mr Chapman and the previous chef, Phil Vickery, he had started to grow for them. Unfortunately they had to sell the property due to the cost of its upkeep and we lost our grower just like that. We were without for nearly a year and returning to scentless and tasteless but perfectly uniform fruit and vegetables but for a chance meeting with John Rowswell of Barrington where his family have farmed since Saxon times and he himself has been growing vegetables since his childhood. When we met he was supplying wholesale vegetables from the markets to pubs and restaurants and selling the vegetables he grew to markets and wholesalers but over the years we've worked together. Although he still buys from markets, his mainstay business is selling what he and his contacts in the area grow to the pubs and restaurants; such is the demand in the west for locally grown products.

Just recently I met Rosie Boycott, who's a successful London journalist and ex-editor of *The Independent*, who has taken on a small organic farm in Dillington, just outside Ilminster, in the grounds of Dillington House. There her young farmer, David Bellows, is growing vegetables, planting grape vines and peach, apricot and mirabell trees in a walled garden where they had

Colourful winter cabbage. Don't worry about the holes, just strip away any damaged leaves. At the very least you know it's probably been grown without the use of pesticides.

originally been grown hundreds of years ago. They also have pigs and intend to take on some South Devon cows and sheep as well, so I now have another string to our fresh produce bow and I wouldn't give them up for all the tea in China. Something just feels right about washing the dirt off the carrot that was pulled that day. As you wash away the dirt you can smell the scent of the carrot getting stronger as you reveal more flesh. Likewise when you slice a celeriac in half and little dew drops of moisture come to the surface and fill the air with the celeriac's fresh smell. Or rubbing fresh mud off the first new potatoes to reveal the pearly white flesh that won't even need to be peeled. You could go on and on about what a pleasure it is to work with great produce like this but I still get chefs phone me and ask me where we buy our vegetables and when I say where they reply, 'Yes we tried them but it all came in with dirt on it'!

Brawn

Brawn is one of those dishes that over time have disappeared from butcher's windows and restaurant menus as people have become more squeamish about what they eat. The moment they connect the meat with the animal, and this always happens when the head is involved, it puts people off. So brawn, generally being made with pig's head, has dropped out of popularity, which is a shame because, like ham, the meat is cured so the dish keeps well and with mustard, cheese, pickles and salads it makes quick savoury lunches or supper. I'm sure if you called it a terrine of pork people would enjoy it with blissful ignorance.

Unless you want to make enough to feed your whole street you'll need only half a pig's head. Ask your butcher to brine it for 48 hours for you as they take up a lot of space, and ask for the head from a smaller pig. If you're going to brine it yourself you'll need 3 litres of water, 400 g of sea salt, 400 g of granulated sugar, 30 g of salt-petre (nitrate) boiled together until totally dissolved then cooled down completely before submerging the head for 48 hours. Then rinse away the brine with fresh water and discard the used brine.

In a large pot cover the head with water and bring to the boil and drain it quickly then recover with fresh cold water add 2 halved onions, 3 peeled and halved carrots, 1 washed and halved leek, 2 bay leaves, a sprig of thyme, 500 ml dry cider, 50 ml cider vinegar and about 20 black peppercorns and simmer the head very gently until the meat falls from the bone without resistance. Drain into another pan through a colander and discard the vegetables, herbs and peppercorns. Wearing rubber gloves to protect you from the heat, pull the soft skin, fat and meat away from the bone until the bones are picked clean. Discard the bones and flake up the flesh and add to it some finely chopped shallot, fresh chopped parsley and 2 or 3 hard boiled eggs, quartered and yolks removed, fresh milled pepper and grated nutmeg and gently mix together. Lay into your terrine or potting mould then bring the stock up to the boil and reduce by half, skimming away any fat and scum that comes to the surface. Taste the stock as it reduces to make sure it is not becoming too concentrated or salty then strain through muslin or a clean wet tea towel and pour over the meat so it just covers (not floods). Leave to set in the fridge for 12–20 hours. Don't mess around de-moulding the terrine, just spoon it straight from the dish and serve with hot English mustard, toast and maybe some gherkins or hot radishes and watercress.

STICKY TOFFEE PUDDING

Sticky toffee pudding is one of those desserts that out of nowhere I suddenly get a yearning for and have to search out a pub or a restaurant where I know I can get my fix. If we make it at work we all gather like hyenas round the trimmings gorging ourselves and murmuring with satisfaction. The recipe here ticks all the boxes – sticky and rich but not so heavy you can't move after a portion. You can either make one big pudding in a deep tray then cut it out or in greased individual moulds for easy portion control; it tastes the same either way.

MAKES A LOT

350 g pitted dates
1⅓ (1.6) litres warm water
1 tsp bicarbonate of soda
100 g butter, softened
350 g caster sugar
350 g self-raising flour
dash of vanilla essence
4 eggs
250 g soft brown sugar
150 g unsalted butter
125 ml double cream

Pre-heat the oven to 180°C. Soak the dates in the water, bring to a boil and add the bicarbonate (do this in a large pan to give it room to foam up) and turn off the heat. In a large mixing bowl mix the butter with the caster sugar. Sift in the flour and add a dash of vanilla essence. Fold in the eggs then slowly fold in the date and water mix until you have a sloppy mess. Line a deep tray or individual moulds with greaseproof paper and fill with the mix. Cover with foil and place in a tray of water and bake until a knife comes out clean; a large one will take about an hour; individual moulds a bit less at about 40 minutes.

Boil the soft brown sugar, butter and double cream together until rich and thick then strain and serve straightaway or chill and serve cold.

SALT BRISKET WITH A WINTER VEGETABLE PICKLE

Ask your butcher for rib roll, the flap of beef that wraps around the rib eye, and prepare it by removing all the gristle and tie it up tight. To salt the brisket you need to make a brine.

1 kg brisket of beef
1 onion, peeled and halved
1 carrot, peeled and halved
1 stick of celery, washed, trimmed and roughly chopped
1 bay leaf
sprig of thyme

FOR THE BRINE

1 kg sea salt
1½ litres water
750 g Demerara sugar
1 tbsp black peppercorns
4 bay leaves
1 sprig of thyme
2 tsp garlic salt
1 tbsp saltpetre

FOR THE VEGETABLE PICKLE

1 small swede
2 large carrots
2 small turnips
2 beetroots
2 medium onions
4 cloves of garlic
2 tsp ground ginger
1 tsp ground mace
½ tsp ground cinnamon
4 cardamom pods

500 g dark soft brown sugar
500 ml cider vinegar
3 tsp salt

To make a brine, dissolve the sea salt in the water then add the Demerara sugar, peppercorns, bay leaves, thyme, garlic salt and saltpetre. Simmer until the sugar dissolves then allow to cool completely. Prick the beef 6 or 7 times with a meat fork to help the brine to penetrate then submerge it in the brine, using a plate to hold it down, and refrigerate for 5–6 days. Rinse in cold water for 5 minutes and pat dry.

Heat up some lard in a braising pan and brown the joint without seasoning. When nicely coloured, turn down the heat and dab away the fat with paper towels. Cover with water and add the onion, carrot, celery and herbs. Cover with a lid and poach very gently until the meat is very soft, between 3 and 4 hours, then turn off the heat and allow to cool until it's just warm. Take the meat from the pan, remove the strings with scissors and roll the beef as tight as possible sealing either end with cling film so it doesn't squirt out of the ends. Carry on rolling until you have a very tight, round sausage mummified in cling film. Chill for a day or so. Reduce down the cooking liquor by about 50 per cent then strain and chill to use as dressing for salad.

To make the vegetable pickle, peel and dice all the vegetables into 1 cm dice and crush the garlic. Place all the ingredients together in a heavy-bottomed pan and simmer on a low to medium heat stirring quite often over a fairly long period until all the liquid has seeped from the vegetables and reduced along with the vinegar. The mix should become dark and thick and the vegetables a little opaque. Pour into a sterile container, allow to cool then refrigerate.

Thinly slice the beef and serve with a spoonful of pickle and some salad leaves dressed with the meat juices.

Rhubarb

First season blush pink champagne rhubarb, if not being shipped over from Holland, is usually associated with Yorkshire and the low-roofed long dark sheds where they are forced by chasing a candlelight to grow tall and tender and quickly. So being a Yorkshireman I've always had a place in my kitchen and on my plate for rhubarb and there are plenty of people growing it in the west now by using straw beds to protect and keep them tender rather than the dark sheds, so it's slightly more tart and requires a little more sugar than the forced Yorkshire varieties.

They come just in the nick of time right at the end of winter when the stored apples are running low and all my preserved fruit has long gone, so it's nice to get an English fruit to brighten up menus and sharpen our palates ready for spring again. And not just in desserts; it can be used like gooseberry to make a sauce for oily fish or in salads as well as classic desserts.

SALAD OF KING PRAWNS WITH RHUBARB, FENNEL AND VANILLA
SERVES 4

1 stalk of rhubarb
½ vanilla pod
1 tbsp icing sugar, plus extra as needed
100 ml grape or rapeseed oil
1 small head of fennel
2 flat leaf lettuce heads, cored, washed and spun
16 cooked, peeled king prawns
1 sprig of chervil

Chop the rhubarb up small and stew in a pan with the vanilla and icing sugar until the rhubarb is completely broken down. Taste and adjust the sugar to your taste. Remove the vanilla pod and cool the mix down completely. Blend in a food processor or with an electric hand blender with the oil until you have a smooth light pink purée then pass and chill down. Very thinly slice the fennel, preferably on a mandolin, otherwise use a sharp knife, then dress the fennel with a little rhubarb purée. On individual plates build up two layers of lettuce, fennel and prawns, 2 prawns each layer, 4 per plate. Drizzle over a little bit of the purée and sprinkle on some chervil leaves.

Rhubarb and Vulscombe Goat's Cheesecake
SERVES 8

3 small sticks of rhubarb
caster sugar
275 ml good quality double cream
100 g icing sugar
225 g plain Vulscombe goat's cheese
½ vanilla pod
1 packet of digestive biscuits
75 g butter, melted

18 cm x 3 cm flan ring

Peel the rhubarb and cut into 5 cm oblongs then cut each oblong in half lengthways. Sprinkle a little sugar in a frying pan on a low heat then put the fruit on top. As it starts to emit its juices turn up the heat and add a little more sugar then allow the fruit to cook in its own juices until it has reduced right down and the fruit is soft. Pour onto a dish and cool down.
Bring the cream, sugar, cheese and vanilla to the boil and simmer until all the cheese has dissolved into the cream. Whisk well then pass through a fine sieve and set aside to cool.
Crush the biscuits in a processor or with a rolling pin and pack the crumbs into your mould on a tray lined with non-stick paper. Brush over the melted butter, this way it won't set too hard, and spread over the rhubarb mix. Wait until the cheese topping is at room temperature then pour over and refrigerate for a few hours before use. This is quite a soft cheesecake as it contains no eggs or gelatine but it has a lovely natural freshness.

Rhubarb Crumble
SERVES 6

175 g plain flour
215 g butter
90 g Demerara sugar
55 g porridge oats
8 sticks of indoor rhubarb or 4 large sticks of outdoor rhubarb
4 tbsp sugar (indoor) or 8 tbsp (outdoor)

Pre-heat the oven to 170°C. Crumb the flour with 115 g of the butter and the Demerara sugar until it has the texture of soft breadcrumbs. If you have a food processor it is much quicker but it's much more aesthetic if you do it by hand. When you've got the desired texture mix in the porridge oats by hand so as not to break them up. Tip onto a non-stick oven tray and toast in the oven until light golden in colour and crunchy to taste. Allow to cool on the tray before you use or store it. (It keeps for 3 or 4 days in a sealed tub.)
Peel and chop enough rhubarb to fill your crumble dish and sprinkle over a fair amount of granulated sugar and the remaining butter diced into little cubes and dotted around. Bake at the same temperature for about 20 minutes until the sugar and butter are molten then cover with the crumble topping and bake for another 20 minutes until the fruit is bubbling up the sides.
Serve with thick custard (see page 104).

What and Who is the Castle Hotel?

England is a wealthy country at the moment with moneymen from all over the world investing their money in our industries like sport, luxury hotels and restaurants. This means that all over England we now have many very luxurious hotels with spas, numerous pools and gyms competing with each other in the leisure and catering industry, but it wasn't always like this.

When the country was less affluent there were less hotels and restaurants because there were less people who could afford to eat in them. So opening and running a smart well-staffed hotel business with huge cellars and well-paid chefs is an easy way to loose a lot of money if you're not prepared to stick by your guns and guard your business closely, and that is what the Chapman family, who own and run the Castle, have done since the 1950s when Peter Chapman and his very young wife Etty took it over as managers. It was then a dank, dust-infested place but Peter used his knowledge of hotels, having been himself born into a family of great hoteliers, and used his passion for fine wines and food to turn the Castle into a landmark establishment for people who enjoyed the luxury of being wined and dined.

In 1976 he managed finally to buy the hotel and the following year his son Christopher, or Kit as he is usually known, returned to help run and eventually take over the business. He has pushed his hotel forward ever since with a succession of chefs attaining Michelin stars, first with Chris Oakes, then Garry Rhodes, Phil Vickery and now me. Mr Chapman, like all hoteliers, wants to run a successful business, pay the bills, and make a profit, but what puts him in the minority is his standards. The goal posts are always moving and his passion for British food and local ingredients was installed a long time before I came and they will be there a long time after me. He has always known the importance of sourcing great local produce that's not stale and travelled. Mrs Chapman, Louise, with her long-standing head housekeeper, Valerie Harper, the breakfast chef of thirty years, Gerry Barge, and Mike Hawkins, the head porter of twenty-odd years, keep the front of house immaculate and with the director and general manager, Kevin McCarthy's strong business mind and impeccable attention to detail overcomes the trials and tribulations of running the ex-Norman fortress, from putting up the enormous Christmas tree to pruning the biggest and most impressive wisteria that you've ever seen and which enrobes the whole of the building, filling Taunton with its perfume when in full bloom.

Running a hotel like this takes so much more than offering cheap rooms with Sky TV to people who are happy to eat from vending machines where making a profit is much more straightforward, 50–100 bedrooms, six full-time staff, no restaurant, no cost of sale, job done. It's a bit different when you're in the same business but with eighty employees so it's been an honour for me to be given a chance to put my stamp on the Castle's history and I hope for a long time in the future that the hotel remains a bastion for West Country produce and British cooking.

Suppliers

This is an alphabetical list of suppliers used by Richard Guest. It is not intended to be an exhaustive listing across the whole of the West Country. Please check local directories or go to www.tasteofthewest.co.uk for suppliers closer to you.

Barrow Boar
Foster's Farm
South Barrow
Yeovil
Somerset BA22 7LN
tel: 01963 440315
email: sales@barrowboar.co.uk
www.barrowboar.co.uk

Bath Soft Cheese
Park Farm
Kelston
Bath BA1 9AG
tel: 01225 331601
email: bathsoftcheese@hotmail.com
www.parkfarm.co.uk

Beech Hayes Farm
Churchinford
Taunton
Somerset TA3 7DW
tel: 01823 601565
email: beechhayes@aol.com

Bonners
37 Silver Street
Ilminster
Somerset TA19 0DW
tel: 01460 52465
email: sales@bonnersthebutcher.co.uk
www.bonnersthebutchers.co.uk

Brown & Forrest
Bowdens Farm
Hambridge
Langport
Somerset TA10 0BP
tel: 01458 251520
email: brownforrest@btinternet.com
www.smokedeel.co.uk

Burcott Mill
Water Powered Flour Mill
Wookey, Nr Wells
Somerset BA5 1NJ
tel: 01749 673118
email: theburts@burcottmill.com
www.burcottmill.com

Creedy Carver
Merrifield Farm
Upton Hellions
Crediton
Devon EX17 1AF
tel/fax: 01363 772682
email: creedycarver@farming.co.uk
www.creedycarver.co.uk

Definitely Devon Clotted Cream
Definitely Devon Ltd.
Rolle Road
Torrington
Devon EX38 8AU
tel: 01805 622018

Deli Farm Charcuterie
Deli Bungalow
Delabole
Cornwall PL33 9BZ
tel: 01840 214106
email: jean@delifarmcharcuterie.co.uk
www.delifarmcharcuterie.co.uk

Denhay Farms Ltd
Broadoak
Bridport
Dorset DT6 5NP
tel: 01308 458963
email: sales @denhay.co.uk
www.denhay.co.uk

Dillington Park Nursery
Dillington House
Ilminster
Somerset TA19 9DT
tel: 01460 57908

D. J. Miles & Co. Ltd
The Vale Yard
High Street
Porlock
Somerset TA24 8PU
tel: 01643 703993
email: info@djmiles.co.uk
www.djmiles.co.uk

Doves Farm Foods Ltd
Salisbury Road
Hungerford
Berkshire RG17 0RF
email: portenquiry@dovesfarm.co.uk
www.dovesfarm.co.uk

Falmouth Bay Oysters
The Docks
Falmouth
Cornwall TR11 4NR
tel: 01326 316600
www.falmouthoysters.co.uk

Gundenham Dairy
North Gundenham
Langford Budville
Wellington
Somerset TA21 0QR
tel: 01823 662704
www.gundenham-dairy.co.uk

Jaspers (Treburley) Ltd
Treburley Abattoir
Treburley
Launceston
Cornwall PL15 9PU
tel: 01579 370461
www.jaspersbeef.co.uk

John Rowswell
Bakers Farm
Barrington, Nr Ilminster
Somerset TA19 0JB
tel: 01460 52381
email: sales@rowswellsfarm.com
www.rowswellsfarm.com

Longman Cheeses
Fir Tree
Galhampton
Yeovil
Somerset BA22 7BH
tel: 01963 441146
www.longman-cheese-sales.co.uk

Lower Preston Farm
Lydeard St Lawrence
Taunton
Somerset TA4 3QR
tel: 01984 656292
fax: 01984 656716

Lynmouth Bay Lobsters
The Glen Lyn Gorge
Lymouth
Devon EX35 6ER
tel: 01598 753207

New Cross Fruit Farm
West Lambrook
South Petherton
Somerset TA13 5HD
tel: 01460 241561
email: whebditch@yahoo.co.uk

Paxton & Whitfield
1 John Street
Bath
Somerset BA1 2JL
tel: 01608 650660
www.paxtonandwhitfield.co.uk

Pete Samway
Sherlands
54 Stonegallows
Taunton
Somerset TA1 5JS
tel: 01823 461374
email: sams@enterprise.net

Phil Bowditch Fish
7 Bath Place
Taunton
Somerset TA1 4ER
tel: 01823 253500

Pitney Farm Shop
Glebe Farm
Woodsbirdshill Lane
Pitney
Somerset TA10 9AP
tel: 01458 253002
email: info@pitneyfarmshop.co.uk
www.pitneyfarmshop.co.uk

Pixford Orchards
Bishops Lydeard
Taunton
Somerset TA4 3HS
tel: 01823 432709

Riverside Butchers
8 Riverside Place
2 St James Street
Taunton
Somerset TA1 1JH
tel: 01823 289097

Rodda's
A and E Rodda and Son
The Creamery
Scorrier
Redruth
Cornwall TR16 5BU
tel: 012098 23373
email: enquiries@roddas.co.uk
www.roddas.co.uk

Roots Deli
7a Bath Place
Taunton
SomersetTA1 4ER
tel: 01823 337233
email: tauntonroots@aol.com
www.tauntonroots.co.uk

S&C Meats
58 East Reach
Taunton
Somerset TA1 3EZ
tel: 01823 333995

St Enodoc Asparagus
Great Kiero Farm
St Minver
Wadebridge
Cornwall PL27 6RP
tel: 01208 863781

Sambava Spices
Unit 2, Roseberry Place
Bath
Somerset BA2 3DU
tel/fax: 01225 426309
email: mail@sambavaspices.com
www.sambavaspices.com

Sara's Dairy
132 East Reach
Taunton
Somerset TA1 3HN
tel: 01823 334734

Sharpham Park Organic Spelt Mill
Sharpham Park
Glastonbury
Somerset BA16 65A
tel: 01458 844 080
email: info@sharphampark.com
www.sharphampark.com

Shipton Mill
Longnewton
Telbury
Glos GL8 8RP
tel: 01666 505050
email: enquiries@shipton-mill.com
www.shipton-mill.com

The Somerset Cider Brandy Company
Ltd.
& Burrow Hill Cider.
Pass Vale Farm
Burrow Hill
Kingsbury Episcopi,
Martock
Somerset TA12 6BU, UK.
tell: 01460 240782
www.ciderbrandy.co.uk

South West Snails
North Nevercleave Farm
Umberleigh
Devon EX37 9AD
tel: 01769 560447
email: southwestsnails@yahoo.co.uk
www.south-west-snails.co.uk

Index